# Lecture Notes in Computer Science　5206

*Commenced Publication in 1973*
Founding and Former Series Editors:
Gerhard Goos, Juris Hartmanis, and Jan van Leeuwen

T0223302

Jörn Altmann   Dirk Neumann
Thomas Fahringer (Eds.)

# Grid Economics and Business Models

5th International Workshop, GECON 2008
Las Palmas de Gran Canaria, Spain, August 26, 2008
Proceedings

 Springer

Volume Editors

Jörn Altmann
International University
Campus 3, 76646 Bruchsal, Germany
E-mail: jorn.altmann@acm.org

Dirk Neumann
University of Freiburg
Platz der Alten Synagoge, 79085 Freiburg, Germany
E-mail: dirk.neumann@vwl.uni-freiburg.de

Thomas Fahringer
University of Innsbruck, Institute of Computer Science
Technikerstraße 21a, 6020 Innsbruck, Austria
E-mail: tf@dps.uibk.ac.at

Library of Congress Control Number: 2008933380


CR Subject Classification (1998): C.2, K.4.4, H.3, J.1


LNCS Sublibrary: SL 5 – Computer Communication Networks
and Telecommunications


| ISSN | 0302-9743 |
|------|-----------|
| ISBN-10 | 3-540-85484-3 Springer Berlin Heidelberg New York |
| ISBN-13 | 978-3-540-85484-5 Springer Berlin Heidelberg New York |

Springer is a part of Springer Science+Business Media

springer.com

© Springer-Verlag Berlin Heidelberg 2008

Typesetting: Camera-ready by author, data conversion by Scientific Publishing Services, Chennai, India
Printed on acid-free paper      SPIN: 12464715      06/3180      5 4 3 2 1 0

# Preface

The Grid computing concept, which allows users to integrate administratively and geographically dispersed computing resources, has been gaining traction in a number of application areas during the past few years. By interconnecting many – heterogeneous, though usually virtualized – computing resources, virtual computer centers or supercomputers can be created, providing a seamless supply of computing resources. Grid computing provides benefits not only for scientific computing (e.g., SETI@home, which interconnects one million computers across 226 countries with a total processing power of 711 TFLOPS) but also in a commercial environment. It is projected that computing Grids can lower the total IT costs of businesses by 30%.

The report "Grid Computing: A Vertical Market Perspective 2005–2010" (by The Insight Research Corporation) estimates an increase of worldwide Grid spending from $714.9 million in 2005 to approximately $19.2 billion in 2010. One of the most prominent activities in academia is the EGEE project being funded with 30 MEuro by the European Commission. EGEE brings together researchers from over 27 countries with the common aim of developing a service Grid infrastructure, which is suited for scientific computing with very high demand for processing power.

Despite existing Grid technology and commercial needs, up to now, not many Grid service offerings exist. One of the few examples is Amazon. It has floated the idea of Cloud Computing with the Elastic Compute Cloud service, which has introduced a business model based on virtualized Grid infrastructures. More sophisticated market places such as zimory.com or strikeiron.com have emerged, selling more complex Cloud services dynamically.

However, even though there are some examples in the commercial area and Grid technology has been adopted strongly in academia (eScience), the general adoption by companies has been slow. The reasons are mainly due to the lack of viable business models coupled with chargeable Grid services and commercial transactions on them. What is needed is a set of mechanisms that enable users to discover, negotiate, and pay for the use of Grid services. According to a report by The451Group, the application of resource trading and allocation models is one of the crucial success factors for establishing commercial Grids.

The 5th International Workshop on Grid Economics and Business Models, GECON 2008, served as a forum for the presentation of current and innovative research results pertaining to the above-mentioned issues with special focus on business models and Grid computing technology. The review process attracted prime research papers on amendments to existing technologies, aiming at the successful deployment of global, commercial service-oriented Grid systems. The workshop received a great deal of attention, obtaining 27 high-quality research papers from researchers and practitioners worldwide. Of those, 10 were accepted, constituting an acceptance rate of 37 %. Each paper was reviewed 3 times at least and in average 3.6 times.

The first paper, "Business Value Chains in Real-Time On-line Interactive Applications" by Mike Surridge, Justin Ferris, and E. Rowland Watkins, presents an in-depth analysis of value chains for the application areas of online gaming and e-learning, an initial implementation, and the implications for constructing value chains using bipartite and bi-directional Service Level Agreements.

The second contribution, entitled "Cost Analysis of Current Grids and its Implications for Future Grid Markets" by Marcel Risch and Jörn Altmann, analyzes the question whether using the Grid is financially advantageous over owning resources. Amazon's EC2 service is used as a reference. The comparison of the costs reveals that Grid is cheaper in the short run but not so in the long run.

In the third paper, "Business Relationships in Grid Workflows" written by Ioannis Papagiannis, Dimosthenis Kyriazis, Magdalini Kardara, Vassiliki Andronikou and Theodora Varvarigou, an approach for modeling strategic business relationships is described. As these relationships affect the offered Quality of Service (QoS) level, a metric for characterizing a service provider's "friendliness" is introduced.

Lior Amar, Ahuva Mu'alem and Jochen Stößer showcase "The Power of Preemption in Economic Online Markets" settings by extending the decentralized local greedy mechanism. This mechanism is known to be 3.281-competitive with respect to the total weighted completion time. The authors show that the preemptive version of this mechanism is even 2-competitive. In addition to this, they provide an in-depth empirical analysis of the average case performance of the original mechanism and its preemptive extension based on real workload traces.

In the fifth contribution "Market Mechanisms for Trading Grid Resources", Costas Courcoubetis, Manos Dramitinos, Thierry Rayna, Sergios Soursos, and George Stamoulis present a market for hardware providers and consumers, who are interested in leasing Grid resources for a certain time period. The proposed market mechanism comprises a stock-market-like mechanism that enables the trading of computational resources on a spot and a futures market. This Grid market is more complicated than the standard spot/futures markets of storable commodities, because of the fact that the computational services traded are perishable and need to be described in terms of quantity and duration.

The contribution of Nikolay Borissov, Arun Anandasivam, Niklas Wirström, and Dirk Neumann titled "Rational Bidding Using Reinforcement Learning: An Application in Automated Resource Allocation" proposes an agent-based bidding procedure for participating in Grid markets. The paper introduces a scenario, which demonstrates the components and methodologies for automated bid generation. In addition to this, the authors introduce a reinforcement learning strategy for agents enabling agents to generate bids and asks rationally. This strategy is evaluated against a truth-telling bidding strategy.

In the seventh contribution, Davidi Maria Parrilli discusses tax issues in decentralized computing environments in his paper titled "Grid and Taxation: the Server as a Permanent Establishment in International Grids". Taxation can be a barrier to the development of international Grids. Based on his analysis of the current taxation approaches, he makes suggestions for amendments.

The eighth paper, "The Pricing Strategy Analysis for the Software-as-a-Service Business Model" by Ma Dan and Abraham Seidman, presents an analytical model of the competition between software-as-a-service and the traditional commercial off-the-shelf software. The authors find that the two distribution channels could coexist in a competitive market in the long run. However, they show that under certain conditions software-as-a-service could gradually take over the whole market for software.

Carmelo Ragusa, Francesco Longo, and Antonio Puliafito describe in their contribution "On the Assessment of the S-Sicilia Infrastructure: a Grid-Based Business System" the S-Sicilia project, a 2-year collaboration between Oracle and the COMETA consortium that targets at setting up a Grid-based business infrastructure to provide business services with guaranteed QoS to companies. It is intended to make it a benchmark infrastructure, with which other scenarios can be compared.

Omer Rana, Martijn Warnier, Thomas Quillinan, and Frances Brazier identify in their paper "Monitoring and Reputation Mechanisms for Service Level Agreements" a lack of research on SLAs. This paper addresses how SLOs may be impacted by the choice of specific penalty clauses. It is devoted to the specification of penalties within the Web Services Agreement (WS-Agreement) negotiation language and how clauses can be enforced based on monitoring the SLAs.

In addition to these papers, we received many paper submissions from research projects on Grid economics, giving an overview of current and ongoing research in this area. Out of these submissions, we selected papers from nine projects (ArguGrid, AssessGrid, BEinGrid, BREIN, D-Grid, Edutain@Grid, Grid4All, GridEcon, and SORMA). These papers can be grouped into three categories. The first category comprises papers on business modeling. The paper contributions in this category come from BEinGrid, Edutain@Grid, and Brein. The second category, which addresses Grid markets, includes papers from SORMA, GridEcon, and Grid4All. In particular, these papers describe market places, market mechanisms, and market-based resource allocation schemes. D-Grid, ArguGrid, and AssessGrid contributed papers to the third category. This category is characterized by papers on Grid architectures.

Finally, we would like to thank the organizers of the 2008 Euro-Par conference, in particular Emilio Luque, for their support in hosting the GECON 2008 workshop in Las Palmas, Spain. We would also like to thank Alfred Hofmann and Ursula Barth from Springer, who ensured a very efficient publication process. Finally, our highest gratitude goes to Sonja Klingert. Without her dedication and substantial efforts in preparing the manuscript, these proceedings would not have been ready on time.

August 2008

Dirk Neumann
Jörn Altmann
Thomas Fahringer

# Organization

GECON 2008 was organized by the International University in Germany, Bruchsal, Germany, Department of Computer Networks and Distributed Systems. It was given organizational support by the University of Freiburg, Germany and the University of Innsbruck, Austria and held in collaboration with EuroPar 2008.

## Executive Committee

| | |
|---|---|
| Chair | Jörn Altmann (Intl. University in Germany, Germany) |
| Vice Chairs | Dirk Neumann (University of Freiburg, Germany) |
| | Thomas Fahringer (University of Innsbruck, Austria) |
| Organization Chair | Sonja Klingert (Intl. University in Germany, Germany) |

## Program Committee

Hermant K. Bhargava (UC Davis, USA)
Rajkumar Buyya (University of Melbourne, Australia)
Costas Courcoubetis (Athens University of Economics and Business, Greece)
Jeremy Cohen (Imperial College London, UK)
Dang Minh Quan (Intl. University of Bruchsal, Germany)
John Darlington (Imperial College London, UK)
Karim Djemame (University of Leeds, UK)
Torsten Eymann University of Bayreuth, Germany)
Wolfgang Gentzsch (D-Grid, Germany)
Kartik Hosenager (University of Pennsylvania, USA)
Chun-Hsi Huang (University of Connecticut, USA)
Junseok Hwang (Seoul National University, South-Korea)
Bastian Koller (HLRS, Germany)
Harald Kornmayer (NEC Laboratories Europe, Germany)
Ramayya Krishnan (Carnegie Mellon University, USA)
Kevin Lai (HP Labs, USA)
Hing-Yan Lee (National Grid Office, Singapore)
Jysoo Lee (KISTI, South Korea)
Steven Miller (Singapore Management University, Singapore)
Omer Rana (Cardiff University, UK)
Rajiv Ranjan (University of Melbourne, Australia)
Thierry Rayna (Imperial College London, UK)
Peter Reichl (Telecommunications Research Center Vienna, Austria)
Simon See (Sun Microsystems, Singapore)
Satoshi Sekiguchi (AIST, Japan)
Burkhard Stiller (University of Zurich, Switzerland)

Yoshio Tanaka (AIST, Japan)
Maria Tsakali (European Commission, Belgium)
Bruno Tuffin (IRISA/INRIA, France)
Dora Varvarigou (National Technical University of Athens, Greece)
Gabriele von Voigt (University of Hanover, Germany)
Kerstin Voss (University of Paderborn, Germany)
Christof Weinhardt (University of Karlsruhe, Germany)
Stefan Wesner (HLRS, Germany)
Phillip Wieder (University of Dortmund, Germany)
Ramin Yahyapour (University of Dortmund, Germany)
Wolfgang Ziegler (Fraunhofer Institute SCAI, Germany)

## Sponsoring Institutions

International University in Germany, Bruchsal, Germany
University of Freiburg, Germany
University of Innsbruck, Austria
Springer LNCS, Heidelberg, Germany
EU-FP6 Project GridEcon (Project No. 033634)
EuroPar 2008, Las Palmas, Spain

# Table of Contents

## Research Projects on Business Modeling

## Research Projects on Market Mechanisms

## Research Projects on Grid Architecture

# Business Value Chains in Real-Time On-Line Interactive Applications

Justin Ferris, Mike Surridge, and E. Rowland Watkins

University of Southampton, IT Innovation Centre,
2, Venture Road, Chilworth, Southampton, SO16 7NP, UK
{jf,ms,erw}@it-innovation.soton.ac.uk

**Abstract.** Grid infrastructure are already being used in the on-line gaming sector to provide large-scale game hosting in a business context. However, the game platforms and infrastructures used do not take advantage of the potential for rich business networks to support indefinite scaling within single game instances, or to simplify the problem of managing the quality of experience and access rights for end customers. The European edutain@grid research project is developing an infrastructure for realising such business networks using bipartite Service Level Agreements. This paper describes the analysis of business value chains and SLA terms for the initial implementation, and provides insights into how these should be formulated, and what challenges this presents to Grid infrastructure implementers.

**Keywords:** Business models, Service Level Agreements, Grid, Trust, Security, Value chains.

## 1 Introduction

The recent maturation of Grid technologies [1] raises the possibility of improving the way that on-line applications such as games and e-learning courses are managed and provided to customers. These applications fall within the broader category of Real-Time On-Line, Interactive Applications (ROIA), a new class of 'killer' application for the Grid. The edutain@grid project [2, 3] is investigating how Grid can improve ROIA provisioning and is developing a novel, sophisticated and service-oriented Grid infrastructure to support secure, reliable and scalable provisioning of ROIA and that supports flexible value chains. To facilitate this work, the project is focusing on exemplar ROIA from two of its partners.

BMT Cordah Ltd provides training courses in search and rescue planning that are used by customers such as the UK Maritime and Coastguard Agency (MCA). The courses are used to train new search and rescue planning staff (around 10% of which leave and have to be replaced annually), and to update existing staff. Currently, courses are run twice per year at a dedicated facility, but it would be better to use distance learning options to reduce costs and the length of time staff have to spend away from their normal stations. This has not been possible up to now because the training depends on the interactive use of simulator models, but edutain@grid will

J. Altmann, D. Neumann, and T. Fahringer (Eds.): GECON 2008, LNCS 5206, pp. 1–12, 2008.

overcome this barrier by allowing students to access simulators securely from remote locations via the Grid.

Darkworks develops on-line multiplayer games for mainstream and niche game distributors. On-line games played over the Internet are a rapidly growing segment of the video games industry, now all the main console vendors support connection to the Internet as standard. It is predicted that in the next few years the on-line game market sector will grow rapidly to billions of Euros, which makes them a 'killer' application capable of justifying massive investment in the Grid. On-line games use virtualised interactive environments very similar to those used in on-line training simulators, posing similar technical challenges to deliver acceptable Quality of Experience. However, on-line games pose additional challenges for the Grid: the end-users are members of the public with little understanding of features such as Grid security and minimal access to technical support, and the number of users can vary by many orders of magnitude during the life of a single game title.

In general, ROIA are soft real-time systems with the potential for very high user interactivity between users. Large numbers of users may participate in a single ROIA instance, and are typically able to join or leave at any time. Thus ROIA typically have extremely dynamic distributed workloads in comparison to more typical Grid-based applications, making them very difficult to host cost-effectively. Also, like other mass entertainment media, on-line games may start out with a small number of users, and go through a very rapid period of growth in popularity whose timing and extent are very hard to predict and may depend on the quality of experience delivered. These factors make hosting ROIA a very challenging (and risky) undertaking. Grid middleware systems such as the Globus toolkit [4], gLite [5], and UNICORE [6], are not well suited to meeting this challenge cost-effectively, because they don't address soft real-time provisioning aspects, and they don't allow the rapid extension of business networks to allow scaling by several orders of magniture beyond the capacity of the initial hoster. Thus initiatives such as Butterfly Grid [7] and Bigworld [8] allows hosters to scale resources according to demand, but do not allow scaling of a single on-line game instance beyond a single hoster.

The edutain@grid project will address these challenges using so-called 'business Grid' developments such as GRIA [9, 10], which currently supports simple Service Level Agreements (SLA) for non-real-time data storage and processing [11]. The project is building on GRIA, extending the commitment models and corresponding resource management technology to address real-time application loads. These are then being used to support extended value chains allowing multiple hosters to participate in the same ROIA instance, and enabling more hosters to be recruited as customer demand increases. In addition, edutain@grid will support demand management mechanisms such as option or variable pricing, and user-friendly security and trust models which are critical for 'business-to-consumer' on-line gaming scenarios.

The rest of this paper is organised as follows. In section 2 we present the analysis of business actors and value chains from the edutain@grid project, and highlight some of the business scenarios that must be supported. Section 3 briefly describes an implementation of the edutain@grid framework to support these value chains, and discusses the initial results and their implications for SLA. Section 4 provides a summary of the overall work on edutain@grid value chains to date, and discusses the direction of future work.

## 2  Business Models in Edutain@grid

To ensure business models for Grid-based ROIA will be economically viable, it is necessary to analyse the value chains (i.e. business actors and value flows) in which ROIA (specifically on-line games and e-learning applications) will be operated and used. The goal of edutain@grid is to support value chains corresponding to commercially viable scenarios, preferably in such a way that the same ROIA application software need not become locked into one particular business scenario. The work of edutain@grid is thus related to efforts in the BEinGRID project, which is performing and analysing Business Experiments (some also using GRIA) to produce a generic value network for Grid [12]. In edutain@grid, this analysis is finer-grained and more focused on the specifics of ROIA provision.

### 2.1  Business Actors

The analysis of value chains revealed an extensive hierarchy of business roles that must be supported by the edutain@grid infrastructure to provide flexibility regarding the business models and value chains supported:

The three main classes of edutain@grid business user are 'providers' who host services through which the ROIA is delivered to users, 'consumers' who access the ROIA by connecting to these services, and 'facilitators' who play other business roles in the creation of ROIA application software, its distribution to providers and consumers, and the operation of ROIA instances. These three main classes and some of their important sub-classes are shown in the actor hierarchy diagram (Figure 1).

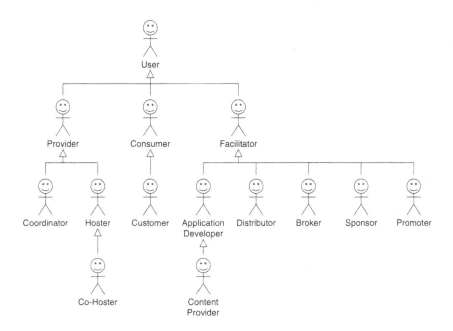

**Fig. 1.** Business Actors in edutain@grid

The providers in edutain@grid actually host servers on which ROIA processes run, thereby making the ROIA available to its users. Three important sub-classes of ROIA providers were identified and will be supported by the project:

- Hoster: is an organisation that hosts core, usually computationally intensive processes that support a ROIA virtual environment including interactions of users with this environment and with each other. In an on-line game, a hoster will run the game simulation processes to which players connect, while in the maritime e-learning scenario a hoster runs the search and rescue simulator.
- Co-hosters: are other hosters participating in the same ROIA instance – where more than one hoster is involved in a single ROIA instance, each hoster will regard the others as 'co-hosters' of the ROIA instance.
- Coordinator: is an organisation that makes a ROIA instance accessible to its consumers, and coordinates one or more hosters to deliver the required ROIA virtual interactive environment.

Note that a co-hoster should not be confused with a coordinator. There is nothing special about a co-hoster. Each hoster for a ROIA instance will consider each other hoster to be a co-hoster. In contrast, a coordinator has quite a different role, it coordinates a set of hosters to provide a ROIA instance to its consumers. Today, on-line game hosters exist, but there are no 'co-hosters' or 'coordinators' because there is only one hoster per game instance. The edutain@grid infrastructure breaks away from this limitation, enabling new business models to manage risks of ROIA hosting and delivery, and provide genuine scalability for ROIA provision.

A consumer in edutain@grid is someone who accesses a ROIA instance – e.g. a player in an on-line game, or a trainee using a search and rescue simulator. Because edutain@grid is not limited to a single application sector, few assumptions can be made about the IT skills or other characteristics of consumers. Indeed, there may be many specialised types of consumers reflecting application-specific roles within the ROIA – e.g. the difference between trainees and tutors using a search and rescue simulator. The edutain@grid framework does not distinguish these application-specific consumer roles, but it does distinguish one special type of consumer known as a 'customer'. The customer actually pays the coordinator to allow them (and in some applications, other consumers) to access the ROIA.

A facilitator in edutain@grid does not run or use ROIA processes directly, but plays some other role in the delivery of ROIA. The most important facilitators in edutain@grid are application developers, whose needs are addressed through the development of an edutain@grid API, and distributors who supply ROIA software to providers and consumers who need mechanisms for software licensing and (in some applications) distribution of run-time software updates.

## 2.2   Service Level Agreements (SLA)

It is important to note that the value chain analysis performed in edutain@grid, is quite different from the business analysis that has come out of other projects such as Gridbus [13]. Gridbus, for example, does not consider the use of value chains, nor analyse the relationships between business actors, but focuses on algorithms for specific business decisions such as brokering within symmetric business networks such as resource-sharing virtual organisations. In edutain@grid, a different approach has been used following the architectural model proposed by the NextGRID project [14, 15] and used with GRIA in the SIMDAT project [11]. Here, each pair of business entities may have a distinctive relationship specified in a bipartite, bi-directional Service Level Agreement (SLA) which is private to the two participants and not exposed to other entities in the value chain. The format of the SLA used in these systems is based on the WS-Agreement specification [16], although a 'discrete offer' protocol is used to establish SLA, rather than using the full WS-Agreement negotiation protocol.

Given that each SLA is in principle different from all the others, it is important to distinguish and clarify the different types of SLA needed by edutain@grid:

- Agreements between customers and coordinators, in which the coordinator agrees to provide access to one or more ROIA global sessions, usually in exchange for payment. For convenience, an agreement of this type will referred to as a *customer account*, but keeping in mind this refers to the terms of use as well as the payment mechanism.
- Agreements between coordinators and hosters, in which the hoster agrees to host ROIA processes to support the coordinator's ROIA global sessions, and to provide accounting information on use of these processes by consumers. An agreement of this type will be referred to as a hosting SLA, but keeping in mind this refers to the payment mechanism as well as the terms of use.
- Agreements between distributors other actors, allowing other actors to receive and use ROIA software. An agreement of this type will be referred to as a software licence. Its terms typically cover how the software is used, rights to access source code or redistribute the software, and optionally payments to the distributor.

How these are used depends on the topology of the value chain through which funds flow from the customers (who ultimately pay for everything) to the other actors.

## 2.3  Value Chains

The simplest value chain considered in edutain@grid is one in which customers pay coordinators for access to the ROIA software as well as services, and the coordinator pays distributors to provide the software and hosters to run the ROIA processes and provide the virtual environment. All revenue thus flows through the coordinator. This topology is shown in Figure 2.

A value network representation of the relationships in this topology is shown in Figure 3. The customer pays the coordinator for access to a ROIA under the terms of the customer account, while the coordinator pays its hoster(s) to host the ROIA and provide accounting under the terms of a hosting SLA. In this value chain the coordinator also pays a distributor for access to ROIA software including the right to distribute it to hosters, and the distributor pays the application developer to produce ROIA software.

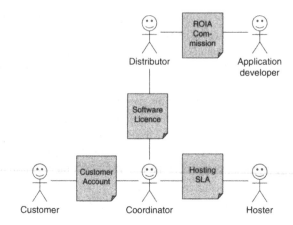

**Fig. 2.** Coordinator-based software licence value chain

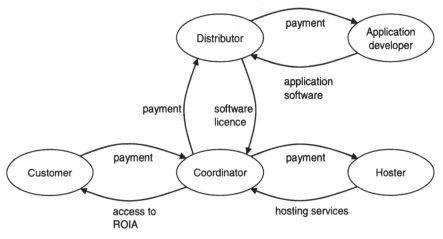

**Fig. 3.** Value network for coordinator-based software licence value chain

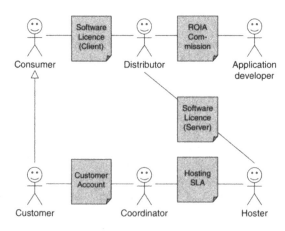

**Fig. 4.** Distributor-based software licence value chain

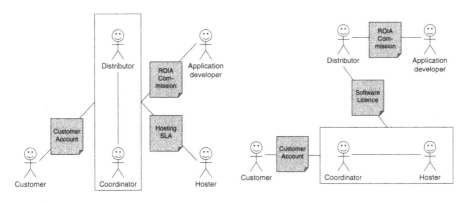

(a) Distributor-Coordinator          (b) Hoster-Coordinator

**Fig. 5.** Collocation of business roles

A more complex topology arises when the distributor provides software to the other actors directly as shown in Figure 4. This topology is more typical of current on-line gaming scenarios in which the software is sold to customers who can then decide for themselves whether to connect to a hoster to join a particular on-line game instance.

Even within a single overall value chain topology there may be a wide range of business models can be encoded in the agreements. For example, in Figure 2 a distributor may charge the coordinator a fixed fee for using the ROIA software, a royalty on the income received from customers, or a percentage of the profits. In Figure 4 the distributor may provide software to hosters for free to encourage the provision of ROIA instances, increasing the value (and hence the price) of the client software for consumers. Thus a wide range of options can be used to balance risks and rewards between the distributor, coordinator and hosters in each case. These will be reflected in the specific terms of the SLA between them.

It is also possible for one business organisation to take more than one of the edutain@grid business roles, as shown in Figure 5. The distributor-coordinator topology shown in Figure 5(a) allows a distributor to form direct relationships with the consumers and hosters using their software, and retain a greater share of the revenue provided by customers. This only works if the distributor is able to market the ROIA to customers, find and negotiate terms with hosters, and run the services needed to support ROIA global sessions – i.e. if they have all the capabilities and relationships needed by edutain@grid coordinators. Similarly, the hoster-coordinator topology shown in Figure 5(b) allows a hoster to retain a greater share of the revenue by acting as their own coordinator. This topology is used by the current generation of on-line game hosters (though with variations in the software distribution), and depends on a hoster being able to market the ROIA directly to customers and take all the responsibility (and risk) of delivering the required Quality of Experience.

As noted in Section 1, one of the innovations provided by edutain@grid is to allow more than one co-hoster to cooperate in providing a single ROIA instance to consumers. Suppose a hoster begins selling access to a massively multiplayer on-line

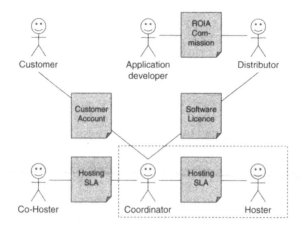

**Fig. 6.** A co-hosted edutain@grid ROIA

game, acting as their own coordinator and using the value chain shown in Figure 5(b). If the game reaches blockbuster status, the number of players may grow beyond the capacity of this hoster, which would lead to degraded Quality of Experience, and rapidly declining participation. The only way the hoster can avoid this is by installing enough capacity to meet the peak demand, but this is risky: if they over-estimate demand they will invest too much and profits will be too low, but if they under-estimate demand the customers will become dissatisfied and the game will only remain a hit and deliver high revenues for a very short time. The edutain@grid project allows a coordinator to split the ROIA instance between more than one hoster, leading to a value chain like the one shown in Figure 6. With this capability, a hoster finding they have a blockbuster on their hands can introduce a second co-hoster to maintain the customer Quality of Experience in exchange for a share of the revenue.

Note this means there is a clear distinction between the coordinator (who sells the game to customers and organises the hosters) and the hosters themselves, even if the same business is acting as the coordinator and one of the hosters (as indicated by the dotted line in Figure 6). The coordinator is the one taking the risk that it may be difficult to maintain customer QoE as demand grows. The share of the revenue they are willing to pass on to hosters (i.e. the price of the hosting SLA) will depend partly on how this risk is shared with hosters through the SLA terms. Hosters will need to focus on managing resources very efficiently, which may limit the number of service level options they can afford to offer [17].

Other value chains may also be created with more facilitator roles. For example, if the number of available hosters (or the number of different hosting options) were to become very large, it may be possible for a business to make money acting as a broker between the coordinator and the hoster. In this scenario, hosting SLA will be set up by the broker, matching the needs of coordinators to the terms offered by hosters. The broker extracts value by charging the hoster: either a commission for each negotiated SLA, or a fee for considering (advertising) the hoster at all. The broker role is economically viable only if the number of actors is too great for direct negotiation between coordinators and hosters to be cost effective. Since this will not be the case initially, the edutain@grid framework is designed to work without brokers but to allow for them when the need arises.

Deciding which value chain topology and business model (SLA terms) makes sense depends on the details of each application and its business context. Even within each application sector, it is unlikely that one topology with one business model will suit every application. Therefore, the edutain@grid business infrastructure must provide sufficient flexibility to support a range of topologies and models, even if each application uses only a single agreement topology and business model.

## 3  Validation Experiments

The edutain@grid project has now produced a first implementation of the framework to support the business actors and value chains presented above for ROIA. The framework is based on a Service Oriented Architecture [18], using GRIA-based services to manage business relationships, along with real-time resource management services from U.Innsbruck and a real-time distributed application framework from U. Muenster. A detailed description of the implementation can be found in [19].

Presently, the framework is being used to perform experiments that investigate which terms in hosting SLAs are most useful for ROIA. The idea is to find terms that coordinators find useful in managing the risks of over/under-estimating user demand, yet allow hosters to retain control over their own resources and implement efficient, ideally autonomic management processes. Support for co-hosting in edutain@grid means that possible interactions and dependencies on co-hosters must be taken into account in this analysis. Consequently, this work must go far beyond existing (even Grid-based) on-line game hosting environments.

The SLA-based management technology used in edutain@grid is based on GRIA, but the SLA terms and metrics typically used with GRIA (based on disk storage and transfer, CPU time, etc [11]) are not very useful (or valuable) in a multi-hosted ROIA scenario. To make use of hosting services with metrics such as these, a coordinator would have to predict how a given ROIA will perform on systems they do not own and with which they are not familiar. To have any chance of doing this, the coordinator will certainly need to control how these systems are allocated and managed, which means the hoster would lose the ability to exploit the systems for other purposes during 'off peak' periods, or to outsource parts of the ROIA to co-hosters if they are unable to handle periods of increased load. Even if the hoster is willing to give up these operational advantages, the coordinator still has to optimise the use of resources not just at one hoster site, but across several co-hosters who will have quite different resources. In short, neither the coordinator nor the hoster is likely to be happy with a hosting SLA expressed in terms of resources. The coordinator will find it hard to manage customer Quality of Experience without deep knowledge of all the resources used by multiple co-hosters, and the hosters will be unable to manage their own resources to maximise returns on their investment from multiple SLA with different coordinators.

Fortunately, GRIA does not force SLA terms to use resource-based metrics – it provides a more general framework which is being further extended in edutain@grid to allow testbed deployments using a wide range of SLA terms. This allows the project partners to conduct realistic experiments in which SLA terms are really used to manage services – the only aspect that is 'simulated' is the settlement of bills based on these terms between the partners. At this stage, edutain@grid experiments are focusing on quite different hosting SLA terms, chosen because they appear to offer the coordinator a good chance of managing ROIA Quality of Experience, but without needing to control (or even understand) the resources and management strategy at each hoster. The terms being investigated in current experiments include:

- the performance of connections between ROIA customers and the hoster, expressed in terms of the virtual environment update rate sustained by the hoster;
- the number of such connections to the hoster;
- the rate at which new connections are made to the hoster.

These metrics relate directly to the concerns of the coordinator – how many customers can their contracted hosters support, and how quickly can new customers join the ROIA? It is already clear that the coordinator can use such 'outcome-related' metrics to manage hosting capacity and control the Quality of Experience seen by their customers. Moreover, hosters can easily measure the number of connections and refuse service if the coordinator (or the application) causes the volume or rate of connections to exceed the limits specified in the hosting SLA.

What is not yet clear is whether the hoster can successfully manage their resources to deliver the required ROIA performance, when the limits on usage are defined in terms of customer behaviour. It is clear that if very few customers are connected to the ROIA, the hoster can use the freedom inherent in such an SLA to reduce the resources allocated – e.g. by running multiple ROIA processes on a single host. However, it is also possible that a ROIA may be come more computationally expensive without a massive increase in customer connections, and since the SLA doesn't specify a limit on resources, the hoster would then be obliged to allocate more resources to maintain the specified ROIA performance. It is also possible for the ROIA itself to induce SLA breaches. For example, imagine an on-line game with (say) 1000 customers provisioned by two co-hosters, each signed to an SLA with a 600 connection limit. It is possible for the ROIA to behave in such a way that all 1000 customers have to transfer their connections to only one of the hosters (e.g. if they all need to gather in one location in the virtual game environment). This would breach the connection limit agreed with that hoster, who would therefore be within their rights to refuse connections, destroying the QoE obtained by customers.

To address these challenges, the project is investigating advanced management models that use forecasts of application and resource load. For example, is may be possible to predict a gathering of on-line gamers in one location, allowing measures to be taken to counteract the negative effects on QoE. At this stage it is not clear what these measures might need to be. One option is to sub-divide the region where customers are predicted to be, and redistribute the pieces between the hosters. Another option is to use 'mirroring', in which replicas of the region are created and customers distributed between them. This technique is already used in single-hoster games to reduce the level of customer interactions, although this does degrade the customers' game experience. The simplest option may be to simply move the region of interest to another, higher-capacity hoster – but would the first hoster notify the coordinator of an impending overload knowing that the work would then be switched to a competitor? To incentivise such behaviour will require a further radical extension of SLA terms beyond those previously used in Grid-based environments.

## 4  Summary and Future Work

The edutain@grid project aims to create a new class of 'killer application' for the Grid: Real-time On-line Interactive Applications (ROIA). This class spans several commercially important applications, including on-line gaming and simulator-based training, both of which are being used in validation case studies in the project.

The project is investigating the need for value chains between business actors, each playing its role to deliver the ROIA to end-customers in a Grid-based environment. The analysis leads to a separation between the roles of the hoster (who hosts ROIA services) and the coordinator (who sells ROIA access to customers and guarantees their Quality of Experience). This separation makes it possible to support co-hosted, and hence more scalable ROIA, as well as conventional single-hosted ROIA (in which a business acts as both hoster and coordinator). The edutain@grid architecture has been designed to be flexible enough to support a wide range of value chain topologies among the roles identified, and to accommodate facilitators such as brokers where such roles are economically viable.

The initial implementation of the edutain@grid framework is now complete, and experiments are being conducted to investigate how business values can be expressed in SLA terms that allow service providers to retain flexibility and control costs, while being attractive to service consumers. Initial findings suggest that the hosting SLA between ROIA coordinators and hosters should be expressed in terms of the outcomes for the coordinator, as more conventional SLA terms based on resource committed by the hoster are of limited value to the coordinator and force the hosters to cede control over aspects of their resource management.

Future work will focus on the analysis of business models constructed using these value chains and SLA terms, and operational management of ROIA and resources to address outstanding challenges such as dynamic ROIA-induced load customer load imbalances. These challenges are already faced in on-line gaming applications, but today the only solution is to restrict customer interactions in the game environment. The edutain@grid approach offers the prospect of Grid-based ROIA with few restrictions, which should also stimulate much greater commercial investment in the Grid itself.

**Acknowledgments.** The work described in this paper is supported by the European Union through EC IST Project 034601 'edutain@grid'.

## References

1. Foster, I., Kesselman, C. (eds.): The Grid2: Blueprint for a New Computing Infrastructure, 2nd edn. Morgan Kaufmann Publishers Inc, Elsevier, Boston (2004)
2. Fahringer, T., Anthes, C., Arragon, A., Lipaj, A., Müller-Iden, J., Rawlings, C., Prodan, R., Surridge, M.: The Edutain@Grid Project. In: Veit, D.J., Altmann, J. (eds.) GECON 2007. LNCS, vol. 4685, pp. 182–187. Springer, Heidelberg (2007)
3. See the edutain@grid website at, http://www.edutaingrid.eu/index.php

4. Foster, I., Kesselman, C.: Globus: A Metacomputing Infrastructure Toolkit. International Journal Supercomputer Applications 11(2), 115–128 (1997)
5. Czajkowski, K., Ferguson, D.F., Foster, I., Frey, J., Graham, S., Sedukhin, I., Snelling, D., Tuecke, S., Vambenepe, W.: The WS-Resource Framework (March 2004)
6. Breuer, D., Erwin, D., Mallmann, D., Menday, R., Romberg, M., Sander, V., Schuller, B., Wieder, P.: Scientific Computing with UNICORE. In: Wolf, D., Münster, G., Kremer, M. (eds.) Procs. of NIC Symposium 2004. John von Neumann Institute for Computing, Jülich. NIC Series, vol. 20, pp. 429–440 (2003)
7. Case Study, I.D.C.: Butterfly.net: Powering Next-Generation Gaming with On-Demand Computing, http://www.ibm.com/grid/pdf/butterfly.pdf
8. Big World Technology, http://www.bigworldtech.com/index/index_en.php
9. Surridge, M., Taylor, S., De Roure, D., Zaluska, E.: Experiences with GRIA — Industrial Applications on a Web Services Grid. In: Proceedings of the First International Conference on e-Science and Grid Computing, pp. 98–105. IEEE Press, Los Alamitos (2005)
10. See for more up to date GRIA news and the latest release, http://www.gria.org
11. Phillips, S.C.: GRIA SLA Service. Cracow Grid Workshop, Poland, 15-18 October (2006)
12. Stanoevska-Slabeva, K., Talamanca, C.F., Thanos, G.A., Zsigri, C.: Development of a Generic Value Chain for the Grid Industry. In: Veit, D.J., Altmann, J. (eds.) GECON 2007. LNCS, vol. 4685, pp. 44–57. Springer, Heidelberg (2007)
13. de Assuncao, M.D., Buyya, R.: An Evaluation of Communication Demand of Auction Protocols in Grid Environments. In: Proceedings of the 3rd International Workshop on Grid Economics & Business (GECON 2006), 16 May, 2006. World Scientific Press, Singapore (2006), http://gridbus.csse.unimelb.edu.au/papers/gecon2006.pdf
14. Snelling, D., Fisher, M., Basermann, A. (eds.): NextGRID Vision and Architecture White Paper. 2006, 30 July (2006), http://www.nextgrid.org
15. Mitchell, B., Mckee, P.: SLAs A Key Commercial Tool. In: Cunningham, P., Cunningham, M. (eds.) Innovation and the Knowledge Economy: Issues, Applications, Case Studies. IOS Press, Amsterdam (2005)
16. Andrieux, A., et al.: Web Services Agreement Specification (WS-Agreement) (March 17, 2007), http://www.ogf.org/documents/GFD.107.pdf
17. McKee, P., Taylor, S.J., Surridge, M., Lowe, R., Ragusa, C.: Strategies for the Service Market Place. In: Grid Economics and Business Models, Procs of the 4th International Workshop, GECON 2007, Rennes, France, August 28, 2007. LNCS, pp. 58–70. Springer, Heidelberg; ISBN 978-3-540-74428-3 (2007)
18. Erl, T.: Service-Oriented Architecture: Concepts, Technology, and Design. Prentice Hall, Englewood Cliffs July (2005)
19. Ferris, J., Surridge, M., Watkins, E.R., Fahringer, T., Prodan, R., Glinka, F., Gorlatch, S., Anthes, C., Arragon, A., Rawlings, C., Lipaj, A.: Edutain@Grid: A Business Grid Infrastructure for Real-Time On-line Interactive Applications. In: 5th International Workshop, GECON 2008, 25-26 August 2008. Las Palmas de Gran Canaria, Spain (2008)

# Cost Analysis of Current Grids and Its Implications for Future Grid Markets

Marcel Risch and Jörn Altmann

International University in Germany, School of Information Technology,
Campus 3, 76646 Bruchsal, Germany
{Marcel.Risch,Jorn.Altmann}@i-u.de

**Abstract.** Commercial Grid markets have been a topic of research for many years. Many claims about the advantages of trading computing resources on markets have been made. However, due to a lack of Grid computing offerings, these claims could not be verified. This paper analyzes the question whether using the Grid is financially advantageous, using the Amazon.com EC2 service as a reference. To perform this analysis, the costs of computing resources in different usage scenarios are calculated, if Grid resources and in-house resources are used. The comparison of the costs reveals that while the Grid is cheaper in the short term, it is not a good investment in the long term and, thus, the existence of a Grid economy will not lead to an end of ownership but rather to a reduction in in-house resources and more efficient resource usage.

**Keywords:** Commercial Grids, Grid Computing, Business Models, Cost Modeling, Capacity Planning, Grid Economics, Utility Computing, Markets.

## 1 Introduction

Commercial Grids have been a focal point of research for many years. The idea of selling idle computing resources on a market for computational power has been advocated since the early 1960s. With the advent of the Internet and the Internet economy, this idea once again received attention during the last years. The advantages of Grid markets have been emphasized with various claims that could not be validated, as a Grid economy did not exist. However, such an economy has now started to develop with the introduction of a number of cluster or cloud computing providers, who sell compute resources on a pay-per-use basis. Using these offers as a basis, we are now able to validate some of the frequently made claims about commercial Grids.

In this paper, we will focus on four claims. They address the financial advantages that companies would gain from using a commercial Grid. Since companies are, in general, seeking ways to gain competitive advantage or to lower their operational costs, the financial advantages of Grids play a major role in promoting Grid usage. Therefore, we will analyze the following four claims:

- *Claim 1:* Companies can reduce the staff for maintaining resources. This idea has been propagated in research and commercial circles [1][2][3].
- *Claim 2:* Companies have large computational power available at their fingertips on a pay-per-use basis [4][5].

J. Altmann, D. Neumann, and T. Fahringer (Eds.): GECON 2008, LNCS 5206, pp. 13–27, 2008.

- *Claim 3:* Companies do not have to purchase the resources and, thus, have no cost of ownership [2][3][4], which is significant for high-performance computing resources.
- *Claim 4:* The advantages of commercial Grids are the reduction in cost [4][5].

Although Claim 1 is difficult to validate for all enterprises, we believe that, due to the difficulty of using Grid resources, it is highly unlikely that an increased Grid usage will result in major savings from personnel reductions in medium-sized companies. There are a number of issues that indicate that the headcount in the in-house IT support staff will remain unchanged. Firstly, the software running on a Grid resource must be maintained and monitored in the same way as the software running on in-house resources. Secondly, the in-house staff must be able to handle many different virtualization tools, such as Xen [6], VMWare [7]. For each of these tools used in a Grid market, the in-house staff must maintain and create the correct images. Since there are as of now no support tools available, the in-house staff must be knowledgeable in may different virtualization tools. Thirdly, any company using the Grid has to perform a detailed cost-benefit analysis to determine whether using the Grid is more cost effective than purchasing in-house resources. Since this analysis requires intimate knowledge of all applications, hardware, and the skill to predict the load levels, experienced staff is needed.

Due to these reasons, we do not believe that the size of in-house IT staff for medium-sized companies can be reduced due to increased Grid usage. Small enterprises, on the other hand, will not only require the computational power, they will also need some software to run on these computers. For these companies, the Grid is more interesting if it offers Software-as-a-Service and not just pure computing power. For large companies, the cost savings through Grid usage are very little. Large companies already benefit from the economies of scale in the operation of their IT resources. IT resources of large enterprises are organized in a few data centers, supported by a sufficiently large number of in-house IT staff. Therefore, any outsourcing of the data center service (i.e. using the Grid) could not result in significant cost savings. Since no type of enterprise is expected to reduce its IT support staff headcount through the use of Grid computing, we will not include the personnel costs in the following parts of this analysis.

Continuing with Claim 2, we can state that this claim is obviously true: All currently existing Grid resource providers have a pricing structure, in which the customer only pays for the computational power used. Furthermore, while there are some limits imposed on the number of resources available, in general, these limits are fairly broad and should not pose any difficulties for users.

Claim 3 is also trivial to verify. Since Grid resources are not purchased but are rather rented to the buyer, the buyer has no costs of ownership. Since Grid resources are not owned by the purchasing company, the purchasing company does not have any costs of ownership.

To perform the analysis of Claim 4, we need to consider the market structure, the type of resources sold and the size of the enterprise using the Grid. Based on this information and evidence gathered in the existing commercial Grid environment, we will determine during the remainder of this paper whether this claim can be supported.

This paper is structured as follows: In section 2, we analyze the potential Grid users, the types of resources available, and the current market structure. In the third section, we present some basic cost information for Grid and in-house resources. In addition, we characterize three companies that are used for comparing Grid and in-house resource costs. These companies need to acquire additional resources, which have the characteristics of one basic instance of an Amazon EC2 resource [8]. In section 4, we present a case-by-case cost analysis for different Grid usage scenarios. In the fifth section, we will analyze the results of the case study and draw some conclusions about the structure of the future Grid market. Finally, we conclude by presenting some open items, which can be explored in future research.

## 2 Analysis Framework

### 2.1 Potential Grid Users

For our analysis, we assume that commercial enterprises mainly use the Grid. These enterprises can be categorized as follows: i) home offices; ii) small enterprises; iii) medium-sized enterprises; and iv) large enterprises. The definitions are standardized in the European Union [9]. In addition to this, we also define the companies in terms of their IT expertise. In general, the smaller the company, the less IT expertise it has. In other words, home offices and small enterprises have less IT expertise than medium-sized or large enterprises. Therefore, their needs for IT solutions differ. Thus, home offices and small enterprises need more complete solutions (e.g. Software-as-a-Service) for their IT needs than medium-sized or large enterprises. Large enterprises, which can perform any kind of IT investment and already benefit from the economies of scale (which Grid computing promises), would not get any additional benefit from participating in a commercial Grid.

Therefore, for our analysis, we only consider medium-sized enterprises. Those companies are characterized by restricted budget for IT investments, and the existence of an IT department.

### 2.2 Resource Types Available on a Grid

In general, any type of compute resource can be sold on a Grid market. However, for the purpose of the analysis, a classification of those resources helps highlighting the characteristics of those resources. Our classification of computing resources resulted in the following four groups:

- High Performance Computers (HPC): Supercomputers for specialized tasks and compute-intensive applications.
- Server clusters: A number of servers, which are located in the same facility and interconnected to ensure high communication speeds between the individual servers. They can be used for high-performance computing as well as for monolithic applications as the computing resources of the next group.
- Servers: Individual servers for running monolithic applications.
- Desktops: Individual workstations for employees.

In this paper, we will focus solely on individual servers, since the existing computing cloud offerings (e.g. Amazon EC2 service) is aimed at companies requiring additional servers. This also makes the comparison between in-house resources and Grid resources easier, since prices for in-house resources can be easily obtained from various hardware manufacturers.

### 2.3 The Market Structure

The structure of the current Grid market is an oligopoly. We have only a few large providers in the market, such as Amazon.com EC2 [8], Sun Grid [10], and Tsunamic Technologies [11]. Because of this market structure and slight differentiation of their services, they can set their prices such that it maximizes profits.

An alternative market structure would be characterized by complete competition between resource providers, who sell their excess resources on a cost basis. In such a market, prices would be generally lower due to competition and the only price fluctuations would be caused by high demand. The demand for resources is higher than the available resources on the Grid.

In this paper, we will focus on the current market and more specifically, on resources obtained from Amazon.com's EC2 service. This provider was chosen for a number of reasons. Firstly, it started its resource sales shortly after the advent of the GridEcon Project [12]. Secondly, the pricing structure is very well described, making it easy to calculate the prices for different usage scenarios. Thirdly, the provider was chosen for its clear specification of the virtual machines, thus ensuring that equivalent servers for in-house installation can be found easily. Lastly, the Amazon EC2 service was chosen due to its popularity: According to 13, this service is now used by about 60,000 customers and generates a revenue of about $131 million.

## 3   Methodology and Data Collection

To determine in which cases the Grid is cheaper than in-house resources, we will use three companies, called $C_1$, $C_2$ and $C_3$, which require additional resources in the form of a single server. Furthermore, we will assume a linear growth of costs for all companies, i.e. if the price for a single server is P, then the cost for n servers will be n*P. Economies of scale are neglected, since it is difficult to estimate both the point at which they set in and the magnitude of the discount.

The three companies will obtain their resources as follows: Company $C_1$ will purchase its server for in-house installation expensively. Company $C_1$ is assumed to be a small company with little purchasing power. Company $C_1$ has higher costs than company $C_2$ which also obtains its resources for in-house installation. Company $C_2$ is assumed to be bigger and, therefore, has higher purchasing power. Company $C_3$ will purchase resources on the Amazon EC2 service.

Since company $C_3$ uses the Amazon EC2 resources, the resources used by the other companies should be comparable. In particular, we will assume that all servers have at least a 2GHz, single-core CPU, at least 2GB of main memory and a hard disk with at least 200GB storage. To match the requirements, company C3 will purchase another 40GB of storage from Amazon's S3 service 14.

The prices for the resources used by companies $C_1$ and $C_2$ were obtained using the online tools of Dell 15, Gateway 16, and HP 17. Based on the prices found, company

$C_1$ has been assigned a server, which is 25% more expensive than the most expensive model. This price was chosen to ensure that $C_1$ has the highest costs and thus, has the largest incentive for using the Grid. Company $C_2$, on the other hand, pays the average price for all resources, thus ensuring that the price paid by $C_2$ is realistically chosen.

The prices that company C3 faces have been obtained from the Amazon EC2 Web site. The actual prices for all resources are described in chapter 4. Since the Amazon.com cost structure emphasizes usage times, we will assume that a server is used continuously for 30 days. This will be the basis for the comparison in chapter 5.

Since the costs of Amazon.com's EC2 depend on the actual usage of the resources, we have to introduce usage scenarios which take the actual usage into account. We have decided on the four scenarios listed below. These were chosen because they illustrate different generic usage patterns that may be encountered by SMEs using the Grid. These scenarios also illustrate the effect the pricing structure has on the overall Grid cost. The term "upload bandwidth" refers to the data transferred out of the Amazon.com EC2 service and the term "download bandwidth" refers to the data transferred into the service.

- *Scenario 1*: Update Server: The server uses a lot of upload bandwidth and little download bandwidth. Such a server would be used for companies with many customers
- *Scenario 2*: Backup Server: The resource uses a lot of download bandwidth and less upload bandwidth. This type of server would be used for off-site backups for important data.
- *Scenario 3*: Computational Server: The resource uses little bandwidth as it is mainly used for computations.
- *Scenario 4*: Medium-Sized Enterprise Web Server: A server that is barely used but hosts a vital program for the company, such as a Web server.

There is one additional alternative to using commercial Grids: Virtual Private Server (VPS) hosting. There are a number of providers of this type of service; however, the resources offered are geared more towards web hosting rather than computation. This is made obvious by the lack of resource specification when it comes to processor speeds. Instead, customers are attracted by the amount of storage offered and the main memory size.

We have compared a number of VPS providers, such as EMC 18, InMotion 19 and Yourserving.com 20. We have found that the resources most comparable to the ones offered by the Amazon.com EC2 service cost between $90 and $170 per month, depending on the subscription length and the provider. Since these costs are significantly above the costs for in-house resources and since the bandwidth allowances are sometimes severely restricted, we have decided that this type of service is not an adequate replacement for in-house resources or for Amazon.com EC2 resources. Therefore, we have ignored this service type in our analysis.

## 4   Cost Calculation

Under normal circumstances, resources will be written off after three years using normal depreciation rules. This means that every month, a depreciation cost is incurred which is added to the other monthly costs. In our cost calculation, we will simplify matters by assuming that depreciation is not used, but rather that the entire cost of an in-house resource has to be paid upfront. This approach easily demonstrates when Grid usage costs reach or exceed the costs for in-house resources.

In this section, we introduce the costs that the three companies face. In addition, we will calculate the monthly costs for each of the two companies that use in-house resources.

## 4.1 Company $C_1$

As we have stated earlier, company $C_1$ obtains its resources expensively. The following is a list of costs that $C_1$ will have to pay for its resources.

- New server: From our research, we have found that an expensive new server costs no more than $650. We will assume that $C_1$ will have to pay $800, which is more than 25% more than the highest price we found.
- Electricity: According to the Energy Information Administration (EIA) 21, the electricity cost for commercial enterprises is at most 14.65 ct/KWh in the contiguous US. For $C_1$, we will assume an electricity cost of 20.00 ct/KWh. To calculate the monthly electricity usage costs, we need to determine the power consumption for the server. Power supplies usually range between 200W and 500W; since the resource used in our calculation is a server which does not require power-hungry components, we will assume that the power supply is in the middle of this range. Therefore, we chose a 350W power supply which means that the server uses 350W/h. This means that one hour of operating the server

$$costs\ 0.350 KWH * 0.20 \frac{\$}{KWH} = 0.07\$ .$$

In the first month, the company will have to pay both the server and the electricity. The costs are shown in Table 1. For the following months, only the electricity costs must be paid which means that the monthly costs are at $50.40.

Table 1. First month costs for $C_1$

|  | Quantity | Price | Total ($) |
|---|---|---|---|
| **Hardware Purchase** | 1 | 800 $ | 800.00 |
| **Electricity** | 720 h | 0.07 $/h | 50.40 |
|  |  |  |  |
| **Total (first month)** |  |  | 850.40 |

## 4.2 Company $C_2$

A similar calculation has to be performed for company $C_2$. This company is able to obtain its resources and electricity cheaper than company $C_1$, thus having a competitive advantage without the Grid. The costs of $C_2$ are divided as follows:

- New server: The average server price for the Amazon EC2-type server was about $500. We will assume that company $C_2$ paid this price for its resources.

– Electricity: Using the EIA table again, we decided to use a more realistic electricity price. Since a large number of IT companies is located in the California, we decided to the use the average commercial electricity price for 2007 as a reference. At time of writing of this paper, the price was 12.76 ct/KWh, which was rounded to 13 ct/KWh for easier computation. Using an online power calculator 22, we determined that a server would use about 200W. This means that one hour of operating the server costs $0.200 KWH * 0.13 \frac{\$}{KWH} = 0.026\$$.

Using this information, we can now calculate the usage costs for the first month for company $C_2$. This information is given in Table 2.

Table 2. First month costs for $C_2$

|  | Quantity | Price | Total ($) |
|---|---|---|---|
| Hardware Purchase | 1 | 500 $ | 500.00 |
| Electricity | 720 h | 0.026 $/h | 18.72 |
| Total (first month) | | | 518.72 |

We can see that company $C_2$ has much lower costs than company $C_1$. In addition, it should be noted that the monthly costs are less than half of the costs incurred by $C_1$, namely only $18.72.

### 4.3  Company $C_3$

Finally, the costs for company $C_3$ need to be introduced. Since $C_3$ uses the Amazon services EC2 8 and S3 14, the total cost incurred for each month depends on the actual usage. In Table 3, the costs for the various items are shown.

Table 3. Costs for using Amazon.com EC2 and S3

| Item | Cost | Restrictions |
|---|---|---|
| Hourly cost | 0.10 $/CPU-hr | None |
| Data Transfer In | 0.10 $/GB | None |
| Data Transfer Out | 0.18 $/GB | First 10 TB/month |
| Data Transfer Out | 0.16 $/GB | Next 40 TB/month |
| Data Transfer Out | 0.13 $/GB | Over 50TB/month |
| Hard Disk Space | 0.15 $/GB-month | Each GB over 160 GB |

## 5  Cost Comparison of Each Scenario

In this section, we determine the costs incurred by using the Grid in each of the four scenarios and compare it with the cost of in-house purchases. These scenarios are defined in the form of usage characteristics.

## 5.1 Scenario 1: Download Server

The download server uses a large amount of upload bandwidth and very little download bandwidth. As a basis for our calculation, we used some data from the SecondLife Blog 23. We assumed that the download server would be used heavily for four days and then be used less for the remainder of the month. Since the blog referred to 70GB of downloads per hour for almost one day which was then followed by several days of 30GB per day, we decided on the following upload quantities: 70GB for the first day, 30GB for the following 3 days and 3.5GB for the remaining 26 days:

$$70\frac{GB}{hr} * 24hr + 30\frac{GB}{hr} * 24hrs * 3 + 3.5\frac{GB}{hr} * 624hr = 6024GB. \quad (1)$$

The result was rounded to 6000GB for the 30 day period to simplify the calculation. The entire cost for the first 30 days of operating a Grid resource is calculated in Table 4.

**Table 4.** Download server costs

|  | Quantity | Price | Total ($) |
|---|---|---|---|
| **CPU-hrs** | 720 | 0.10 $/h | 72 |
| **Hard Disk Space** | 40 | 0.15 $/GB | 6 |
| **Upload Data** | 6000 | 0.18 $/GB | 1080 |
| **Download Data** | 100 | 0.10 $/GB | 10 |
| **Total** | | | 1168 |

It can be easily seen that the Grid in this case is extremely expensive, mainly due to the high upload costs. Comparing this value with the prices obtained by companies $C_1$ and $C_2$, we can see that $C_3$ pays 125% more than the amount paid by $C_2$ and 37% more than $C_2$.

However, in this scenario, we assume that $C_1$ and $C_2$ have sufficient bandwidth to satisfy the download requirements. Since this amount of bandwidth is usually not available for medium-sized companies, both $C_1$ and $C_2$ would have to purchase additional bandwidth. In order to support 70GB/day in uploads; they would need about 14 lines of an AT&T 6Mbit download line service 24. This costs $60 per line and therefore, the total cost for 14 lines would be $840 per month. Alternatively, a Verizon 15Mbit upload line could be purchased for about $240 per month 25.

In both cases, the monthly cost for companies $C_1$ and $C_2$ would increase. However, in the long-term the Grid would still be more expensive. This can be demonstrated by showing the cost graphs of all companies. In Fig. 1, we show the cost graphs over time if both $C_1$ and $C_2$ use the more expensive Internet access service. If the companies would use the less expensive option the slope of the curve would be even lower.

As we can see, even with the expensive Internet access, the costs of the Grid are higher than for in-house resources after three months. It should be noted however, that the Internet prices require a one-year subscription. If the company requires the high download bandwidth for one month only, then the Grid would be much cheaper, since the Internet connection would cost at least $2900 for a one-year subscription.

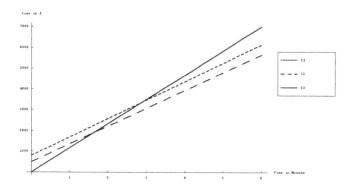

**Fig. 1.** Price comparison with expensive internet

## 5.2 Scenario 2: Backup Server

A backup server has a high number of downloads and a low number of uploads, assuming that the data stored in the backup server is rarely needed. Since the upload bandwidth is not used as much as in the first case, the companies using in-house resources would not have to resort to purchasing additional Internet connectivity. For company $C_3$, we will assume that it performs uploads of 500GB every month. This corresponds to loosing two complete sets of data and making some minor corrections. Furthermore, we assume that the company downloads about 3000GB. This corresponds to backing up 100GB every day and replacing copies after two days. The monthly cost calculation can be seen in Table 5.

**Table 5.** Monthly costs of a backup server

|  | Quantity | Price | Total ($) |
|---|---|---|---|
| **CPU-hrs** | 720 | 0.10 $/h | 72 |
| **Hard Disk Space** | 40 | 0.15 $/GB | 6 |
| **Upload Data** | 500 | 0.18 $/GB | 90 |
| **Download Data** | 3000 | 0.10 $/G | 300 |
| **Total** | | | 468 |

In this case, the Grid is cheaper than in-house resources in the beginning as well. However, as the monthly costs are much higher when using the Grid, company $C_3$ soon pays more than the companies purchasing in-house resources. After about 1.5 months, company $C_2$ will pay less than company $C_3$; after 2.5 months company $C_1$ will pay less than company $C_3$. This development is shown in Fig. 2.

The figure illustrates how much more expensive the Grid is in the long run. However, it should be noted that this calculation is only valid if the company who uses in-house resources can host the new server. If the new server has to be hosted at a different location, which is not owned by the company, or if such a location has to be built or bought, then the Grid will be cheaper, since the costs for the new location will be much higher than the monthly Grid costs.

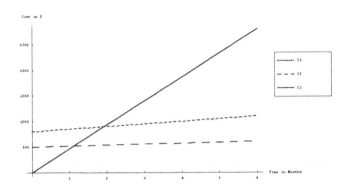

**Fig. 2.** Price comparison for backup servers

### 5.3  Scenario 3: Computational Server

So far, we have only examined resources that require large amounts of bandwidth. However, bandwidth is one of the main cost drivers of the Amazon EC2 service. Therefore, we will now focus on a server which requires less bandwidth and is largely used for compute-intensive tasks. We assume that the server requires 100GB upload and 100GB download, since this server may be part of a computationally large work-flow where the individual subjobs transfer data between each other. The monthly Grid costs are detailed in Table 6.

**Table 6.** Computational Server monthly costs

|  | Quantity | Price ($) | Total ($) |
|---|---|---|---|
| **CPU-hrs** | 720 | 0.10 $/h | 72 |
| **Hard Disk Space** | 40 | 0.15 $/GB | 6 |
| **Upload Data** | 100 GB | 0.18 $/GB | 18 |
| **Download Data** | 100 GB | 0.10 $/GB | 10 |
| **Total** |  |  | 106 |

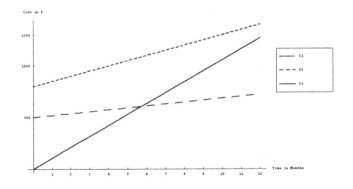

**Fig. 3.** Price comparison for computational servers

Although the expenses for Internet access are still significant, the monthly cost is much lower than that of the previous scenario. Even when using less bandwidth, the Grid is still more expensive than in-house resources in the medium-term. The cost difference between the bandwidth-intensive servers and this server is reflected by the fact that the breakeven point between Grid resources and the in-house resources has been moved to a later date: for company $C_2$, the breakeven is reached after slightly less than six months, for company $C_1$ the breakeven is reached after a little more than 14 months. This is illustrated in Fig. 3 below.

### 5.4 Scenario 4: SME Web Server

In this case, we assume that a small, little-known company uses the Grid to set up a Web server. Since the company is not known, there will be very little traffic on the server, and therefore, these will be almost no bandwidth used. However, since Amazon.com charges the user for each started GB of bandwidth used, we will take some minimal traffic into account. During the first month, we will assume some higher download usage, since the machine image will have to be transferred. For the subsequent months, we will assume that only web traffic will be incurred. For this traffic, we will assume that each web page has a size of about 100 KB and that the ten pages are request per day. This means that about 30MB of data transferred out of Amazon.com.

Furthermore, we will assume that the company will not purchase additional hard disk space on Amazon's S3 service. Only the costs for the subsequent months are shown in Table 7, the costs for the first month are only slightly and can therefore be neglected.

**Table 7.** SME web server first month costs

|  | Quantity | Price | Total ($) |
|---|---|---|---|
| **CPU-hrs** | 720 | 0.10 $/h | 72.00 |
| **Upload Data** | 1 | 0.18 $/GB | 0.18 |
| **Download Data** | 1 | 0.10 $/GB | 0.10 |
| **Total** | | | 72.28 |

These costs are significantly lower than those for of the previous scenarios. Thus, the Grid price in this case is much more competitive than in the previous cases. This fact is illustrated in Fig. 4 below.

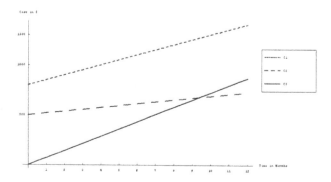

**Fig. 4.** Cost comparison for a SME web server

Compared to the resources bought by company $C_2$, the Grid becomes more expensive after about 9 months. Since company $C_1$ has higher costs, the breakeven will not be reached until about month 35. Therefore, we can conclude that the Grid is cheaper in the medium- to long-term if the in-house resources are very expensive. However, if the in-house resources are cheap, then the Grid is only cheaper in the medium-term.

# 6  Analysis

This section will consist of two parts: in the first part, we will discuss the remaining claim using the information provided in section five. In the second part, we will determine the implications that the analysis results have on the future Grid market.

## 6.1  Claim Analysis

In the introduction to this paper, we have given four claims about Grid economies. Of these we have already addressed three claims, namely the claim that companies have large computational power available at a pay-per-use model, the claim that companies can reduce their in-house staff, and the claim of no cost of ownership.

In the last claim, it was asserted that the Grid reduces the cost for hardware resources. This claim has been the starting point for the detailed cost analysis in the previous section. From our calculations, we can state that using the Grid is not always cheaper than using in-house resources. In fact, every company must determine for itself at which point the Grid becomes too expensive. In general, the cost-effectiveness of the Grid depends on two parameters: the usage duration and the usage intensity. Using these parameters, we can enumerate some cases, in which the Grid usage would be advantageous:

- To cover short, infrequent demand peaks. These peaks should not occur more often than once every several months, or once every year. The peaks last for a few weeks at most.
- If the data backup should be made in a physically different location, which cannot be afforded by a company otherwise.
- Lightly used resources over a short to medium-term period.

Since there are cases, in which the currently existing Grid market is not cheaper than in-house resources, we can conclude that the existence of a Grid economy will not lead to an end of ownership. But, companies will be able to reduce their resource infrastructure by covering infrequent usage peaks with Grid resources. However, regularly occurring peaks must still be provided for using in-house resources. Consequently, there will still be in-house resources that remain idle for some periods of time. Two general statements can be made, based on our calculations:

- *For heavily used resources*: If the resource requirements exceed the in-house capacity for less than two months during a depreciation period of three years, then the current Grid market is cheaper. Therefore, given the current resource prices, the usage duration is the main decision factor for which resources should be bought. If the resource is used for less than 6% of the three years (depreciation period), it should be bought on the Grid.

– *For less heavily used resources*: If the resource requirements exceed the in-house capacity for less than six months during the three year depreciation period, then the current Grid market is cheaper. Therefore, if the resource is used for less than 17% within a period of three years, it should be bought on the Grid.

## 6.2 Implications for the Future Grid

We have determined that companies will still have excess of in-house resources. Therefore, a solution needs to be found as to what can be done with these resources when they are idle. There are two courses of action open to companies: They either turn off the resources to conserve electricity and thereby reduce expenditures, or, they sell the excess resources on a Grid market for commodity goods. The first option is sub-optimal, since only the electricity costs are reduced. Since electricity at this point remains cheap, the savings will be fairly low. The second course of action, on the other hand, will allow companies to recoup most of their costs, including maintenance and depreciation costs. This added income would allow the company to leave its resources switched on while at the same time ensuring that no money is lost due to idle resources.

A Grid market for commodity goods, in which companies can sell their idle resources, would be characterized by intense competition between resource sellers. The advantages of such a market are numerous: Due to the intense competition, the prices would be lower than in the current Grid market, which is a seller's market. This lower price would, in turn, encourage buyers to purchase more Grid resources, since the difference in cost between the Grid resources and their in-house resources is relatively small. It would also lower the barrier of entry to the Grid for new users. In addition, Green IT objectives are met, since resources are used to their full capacity and, therefore, resources rarely sit idle any longer.

A Grid market as described above has to fulfill some requirements: Firstly, it has to sell commodity goods, which are comparable and substitutable. Therefore, the market allows for a competitive market environment. Secondly, the Grid market has to be able to manage many providers and buyers in a single platform. It must be able to handle a large volume of trades and store large amounts of data about these trades. Due to the competition, resource providers will use marginal pricing for their resources to remain competitive. Only congestion which is caused by short term high demand peaks will cause high prices.

For such a market to operate smoothly, some support services need to be developed. These services are especially important for companies that have little or no Grid expertise. This idea has been at the heart of the GridEcon project which has developed a framework to support services for SMEs with little Grid expertise. These services include various brokers (e.g. Risk Broker, Workflow Broker, and Insurance Broker) as well as services such as a Capacity Planning Service. The goal of these services is to simplify the transition to the Grid and its usage as much as possible.

## 7 Conclusion

In this paper, we have discussed four claims about Grid computing, and analyzed one in detail. We have found that the Grid is not always cheaper than in-house resources. Since, at present, only few Grid resource providers exist in the market, they can easily generate profits. Therefore, the effects of the economies of scale are negated. Therefore, any company considering the use of Grid resources should carefully calculate whether the Grid is actually cheaper than in-house resources.

From the analysis of the costs of the current Grid (which is a set of data centers of servers), we have determined that the existence of a Grid will not lead to an end of ownership but will lead to a decrease in over-provisioning of computing resources. We expect that rare demand peaks will be covered using Grid resources.

Since, under the current market structure, companies still have to over-provision, they will have to face the question of what to do with idle resources. Selling these resources on a Grid market is the best option, since all incurred costs can be recouped. If many companies sell their idle resources on a market, this will lead to strong competition, which will force prices to remain low unless there is a severe resource shortage. The low prices will attract more buyers, thereby increasing supply and demand. During times of high demand, companies may even be able to make small profits due to the increased prices they can charge.

The workings of this competitive market need to be studied further, with special attention paid to price setting, the price development over time, the actions taken by resource sellers and buyers, and the effects these actions have on the market. This also leads to the question of how companies will act and react to price fluctuations.

In addition, the analysis performed in this paper can also be repeated for other resource types, such as differentiated goods. The results could form the basis for a Grid markets for differentiated goods.

# References

1. Southern Partnership for Advanced Computational Infrastructures (SPACI),
   http://www.spaci.it/content.php?loc=projects&pg=prj.php&cat=gm&id=10
2. Yeo, C.S., Buyya, R., Assunção, M.D., Yu, J., Sulistio, A., Venugopal, S., Placek, M.: Utility Computing on Global Grids. In: Bidgoli, H. (ed.) The Handbook of Computer Networks, ch. 143. John Wiley & Sons, New York (2007)
3. Fujitsu Siemens Computers, http://www.fujitsu-siemens.it/it_trends/grid_computing.html
4. Altmann, J., Courboubetis, C., Darlington, J., Cohen, J.: GridEcon – The Economic-Enhanced Next-Generation Internet. In: Veit, D.J., Altmann, J. (eds.) GECON 2007. LNCS, vol. 4685, pp. 188–193. Springer, Heidelberg (2007)
5. Altmann, J., Ion, M., Mohammed, A.A.B.: Taxonomy of Grid Business Models. In: Veit, D.J., Altmann, J. (eds.) GECON 2007. LNCS, vol. 4685, pp. 29–43. Springer, Heidelberg (2007)
6. XenSource, Inc., http://xen.org
7. VMware, Inc., http://www.vmware.com
8. Amazon Elastic Compute Cloud (Amazon EC2),
   http://www.amazon.com/gp/browse.html?node=20159001
9. Enterprise – SME Definition,
   http://ec.europa.eu/enterprise/enterprise_policy/sme_definition/index_en.htm
10. Sun Grid, http://www.sun.com/service/sungrid/index.jsp

11. Tsunamic Technologies Inc., `http://www.clusterondemand.com`
12. GridEcon, `http://www.gridecon.eu`
13. Schonfeld, E.: Who Are The Biggest Users of Amazon Web Services? It's Not Startups., `http://www.techcrunch.com/2008/04/21/who-are-the-biggest-users-of-amazon-web-services-its-not-startups`
14. Amazon Simple Storage Service (Amazon S3), `http://www.amazon.com/gp/browse.html?node=16427261`
15. Dell, `http://www.dell.com`
16. Gateway, Inc., `http://www.gateway.com`
17. Hewlett-Packard Development Company, L.P., `http://www.hp.com`
18. EMC Telecom Corporation, `http://www.emcwebhosting.com/vps_hosting_extreme_linux.php`
19. InMotion Hosting, Inc., `http://www.inmotionhosting.com/vps_hosting.html`
20. Yourserving.com, `http://yourserving.com/vps_server`
21. Energy Information Administration, Average Retail Price of Electricity to Ultimate Customers by End-Use Sector, by State, `http://www.eia.doe.gov/cneaf/electricity/epm/table5_6_b.html`
22. Journey Systems, LLC., Power Calculator, `http://www.journeysystems.com/?powercalc`
23. Linden Research, Inc., SecondLife Blog, `http://blog.secondlife.com/2006/10/26/amazon-s3-for-the-win`
24. AT&T, `https://swot.sbc.com/swot/dslMassMarketCatalog.do?do=dslProductPage&offerId=90027&serviceType=DYNAMICIP`
25. Verizon, `http://www22.verizon.com/content/businessfios/packagesandprices/packagesandprices.htm`

# Business Relationships in Grid Workflows

Ioannis Papagiannis, Dimosthenis Kyriazis, Magdalini Kardara,
Vassiliki Andronikou, and Theodora Varvarigou

Dept. of Electrical and Computer Engineering, National Technical University of Athens,
9, Heroon Polytechniou Str, 15773 Athens, Greece
el03272@mail.ntua.gr,
{dkyr,mkardara,vandro,dora}@telecom.ntua.gr

**Abstract.** Although initially designed to cover the needs of computationally-intensive applications, Grid technology of nowadays aims at providing an infrastructure that can also serve the needs of the business domain. Taking into consideration that the available service providers may have business / strategic relationships, this paper focuses on describing an approach for modeling these relationships. Furthermore and since these relationships may affect the parameters regarding the offered Quality of Service (QoS) level, we present a metric for characterizing a service providers "friendliness". The latter can be used to promote the most positively influential providers and put aside those with a negative influence during a QoS-based selection process in Grid workflow management systems.

**Keywords:** Grid Computing, Quality of Service, Business Relationships, Workflows.

## 1 Introduction

Although initially designed to cover the computational needs of high performance applications [1], [2], Grid technology of nowadays aims at providing the infrastructure for the general business domain. Advanced infrastructure requirements combined with innate business goal for lower costs have driven key business sectors such as multimedia, engineering, gaming, environmental science, among others towards adopting Grid solutions into their business. Furthermore, complex application workflows are emerging along with specification languages used to enable the workflow description and execution on Grid environments. The final success of this business orientation of Grid technology however will primarily depend on its real adopters; the end users whose main demand refers to the offered level of quality.

Since workflow is a wide concept in technology, the terminology regarding workflow definitions that is used in the remainder of this paper is defined. Regarding the general definition, Workflow Management Coalition (WfMC) provides the following definition [3]: "Workflow is the automation of a business process, in whole or part, during which documents, information or tasks are passed from one participant to another for action, according to a set of procedural rules". A Workflow Model / Specification is used to define a workflow both in task and structure level. There are

J. Altmann, D. Neumann, and T. Fahringer (Eds.): GECON 2008, LNCS 5206, pp. 28–40, 2008.

two types of workflows, namely Abstract and Concrete [4], [5] while concrete work-flows are also referred to as executable workflows in some literature [6]. In an abstract model, the tasks are described in an abstract form without referring to specific Grid resources for task execution since it provides the ability to the users to define workflows in a flexible way, isolating execution details. Furthermore, an abstract model provides only service semantic information on how the workflow has been composed and therefore the sharing of workflow descriptions between Grid users is feasible, which is of major importance for the participants of Virtual Organizations (VOs) [1]. Abstract models can be composed with systems like the one presented in [7]. In the concrete model, the tasks of the workflow bind to specific resources and therefore this model provides service semantic and execution information on how the workflow has been composed both for the service instances and for the overall composition (e.g. dataflow bindings, control flow structures).

This shift from science Grids to business Grids in parallel with the replacement of simple job executions to complex workflow management [3] and enactment in Grids resulted in advanced requirements in the field of workflow mapping with regard to QoS metrics / resources' special attributes (e.g. performance profile). Based on the fact that each workflow contains processes that can be executed from a set of service providers / instances (candidates), which are annotated with QoS information, workflow mapping refers to the mapping of the aforementioned workflow processes to Grid provided services taking into account the QoS metrics in order to provide a selection of candidates guaranteeing end-to-end QoS for the submitted workflow. In the bibliography, it is referred as Workflow QoS Constraints and remains one of the key factors in a Grid Workflow Management System and more specifically in the Workflow Design element [8].

As presented in the Related Work section of this paper, there are many approaches that address the QoS issue in Grid environments while in one of our previous works [9] we have presented in detail a QoS-aware workflow mapping mechanism. However, the business relationships between the service providers are not taken into consideration during the selection process. In greater detail, the service providers may have business relationships that can be Cooperating, non-Cooperating or even Antagonistic, Cheating, or Malicious. These relationships affect the workflow mapping since the QoS metrics of a service provider may change based on a selection of another provider. In many occasions, a service provider may alter his offered services' QoS values based on the selection of another service provider depending on their business relationships.

What we discuss and present later on is a modeling of the business relationships within Grid workflows and an approach that provides a metric for defining a service provider's "friendliness" based on the relationships that a service provider has with others. The aforementioned metric can be used by QoS-based selection mechanisms to take into account business relationships during the selection process and meet the user's QoS requirements.

The remainder of the paper is structured as follows. Section 2 presents related work in the field of QoS-based workflow management in Grids. Section 3 introduces the concept of Business Relationships in workflows and provides a modeling approach for them while a proposal for defining a metric to characterize a service provider's friendliness, is included thereafter in Section 4. Finally, Section 5 concludes with a discussion on future research and potentials for the current study.

## 2  Related Work

There are various approaches for QoS-based workflow management in Grid environments. In some cases, the selection process is based on the Service Level Agreement (SLA) negotiation process, as discussed in [11], [12] and [13]. The end-user's constraints and preferences are passed to several service providers through the functionality offered by a broker (usually the SLA Management Service) for allocating the appropriate service providers. The Globus Architecture for Reservation and Allocation (GARA) [14] addresses QoS at the level of facilitating and providing basic mechanisms for QoS support, namely resource configuration, discovery, selection, and allocation. Outcomes of the research on QoS-based selection for workflows are also presented in [15], [16] and [17]. The first one proposes an algorithm that minimizes cost in the time constraint while the second work presents a system that is able to meet pre-defined QoS requirements during the workflow mapping process. Authors of [17] discuss a system that based on event condition action rules, maps workflow processes to Grid resources taking into account QoS information. A workflow QoS specification and methods to predict, analyze and monitor QoS are presented in [18] and [19]. The work is focused on the creation of QoS estimates and the QoS computation for specific metrics – time, cost, fidelity and reliability with the use of two methods: analysis and simulation. In this case, the parameters are handled one by one similar to [15] and [20] and not in a combined way while the overall estimation emerges from the individual tasks.

Authors in [22] present the ASKALON tool which comprises four components along with a service repository to support performance-oriented development of parallel and distributed (Grid) applications. Literatures [23], [24] and [25] discuss the ICENI environment in which a graph based language is used to annotate component behaviors and perform optimizations based on the estimated execution times and resource sharing. The gathered performance information is taken into account during the resource selection while the mapping of work onto resources through a workflow enabled scheduler (which is able to make use of performance information) is also supported. Moreover, a three-layered negotiation protocol for advance reservation of the Grid resources and a mechanism that optimizes resource utilization and QoS constraints for agreement enforcement is presented in [26].

An interesting work for workflow mapping based on SLAs is discussed in [27]. The authors present a mechanism for assigning sub-jobs of a workflow to Grid resources in a way that meets the user's deadline and provides the cheapest solution. Moreover, an agent-based method for service composition is described in [28], where an enhanced service composition model allows for service requestors, providers and brokers to profit from the dynamic composition of Grid resources and services into executable workflows.

The difference between the systems presented in this section and our proposed scheme lies on the fact that while the ones presented here yield very good results for QoS-based selection, they consider as QoS parameters during the selection process either the parameters published by the service providers (via SLAs) or those obtained from monitoring tools over the resources. However, they do not tackle an issue that may affect the selection process and refers to changes in the QoS values due to business relationships. This kind of information cannot be obtained with monitoring tools since these work during the execution of a process whilst algorithms and methods have not been published for QoS-based selection with a priori knowledge of the effects of service providers' business relationships.

# 3  Business Relationships

Following, we describe an approach for modeling the business relationships and take into account this information during the QoS-based selection for Grid workflows.

## 3.1  Modeling Business Relationships

Firstly, one of the issues that has to be resolved is how the strategic relationships are modeled on the service provider's space. The proposed approach looks at strategic relationships from an external perspective as it focuses on how the selection of a provider affects other providers. As a result, we model each strategic relationship as a directed edge on the problem's graph from a service provider A to a service provider B. The source of the edge is the provider that stimulates the relationship and the destination is the provider that alters its service parameters in response to the selection of the source.

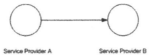

Service Provider A            Service Provider B

**Fig. 1.** A Strategic relationship between two service providers

In the example presented on the above figure (Fig. 1), service provider A triggers a change to provider B's QoS parameters and thus, we have an edge from node A to node B. In the case that the selection of provider B changes the parameters of provider A we require the existence of a second edge with the opposite direction.

The above modeling is characterized "external" as it puts the stimulator instead of the actual affected node in the center of attention. On the whole service instances space, the instances that affect a great number of other instances will appear as the source of numerous vectors and as a result their total effect on other instances can be measured. The opposite approach, deriving all edges from the affected service instance, has the disadvantage of taking the focus off the influential service instances and it is not suitable for a forward-looking heuristic algorithm.

A constraint that needs to be underlined is that all business relationships should reference service providers from different workflow processes. A business relationship, either positive or negative, from a service provider to another on the same workflow process is not feasible as those two services will never be selected together on the final concrete workflow.

## 3.2  Measuring a Strategic Relationship's Influence

In order to design a function that characterizes a service instance's influence, we need to have a way to express the influence of a specific strategic relationship. In this section we propose a metric that rates that influence from various perspectives in an effort to express all of its aspects, relative and absolute. This metric may be applied to the QoS parameters of each service instance and as part of this study we consider as initial representative parameters the following: Cost, Execution Time and Availability. Based on that, the metric should tackle three (3) distinct influence aspects: the influence on cost, on execution time and on service availability. These metrics are all derived from the following equations.

We denote:

$$SRI_{cost/time/availabilty}(\text{trigger, affected, levels}) \qquad (1)$$

as a metric for a Strategic Relationship's Influence, where: *trigger* refers to the service provider that triggers a strategic relationship, *affected* refers to the service provider that alters its QoS parameters, and *levels* refers to the set of processes that we measure the influence of the relationship on.

The SRI metric consists of two addends, each one representing two distinct parts of a relationship's influence:

$$SRI(trigger, affected, levels) = Immediate\ Influence(trigger, affected) + \\ Future\ Influence(affected, levels) \qquad (2)$$

### 3.3  A Strategic Relationship's Immediate Influence

The first addend that we define here is the *Immediate Influence*. This influence is defined as the actual advantage or disadvantage that a service provider gains by selecting the triggering provider. This Immediate Influence is measured in terms of the QoS parameters effect on the affected provider. The Immediate Influence needs not only to take account of the actual QoS parameters changes but also to express the potential of the original values.

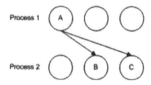

**Fig. 2.** Calculating the Immediate Influence of different Strategic Relationships

In the above example (Fig. 2), service provider A influences both service providers B and C. Since we want to measure each relationship's Immediate Influence, the first issue we need to take account of is how much node B or C alters their QoS parameters. Regarding service provider A, its QoS parameters are not altered but based on the strategic relationships a value that will characterize its "friendliness" will be calculated (as described in Section 4 of this paper). The service providers for which their QoS parameters' values may change are the ones that have "incoming" relationships, in Fig. 2 these are the providers B and C.

Moreover, a simple improvement measure is not enough as it might provide a false perception of a relationship's actual influence. In the above example, the two relationships may provide a similar amount of benefit to both providers (B and C) and thus the relationships seem equally influential. In fact, provider C may be an extremely inefficient provider and thus the influence on him is actually unimportant compared to the influence on an already efficient provider, as B may be.

From the above, we denote *I.I.*(trigger, affected) as the Immediate Influence of a specific strategic relationship and we have:

$$II_{\frac{cost}{time}} = \frac{Old\ Value - New\ Value}{Old\ Value}\, e^{Slope \frac{Max\ Value - Old\ Value}{Max\ Value - Min\ Value}} \tag{3}$$

and

$$II_{availability} = \frac{New\ Value - Old\ Value}{Old\ Value}\, e^{Slope \frac{Old\ Value - Min\ Value}{Max\ Value - Min\ Value}} \tag{4}$$

where: *Value* is the corresponding QoS parameter's value of the affected service provider: *OldValue* refers to the value of a parameter without taking into account a business relationship while *NewValue* is the one that emerges from such a relationship; and *Minimum* and *Maximum* values are referring to the corresponding QoS parameter's values inside a service process.

The first fractional factor represents the relational change in the parameter's value. The better the change the bigger the benefit from this strategic relationship. The second factor has a double role. The first one is to amplify the I.I. values of those service providers that already were close to the best of their process. The second is to express the user's interest on that specific parameter by multiplying with a slope factor that will be better clarified later on. The differentiation between cost/time and availability derives from the fact that better availability values are the largest ones, in contrast to what happens with cost and time.

The values that the I.I. metric has are positive when the service parameter is improved by the strategic relationship and negative otherwise. In case that there are no changes, the I.I. becomes zero. Additionally, the changes on critical service providers will be represented by large absolute I.I. values, either positive or negative.

### 3.4  A Strategic Relationship's Future Influence

As seen in the previous section, when calculating a SRI, the first and most basic influence that we must take account of is the Immediate one. Unluckily, this influence alone is not enough to capture a relationship's effect to the whole set of processes.

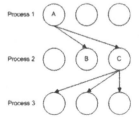

**Fig. 3.** A strategic relationship with Future Influence

The above figure adds to Figure 2 a new process with new service providers. We still want to calculate the SRI of both relationships from node A to nodes B and C. Let's assume that B and C are two identical service provider that improve their parameters in the exact same way. As a result, their I.I. values will be identical. On a second look on the whole graph, we can see that the relationship from A to C is actually better than the relationship from A to B, not because of immediate improvements but in terms of future benefit. If all of the providers in process 3 improve their QoS parameters then the SRI in the A-C relationship must be higher than the A-B one. A Strategic Relationship's Future Influence tries to capture that exact effect.

The first issue we must take into account while calculating a relationship's Future Influence is which future relationships we should take into account.

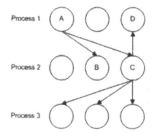

**Fig. 4.** An indifferent relationship on Future Influence calculation

Figure 4 represents the same process space as Figure 3 but also adds a new relationship from provider C to provider D. The question is: when calculating the *Future Influence* of the relationship A-C should the relationship C-D be taken into consideration? The answer is no. The Future Influence of the A-C relationship wants to capture the further potential of a relationship, in case that the source provider is actually selected. As a consequence, the fact that the provider C can actually improve another provider on process 1 is actually indifferent to relationship A-C as relationship A-C requires that provider A is selected. Additionally, any relationships that service provider C has with other process levels where a selection is finalized are also discarded in the calculation as they cannot influence the selection process.

This Future Influence is not restricted to a single level. On the contrary, any of the providers in process 3 may have interesting influence that should be taken into consideration. Those relationships in further levels are of course of diminishing interest and their effect should be reduced gradually. Additionally, when calculating the future effects on further levels, all provider choices in processes towards them should be considered finalized. In the above example, let's assume that any of the providers in process 3 has strategic relationships with some of providers in processes 1-2 and in a new process 4. We still are counting the SRI of relationship A-C. When we will be calculating the Future Influence of providers in process 3, choices in processes 1 and 2 are considered finalized and we should only take care of those relationships from process 3 towards process 4. The above restrictions guarantee that the calculation of the Future Influence will finalize after as many iterations as the current active processes.

Another interesting issue that arises from the calculation of a strategic relationship's Future Influence is how to actually summarize a provider's Future Influence with multiple future relations. In the above example, that exact issue appears on provider C when calculating the SRI of relationship A-C. That provider has 3 strategic relationships of interest; some of which may be beneficial while others may prove harmful. Moreover, in a wider example, a small number of relationships may be very harmful while the vast majority is beneficial. If such is the case, the overall Future Influence should not be overwhelmed by the minority of harmful relationships but should reflect the fact that relationships are mostly beneficial.

Finally, one issue remains that concerns the actual weight of Future Influence compared to Immediate Influence in a strategic relationship. On the previous example, let's assume that providers B and C have equal initial QoS parameters. Moreover, the strategic relationship A-B is greatly beneficial to provider B while the relationship A-C does nothing but little changes to provider C. The problem that arises is how to compare a relationship like A-B with large Immediate Influence to a relationship like A-C with little Immediate but great Future Influence. In other words, the problem that arises is when Future Influence is important enough to actually be compared to the Immediate one. The answer to this problem derives from the observation that the more choices there are in the future processes, the harder it should be to create a, comparable to Immediate, Future Influence. On the other hand, the more affected services there are in a given set of possible relations, the more Future Influence becomes important.

Denoting F.I.(affected, levels) as the Future Influence of an affected node towards a set of process levels that we are measuring it on, we have:

$$F.I.(affected, levels) =$$

$$\frac{1}{\frac{Num[remLevels]}{2}} \sum_{\forall n \in adj(affected,remLevels)} \left( F_{balancing} SRI(affected, n, remLevels) \right) \quad (5)$$

$$F_{balancing} = \begin{cases} F_{bpositive}, & SRI(affected, n, remLevels) > 0 \\ F_{bnegative}, & SRI(affected, n, remLevels) < 0 \end{cases} \quad (6)$$

$$F_{bpositive} = \frac{Num[c=adj(affected,remLevels):SRI(affected,c,remLevels>0)]}{Num[adj(affected,remLevels)]} \quad (7)$$

$$F_{bnegative} = \frac{Num[c=adj(affected,remLevels):SRI(affected,c,remLevels<0)]}{Num[adj(affected,remLevels)]} \quad (8)$$

where: remLevels is the set (levels-level(affected)) that represents the remaining process levels that F.I. is calculated on, Num[] returns the current number of service providers in a given set of processes, and adj(affected,remLevels) is the set of adjacents to the affected node inside a set of processes.

The above equations describe the calculation of a given relationship's Future Influence. The first thing to notice is that F.I. is a recursive procedure that requires the calculation of all future relationship's SRIs. This calculation is bounded inside the affected node's relationships to process levels that have not already been visited. As the algorithm visits various levels, each one of them is considered visited and the calculation eventually finalizes.

Addition of the SRIs from affected providers' future relationships is preceded by balancing the results. This step uses two balancing Factors, *Fbpositive*, *Fbnegative* and multiplies accordingly each positive or negative SRI. These factors represent the F.I. balance between positive and negative F.I.s and amplifies those that outvote. These factors can diminish the minority's relationships Future Influence, and thus the metric is not affected by isolated, possibly malevolent, relationships. To achieve this, Fbalancing is calculated as the number of each category's (negative or positive) relationships divided by the total number of relationships.

After balancing each subsequent SRI, the metric adds those results and the final outcome is divided by a new balancing factor. As described previously, this balancing factor actually represents the relation between each relationship's Immediate and Future Influences. By dividing with the half size of still existing provider choices, we decrease greatly the F.I.'s importance. This decrease is greater when we are making choices for the first processes but gets smaller as the process space is reduced. In other words, when we are making early Influence calculations we are primarily interested in Immediate gains, while, when the choices diminish, Future Influence becomes more and more important. From another perspective, this division factor represents the exact number of future relationships required to surplus the Immediate Influence. Thus, better results appear when this number is equal to half the possible future relationships and that is the reason behind division by two.

## 4  Friendliness of a Service Provider

Up until now, we have created a metric that represents the true value of a business relationship. That metric that was called S.R.I. has a wide set of beneficial properties that we will take advantage of in order to create a well performing heuristic function that defines the friendliness of a service provider based on the business relationships. This heuristic function takes the focus of strategic relationships and puts it on service providers themselves. Its main goal is to utilize the properties of each provider's strategic relationships and characterize the provider according to his potential for future workflow execution benefit. This new metric that will be calculated for every service provider is called *Service Provider Friendliness* (S.P.F.) and we will outline some of its interesting properties.

The first interesting issue that should be resolved when calculating a SPF is which strategic relationships we should take into account.

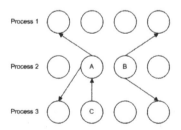

**Fig. 5.** Calculating the SPF for service providers A and B

In the example in Figure 5 we want to calculate a metric that will outline which of providers A and B is more appropriate for selection in process 2. This metric that is called SPF should consider the SRIs of each provider's strategic relationships in order to calculate a result. In the above example let's assume that A and B provide similar QoS parameters with provider B being overall slightly better. Providers A and B influence two other providers which are identical and are influenced in the exact same manner from A and B. Additionally, provider A can be influenced from provider C. The problem here is which provider, A or B, is preferable. If we take into account the relationship C-A we can say that provider A is actually the better future choice. But if we look closer, provider B can actually give better QoS parameters now and provide equal future expansion potential. As the algorithm runs next on process level 3, no one can guarantee that provider C will make its final choice there as the SRI metric is indifferent of the triggering provider's parameters. So we cannot add value to provider A and thus, provider B should be the preferable choice on process 2. To summarize, the calculation of Service Provider Friendliness should be unaware of any strategic relationships that can influence this provider and should only take account of providers that can be influenced.

Another interesting issue that reappears on SPF as it did in SRI is how we can tackle providers with mixed type influences.

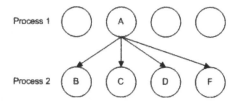

**Fig. 6.** Handling mixed types of Strategic Relationships

In the above figure, provider A influences all providers in process 2, with SRIs -10, 3, 3, 3 accordingly. Provider A actually has good future strategic potential, even though it can be destroyed by a single negative one. In order to minimize the minority's effect, balancing factors need to be used again that should take account of how positive and negative influences are distributed.

Considering those issues, we denote SPF as Service Provider Friendliness and we have:

$$SPF_{cost|time|availability}(provider, levels) =$$

$$\frac{\sum_{levels}(Affected\ Nodes * \overline{SRI}_{cost|time|availability}(provider) * F_{balancing})}{Num[levels]} \quad (9)$$

$$F_{balancing} = \begin{cases} F_{bpositive}, & SRI(provider) > 0 \\ F_{bnegative}, & SRI(provider) < 0 \end{cases} \quad (10)$$

$$F_{bpositive} = \frac{Num[c=adj(provider,curLevel):SRI(provider)>0]}{Num[adj(provider,curLevel)]} \quad (11)$$

$$F_{bnegative} = \frac{Num[c=adj(provider,curLevel):SRI(provider)<0]}{Num[adj(provider,curLevel)]} \qquad (12)$$

where: *provider* is the service provider we are calculating the SPF for, *levels* is the set of process levels that we are calculating the SPF on, *curLevel* is the current process level from the given set of levels, *Affected Nodes* is the number of adjacent to provider nodes in the current level, Mean *SRI* is the arithmetic mean of SRIs for the strategic relationships that are triggered from provider and affect other service providers only in the current level, and the Balancing Factors are calculated as in F.I. and they count SRI types per level.

To calculate the SPF for a service provider, each provider's strategic relationships are separated on a per process basis. For each process, we balance each relationship's SRI and we calculate the arithmetic mean of the results. In order to express that more relationships with the same mean SRI are better than less, we multiply with the actual number of the affected services per process. After we have completed the calculation for each affected process level, the final result is the average mean of the per process results.

Examples of situations where this work may be applied refer to various business cases in which the service providers may have business relationships. A first example of such a business case can be found at the mobile telephony world. The service providers have business relationships: Antagonistic in the same country and Cooperating for different countries for the roaming service. Another example refers to the travel agencies since nowadays many airline companies have strategic relationships with hotels, car rental companies etc.

The above metric (SPF) is a heuristic function that can be used from QoS-based selection mechanisms for workflows in order to characterize each provider's future strategic potential. It should be calculated for each QoS parameter type (in this study: availability, cost and execution time). This metric includes the necessary characteristics as it takes advantage of various relationship parameters in a consistent way and it is reliable enough to avoid possible malevolent relationships between antagonistic service providers.

## 5 Conclusions

In this paper we have presented an approach for modeling business / strategic relationships in Grid workflows and formulated an appropriate metric that can be used to promote the most positively influential service providers and put aside those with a negative influence during a QoS-based selection process. The latter is of major importance since taking into account this metric allows:

- The definition of a concrete workflow that meets the user's cost constraints; which might not be feasible without considering the business relationships.
- The definition of a concrete workflow offering higher level of end-to-end QoS since the cost difference obtained due to the business relationships of the service providers may be used to select service instances with higher QoS values of other parameters (e.g. lower execution time).

Notwithstanding, it is within our future plans to attempt to include the metrics proposed in this paper within a QoS-based selection mechanism for the definition of concrete workflows. Furthermore, within a business Grid, it is general accepted that each trading must be legalized with a contract, the SLA. The service provider's friendliness is not included in the SLAs but is calculated and doesn't affect the compensation terms / fines in the cases of QoS violations. A topic of future research would be to take into account a service provider's friendliness in the aforementioned cases. Concluding, Grids have not yet adopted an effective scheme that will facilitate end-to-end QoS provisioning taking into consideration possible business relationships between the service providers. In that rationale, we have shown the importance of a metric that characterises the "friendliness" of a provider, the use of which is expected to significantly increase the effort to address in a dynamic way the business relationships in Grid workflows.

# References

1. Foster, I., Kesselman, C., Tuecke, S.: The Anatomy of the Grid: Enabling Scalable Virtual Organizations. International Journal Supercomputer Applications 15(3) (2001)
2. Leinberger, W., Kumar, V.: Information Power Grid: The new frontier in parallel computing? IEEE Concur. 7(4), 75–84 (1999)
3. Workflow Management Coalition, Terminology & Glossary, Document Number WFMC-TC-1011, Issues 3.0 (February 1999)
4. Deelman, E., Blythe, J., Gil, Y., Kesselman, C.: Workflow Management in GriPhyN, The Grid Resource Management. Kluwer, Netherlands (2003)
5. Deelman, E., Blythe, J., Gil, Y., Kesselman, C., Mehta, G., Patil, S., Su, M.H., Vahi, K., Livny, M.: Pegasus: Mapping Scientific Workflow onto the Grid. In: Across Grids Conference 2004, Nicosia, Cyprus (2004)
6. Ludäscher, B., Altintas, I., Gupta, A.: Compiling Abstract Scientific Workflows into Web Service Workflows. In: 15th International Conference on Scientific and Statistical Database Management, Cambridge, Massachusetts, USA, July 09-11, pp. 241–244. IEEE CS Press, Los Alamitos (2003)
7. Bubak, M., Gubała, T., Kapałka, M., Malawski, M., Rycerz, K.: Workflow composer and service registry for grid applications. Future Generation Computer Systems 21(1), 79–86 (2005)
8. Yu, J., Buyya, R.: A Taxonomy of Workflow Management Systems for Grid Computing. Journal of Grid Computing 3(3 - 4), 171–200 (2005)
9. Kyriazis, D., Tserpes, K., Menychtas, A., Litke, A., Varvarigou, T.: An innovative Workflow Mapping Mechanism for Grids in the frame of Quality of Service. Future Generation Computer Systems (2007)
10. Spooner, D.P., Cao, J., Jarvis, S.A., He, L., Nudd, G.R.: Performance-aware Workflow Management for Grid Computing. The Computer Journal (2004)
11. Bochmann, G., Hafid, A.: Some Principles for Quality of Service Management, Technical report, Universite de Montreal (1996)
12. Al-Ali, R.J., Amin, K., von Laszewski, G., Rana, O.F., Walker, D.W., Hategan, M., Zaluzec, N.J.: Analysis and Provision of QoS for Distributed Grid Applications. Journal of Grid Computing, 163–182 (2004)
13. Padgett, J., Djemame, K., Dew, P.: Grid-based SLA Management. LNCS, pp. 1282–1291. Springer, Heidelberg (2005)

14. Foster, I., Kesselman, C., Lee, C., Lindell, B., Nahrstedt, K., Roy, A.: A Distributed Resource Management Architecture that Supports Advance Reservation and Co-Allocation. In: Proceedings of the International Workshop on QoS, pp. 27–36 (1999)
15. Yu, J., Buyya, R., Tham, C.K.: QoS-based Scheduling of Workflow Applications on Service Grids., Technical Report, GRIDS-TR-2005-8, Grid Computing and Distributed Systems Laboratory, University of Melbourne, Australia (2005)
16. Guo, L., McGough, A.S., Akram, A., Colling, D., Martyniak, J., Krznaric, M.: QoS for Service Based Workflow on Grid. In: Proceedings of UK e-Science 2007 All Hands Meeting, Nottingham, UK (2007)
17. Khanli, L.M., Analoui, M.: QoS-based Scheduling of Workflow Applications on Grids. In: International Conference on Advances in Computer Science and Technology, Phuket, Thailand (2007)
18. Cardoso, J., Sheth, A., Miller, J.: Workflow Quality of Service. In: Proceedings of the International Conference on Enterprise Integration and Modeling Technology and International Enterprise Modeling Conference (ICEIMT/IEMC 2002). Kluwer Publishers, Dordrecht (2002)
19. Cardoso, J., Miller, J., Sheth, A., Arnold, J.: Modeling Quality of Service for Workflows and Web Service Processes., Technical Report, LSDIS Lab, Department of Computer Science University of Georgia (2002)
20. Buyya, R., Abramson, D., Venugopal, S.: The Grid Economy. Proceedings of the IEEE 93(3), 698–714 (2005)
21. Buyya, R., Murshed, M., Abramson, D.: A Deadline and Budget Constrained Cost-Time Optimization Algorithm for Scheduling Task Farming Applications on Global Grids. In: Proceedings of the 2002 International Conference on Parallel and Distributed Processing Techniques and Applications(PDPTA7 2002) (2002)
22. Fahringer, T., Jugravu, A., Pllana, S., Prodan, R., Seragiotto Jr, C., Truong, H.L.: ASKALON: a tool set for cluster and Grid computing. Concurrency and Computation: Practice and Experience 17(2-4), 143–169 (2005)
23. Mayer, A., McGough, S., Furmento, N., Lee, W., Newhouse, S., Darlington, J.: ICENI Dataflow and Workflow: Composition and Scheduling in Space and Time. In: UK e-Science All Hands Meeting, Nottingham, UK, pp. 894–900. IOP Publishing Ltd., Bristol (2003)
24. McGough, S., Young, L., Afzal, A., Newhouse, S., Darlington, J.: Performance Architecture within ICENI. In: UK e-Science All Hands Meeting, Nottingham, UK, pp. 906–911. IOP Publishing Ltd., Bristol (2004)
25. McGough, S., Young, L., Afzal, A., Newhouse, S., Darlington, J.: Workflow Enactment in ICENI. In: UK e-Science All Hands Meeting, Nottingham, UK, pp. 894–900. IOP Publishing Ltd., Bristol (2004)
26. Siddiqui, M., Villazon, A., Fahringer, T.: Grid capacity planning with negotiation-based advance reservation for optimized QoS. In: Proceedings of the 2006 ACM/IEEE Conference on SuperComputing SC (2006)
27. Quan, M.D.: Mapping heavy Communication Workfows onto Grid Resources within SLA Context. In: Proceedings of the Second International Conference on High Performance Computing and Communications (HPCC 2006), Munich, Germany (2006)
28. Curcin, V., Ghanem, M., Guo, Y., Stathis, K., Toni, F.: Building next generation Service-Oriented Architectures using argumentation agents. In: Proceedings of the 3rd International Conference on Grid Services Engineering and Management (GSEM 2006), Erfurt, Germany, September, 2006. Lecture Notes in Informatics, p. 88 (2006)

# The Power of Preemption in Economic Online Markets*

Lior Amar[1], Ahuva Mu'alem[2], and Jochen Stößer[3]

[1] Institute of Computer Science, The Hebrew University of Jerusalem,
Jerusalem, 91904 Israel
lior@cs.huji.ac.il
[2] Social and Information Sciences Laboratory (SISL), California Institute of
Technology, 1200 E. California Blvd., Pasadena, CA 91125, USA
ahumu@yahoo.com
[3] Institute of Information Systems and Management (IISM),
Universität Karlsruhe (TH), Englerstr. 14, 76131 Karlsruhe, Germany
stoesser@iism.uni-karlsruhe.de

**Abstract.** In distributed computer networks where resources are under decentralized control, selfish users will generally not work towards
one common goal, such as maximizing the overall value provided by the
system, but will instead try to strategically maximize their individual
benefit. This shifts the scheduling policy in such systems – the decision
about which user may access what resource – from being a purely algorithmic challenge to the domain of mechanism design.

In this paper we will showcase the benefit of allowing *preemption* in such
economic online settings regarding the performance of market mechanisms
by extending the Decentralized Local Greedy Mechanism of Heydenreich
et al. [11]. This mechanism was shown to be 3.281-competitive with respect to total weighted completion time if the players act rationally. We
show that the *preemptive version* of this mechanism is 2-competitive. As
a by-product, preemption allows to relax the assumptions on jobs upon
which this competitiveness relies. In addition to this worst case analysis, we provide an in-depth empirical analysis of the *average case performance* of the original mechanism and its preemptive extension based on
real workload traces. Our empirical findings indicate that introducing preemption improves both the utility and the slowdown of the jobs. Furthermore, this improvement does not come at the expense of low-priority jobs.

**Keywords:** Mechanism Design, Online Scheduling, Preemption.

## 1 Introduction

The aim of this paper is to study the benefit of allowing preemption in economic
online settings. In distributed computer networks where resources are under

---

* This work has been supported in parts by the EU IST program under grant 034286
"SORMA". Jochen Stößer was additionally funded by the German D-Grid initiative
under grant "Biz2Grid".

J. Altmann, D. Neumann, and T. Fahringer (Eds.): GECON 2008, LNCS 5206, pp. 41–57, 2008.
© Springer-Verlag Berlin Heidelberg 2008

decentralized control, selfish users will generally not work towards one common goal, such as maximizing the overall value provided by the system, but will instead try to strategically maximize their individual benefit. This shifts the scheduling policy in such systems – that is the decision about which user may access what resource – from being a purely algorithmic challenge to the domain of mechanism design [17]. In mechanism design, scheduling (or "allocation") algorithms are combined with pricing rules so as to align the users' individual goals with the designer's overall goal.

Until recently, only few grid and cluster systems provided preemptive migration (e.g. [2]), which is the ability of dynamically moving computational jobs across machines during runtime. The emerging technology of virtualization becomes an important building block in grids (e.g. [7]). Virtualization provides off-the-shelf support for virtual machine migration, thus making the use of preemption and migration more accessible. The power of migration was studied in [1] in the context of online fair allocations in heterogenous organizational grids: under mild assumptions it was shown that several natural fairness and quality of service properties cannot be achieved without the ability to preempt jobs during runtime.

**Our Contribution.** In this paper we will showcase the benefit of allowing *preemption* in economic online settings regarding the performance of online market mechanisms. Online mechanisms continuously assign jobs to machines as new jobs enter the system and/or machines become idle. The advantage of online mechanisms compared to periodic mechanisms is increased responsiveness. On their downside, however, online mechanisms have to make allocation decisions with less information and these decisions may prove unfortunate as new information (e.g. new jobs) is released. Preemption can mitigate such unfortunate decisions by allowing the allocation mechanism to suspend a running job in favor of some more desirable job and to possibly continue this suspended job later on the same machine.

The results of our paper show that the performance of economic online mechanisms can be improved by performing preemptions, which has largely been neglected in the existing literature on market mechanisms. E.g. the Decentralized Local Greedy Mechanism of Heydenreich et al. [11] was shown to be 3.281-competitive with respect to total weighted completion time if the players act rationally. We analytically show that the *preemptive version* of this mechanism is 2-competitive. As a by-product, preemption allows to relax the assumptions on jobs upon which this competitiveness relies. At the core of this paper, we provide an in-depth empirical analysis of the *average case performance* of the original mechanism and its preemptive extension based on real workload traces. Our empirical findings indicate that introducing preemption improves both the utility and the slowdown of the jobs. Furthermore, this improvement does not come at the expense of low-priority jobs.

**Structure of this Paper.** We introduce the characteristics of job agents and machines in Section 2. In Section 3, we present an economic online mechanism by Heydenreich, Müller and Uetz [11] which constitutes the baseline model for our investigation. In Section 4 and at the core of this paper, we show how the mechanism's competitive (i.e. worst-case) ratio improves if preemption of jobs is introduced. In Section 5 we empirically analyze the average case with real workload traces. Section 6 discusses related work. Section 7 concludes the paper and points to future work.

## 2   The Setting

We face the problem of having to schedule a set of jobs with arbitrary release dates onto $n$ parallel *homogeneous* machines with the aim of minimizing total weighted completion time $\sum_{j \in J} w_j C_j$, where $J$ is the set of jobs to be scheduled. $C_j$ denotes job $j$'s completion time, i.e. the point in time when $j$ leaves the system. Job $j \in J$ is of type $\theta_j = (r_j, p_j, w_j) \in \mathbb{R}^+ \times \mathbb{R}^+ \times \mathbb{R}^+$, where $r_j$ denotes $j$'s release date, $p_j$ its runtime, and $w_j$ is its weight, which can be interpreted as $j$'s waiting cost, that is the cost of remaining in the system for one additional unit of time.

We consider a setting in which each agent submits a single job and we will thus use the terms "agent" and "job" interchangeably in the remainder of this paper. While the machines are obedient, the jobs are rational and selfish. Each job $j \in J$ aims at maximizing its individual (ex post) utility

$$u_j(C_j, \pi_j | \theta_j) = -w_j C_j - \pi_j, \tag{1}$$

where $\pi_j$ is $j$'s payment. Job $j$ may decide to strategically misreport about its type, i.e. it may report $\tilde{\theta}_j = (\tilde{r}_j, \tilde{p}_j, \tilde{w}_j) \neq (r_j, p_j, w_j)$ in order to improve its utility compared to truthful reporting. Obviously, $\tilde{r}_j \geq r_j$. Furthermore, $\tilde{p}_j \geq p_j$ since any excess runtime can easily be detected and punished by the system. We henceforth assume that jobs are numbered according to their time of arrival, i.e. $k < j \Rightarrow \tilde{r}_k \leq \tilde{r}_j$.

## 3   Baseline Model – A Decentralized Local Greedy Mechanism

Heydenreich et al. [11] examine the setting at hand *without* preemption, that is $P|r_j| \sum w_j C_j$ in the classic notation of Graham et al. [9]. They propose a *Decentralized Local Greedy Mechanism* (*DLGM*) which will be presented now for the ease of exposition:

**Step 1 – Job report:** At its chosen release date $\tilde{r}_j$, job $j$ communicates $\tilde{w}_j$ and $\tilde{p}_j$ to every machine $i \in N$.

**Step 2 – Tentative machine feedback:** Based on the received information, the machines communicate a tentative machine-specific completion time $\hat{C}_j(i)$ and a tentative payment $\hat{\pi}_j(i)$ to the job. The tentativeness is due to the fact that later arriving jobs might overtake job $j$. This leads to a final ex post completion time $C_j(i) \geq \hat{C}_j(i)$ and a final ex post payment $\pi_j(i) \leq \hat{\pi}_j(i)$ as compensation payments by overtaking jobs might occur (see Step 3 below).

The local scheduling on each machine follows Smith's ratio rule [20], which has been shown to be optimal for $1|| \sum w_j C_j$ with one single machine and without release dates. Jobs are assigned a priority according to their ratio of weight and processing time: Job $j$ has a higher priority than job $k$ if (1) $\tilde{w}_j/\tilde{p}_j > \tilde{w}_k/\tilde{p}_k$ or (2) $\tilde{w}_j/\tilde{p}_j = \tilde{w}_k/\tilde{p}_k$ and $j < k$, and is inserted in front of $k$ into the waiting queue at this machine. For obtaining the tentative completion time, the remaining processing time of the currently running job and the runtimes of the higher-prioritized jobs in the queue as well as $j$'s own runtime have to be added to $\tilde{r}_j$. The tentative payment equals a compensation of utility loss for all jobs which would be displaced if $j$ was queued at this machine.

**Step 3 – Queueing:** Upon receiving information about its tentative completion time and required payment from the machines, job $j$ makes a binding decision for a machine. $j$ is queued at its chosen machine $i$ according to its priority and pays $\tilde{w}_k \tilde{p}_j$ to each lower ranked job $k$ at this machine.

For evaluating and comparing market mechanisms, we need to define the user behavior, i.e. the agents' strategies $s$, and a metric. We will start with the former.

Under *DLGM*, $j$'s strategy consists of reporting its type *and* choosing a machine. Let $\tilde{s}$ be the vector containing the arbitrary strategies of all agents, and let $\tilde{s}_{-j}$ be the vector containing the arbitrary strategies of all agents except $j$. Given the tentative machine feedback, let $\hat{u}_j(s, \theta_j)$ be job $j$'s *tentative utility* at time $\tilde{r}_j$. Heydenreich et al. [11] use the concept of myopic best response equilibria in order to model the behavior of rational and selfish agents:

**Definition 1.** *A strategy profile* $s = (s_1, \cdots, s_n)$ *is called a* myopic best response equilibrium *if, for all* $j \in J$, $\theta_j$, $\tilde{s}_{-j}$, *and all strategies* $\tilde{s}_j$ *which* $j$ *could play instead of* $s_j$,

$$\hat{u}_j((s_j, \tilde{s}_{-j}), \theta_j) \geq \hat{u}_j((\tilde{s}_j, \tilde{s}_{-j}), \theta_j). \tag{2}$$

**Theorem 1 (Theorem 9 in [11]).** *Given the types of all jobs, the strategy profile where each job* $j$ *reports* $\bar{\theta}_j = \theta_j$ *and chooses a machine which maximizes its tentative utility* $\hat{u}_j(C_j, \pi_j|\theta_j)(i) = -w_j\hat{C}_j(i) - \hat{\pi}_j(i)$ *is a myopic best response equilibrium under* DLGM.

That is, without knowledge about the future and other jobs' types, each job maximizes its *tentative* utility by truthfully reporting its characteristics and choosing the best available machine. Furthermore, if the player *truthfully* report his type, then his ex-post utility *equals* his tentative utility since whenever the job's tentative completion time changes, the job is immediately compensated for the exact loss of his utility.

Since we now know how agents act in this model, we can evaluate the performance of *DLGM* as regards efficiency. A common metric for a mechanism's performance is its *competitive ratio* in its strategic equilibrium, in this case the myopic best response equilibrium. In our setting, a mechanism's competitive ratio is defined as the largest possible ratio of the total weighted completion time generated by the specific mechanism if all agents play their equilibrium strategy divided by the theoretical minimum of an omniscient offline mechanism which knows all the jobs' true types when making its allocation decisions. We state one of the main results of Heydenreich et al., as this becomes the baseline for our later analysis:

**Theorem 2 (Theorem 10 in [11]).** *Suppose every job is rational in the sense that it truthfully reports $r_j$, $p_j$, $w_j$ and selects a machine that maximizes its tentative utility at arrival. Then* DLGM *is 3.281-competitive for the scheduling problem* $P|r_j| \sum w_j C_j$.

This theorem essentially captures *DLGM*'s performance without using preemption.

## 4 Adding Preemption

We will now examine the impact of introducing preemption to *DLGM* on the mechanism's competitive ratio. We will henceforth refer to this extended *DLGM* as *Preemptive DLGM* or *P-DLGM*.

We introduce the following notation. Let $p_j$ continue to denote $j$'s total runtime, but let $p_j(t)$ be its *remaining* runtime at time $t$. In contrast to *DLGM*, *P-DLGM* uses a *dynamic extension* of Smith's ratio rule, i.e. at time $t$, we order jobs according to the ratio of their weight and the remaining runtime $(\tilde{w}_j/\tilde{p}_j(t))$. Hence, let $H_j(t) = \{k \in J \mid \tilde{w}_k/\tilde{p}_k(t) > \tilde{w}_j/\tilde{p}_j(t)\} \cup \{k \leq j \mid \tilde{w}_k/\tilde{p}_k(t) = \tilde{w}_j/\tilde{p}_j(t)\}$, i.e. $H_j(t)$ contains all jobs with higher priority than job $j$ at time $t$, including $j$ itself. We further introduce $L_j(t) = J \setminus H_j(t)$, i.e. the set containing all jobs with a lower priority than $j$. We denote $j \rightarrow i$ if job $j$ is assigned to machine $i$. Finally, we denote the *actual* (ex post) end time of $j$, i.e. the time when $j$ leaves the system, by $E_j$. Consequently, at time $\tilde{r}_j$, all jobs $k$ with $k < j$ and $E_k > \tilde{r}_j$ are present in the system.

*P-DLGM* comprises the following three steps:

**Step 1 – Job report:** At its chosen release date $\tilde{r}_j$, job $j$ communicates $\tilde{w}_j$ and $\tilde{p}_j$ to every machine $i \in N$.

**Step 2 – Tentative machine feedback:** Based on the received information, the machines communicate a tentative machine-specific completion time and a tentative payment to the job.

The tentative completion time of job $j$ at machine $i$ is determined as

$$\hat{C}_j(i) = \tilde{r}_j + \tilde{p}_j + \sum_{\substack{k \in H_j(\tilde{r}_j) \\ k \rightarrow i \\ k < j \\ E_k > \tilde{r}_j}} \tilde{p}_k(\tilde{r}_j), \tag{3}$$

i.e. the projected time that job $j$ spends on machine $i$ equals the sum of $j$'s own runtime and the remaining runtimes of all jobs which are queued at in front of $j$ at $i$ at time $\tilde{r}_j$.

The tentative compensation payment of job $j$ at machine $i$ is determined as

$$\hat{\pi}_j(i) = \tilde{p}_j \sum_{\substack{k \in L_j(\tilde{r}_j) \\ k \to i \\ k < j \\ E_k > \tilde{r}_j}} \tilde{w}_k, \qquad (4)$$

i.e. $j$'s runtime multiplied by the aggregate weights of all jobs which are displaced at machine $i$ due to the addition of $j$ at time $\tilde{r}_j$. This comprises the currently waiting jobs and, due to allowing preemption, possibly also the currently running job.

**Step 3 – Queueing:** Upon receiving information about its tentative completion time and required payment from the machines, job $j$ makes a binding decision for a machine. Job $j$ is queued at its chosen machine $i$ according to its priority or preempts the currently running job – which is then put back into this machine's local queue – and pays $\tilde{w}_k \tilde{p}_j$ to each lower ranked job $k$ at this machine.

Note that in our extension to the basic *DLGM* we assume zero preemption cost, that is jobs can be suspended in negligible time. This is a reasonable assumption since – in contrast to migrations where jobs are transferred between *different* machines over the network (a setting investigated in [1]) – in our mechanism jobs are suspended on one single machine.

We are now ready to state our main results:

**Lemma 1.** *Given the types of all jobs, the strategy profile where each job $j$ reports $\tilde{\theta}_j = \theta_j$ and chooses a machine which maximizes its tentative utility $\hat{u}_j(C_j, \pi_j | \theta_j)(i) = -w_j \hat{C}_j(i) - \hat{\pi}_j(i)$ is a myopic best response equilibrium under P-DLGM and its ex post utility equals its tentative utility.*

*Proof.* Due to the dynamic extension to Smith's ratio rule, the proof to Lemma 1 reduces to the proofs to Theorem 9 in [11] as the dynamic priorities can be plugged into the latter. Consequently, the proof to this theorem and its supporting lemmata and theorems do not change if preemption is introduced. The full proof will be included the full version of this paper.

**Theorem 3.** *Suppose that every job $j$ plays its myopic best response strategy according to Lemma 1. Then P-DLGM is 2-competitive for the scheduling problem $P|r_j, pmtn| \sum w_j C_j$.*

Refer to Appendix A for the detailed proof to this theorem.

Note that Megow and Schulz [14] also give an allocation algorithm that is 2-competitive for $P|r_j, pmtn| \sum w_j C_j$. However, they do not consider strategic agents and thus do not give a pricing scheme for this algorithm. Furthermore, they use *static priorities* when ordering jobs which are independent of the jobs' progress and the allocation algorithm is *centralized* as opposed to our decentralized setting. Most importantly, the latter leads to Megow and Schulz using migration (i.e. the moving of jobs across machines) whereas *P-DLGM* only uses preemption (i.e. suspended jobs are continued on the same machine).

One may argue that the bounds in Theorems 2 and 3 relate to different optimization problems. However, exactly this difference – introducing preemption – is our main point in this paper, which is captured by the following theorem:

**Conclusion 1.** *Suppose that every job $j$ plays its myopic best response strategy according to Lemma 1. Then preemptions allow us to improve the upper (worst-case) bound on the objective value $\sum w_j C_j$ generated by a market mechanism from 3.281 to 2.*

*Proof.* Take Theorems 2 and 3 as well as the fact that the objective value $Z_{pmtn}^{OPT}$ of the optimal solution to $P|r_j, pmtn| \sum w_j C_j$ will always be less than or equal to the objective value $Z^{OPT}$ of the optimal solution to $P|r_j| \sum w_j C_j$. Consequently, if $Z$ is the objective value generated by *P-DLGM*, then $Z \leq 2Z_{pmtn}^{OPT} \leq 2Z^{OPT}$.

The performance ratio of the basic *DLGM* relies on the artificial assumption that *critical jobs*, that is jobs with long runtimes, are only released to the system later in the scheduling process. To achieve this, Heydenreich et al. [11] impose the restriction $r_j \geq \alpha p_j$, and optimize the performance ratio $\rho$ over $\alpha$ to obtain $\rho = 3.281$. With preemption, we cannot only lower this upper bound to $\rho = 2$, but additionally we can omit this artificial restriction.

As mentioned above, it was shown in [11] that there is no payment scheme which can complement *DLGM* so as to make truthtelling a dominant strategy equilibrium where revealing the true job type and choosing the best machine is not only the tentatively optimal strategy but is also optimal from an ex post perspective. This result applies also for *P-DLGM*.

**Proposition 1.** *It is not possible to turn* P-DLGM *into a mechanism with a dominant strategy equilibrium in which all jobs report truthfully by only modifying the payment scheme.*

*Proof.* The proof follows from Theorem 14 in [11]. It relies on a simple example to show that, under *DLGM*, jobs may improve their ex post completion time by reporting $\tilde{w}_j < w_j$, which contradicts weak monotonicity, a necessary condition for truthfulness [11, 12]. In the example, all jobs arrive at the same time. Consequently, no preemption can occur and this example as well as the supporting lemmata thus also hold with preemption.

An interesting open question for future research remains: Is there any truthful mechanism (in dominant strategies) at all for this setting?

# 5   Empirical Analysis

## 5.1   Experimental Setup

In the previous section, we have shown that *P-DLGM* yields a better *worst-case* performance than *DLGM*. In this section, we want to analyze the *average case* by means of an empirical analysis based on real workload traces.

**Table 1.** Workload traces

| Trace | Timeframe | Jobs (original) | Jobs (serialized) | CPUs | Runtime Mean (sec.) | CV (%) |
|---|---|---|---|---|---|---|
| WHALE | Dec'05 – Jan'07 | 196,417 | 280,433 | 3,072 | 35,658 | 237 |
| REQUIN | Dec'05 – Jan'07 | 50,442 | 466,177 | 1,536 | 45,674 | 411 |
| LPC-EGEE | Aug'04 – May'05 | 219,704 | 219,704 | 140 | 3,212 | 500 |
| DAS2-FS4 | Feb'03 – Dec'03 | 32,626 | 118,567 | 64 | 2,236 | 961 |

We have implemented a simulator to study online mechanisms for the scheduling in distributed computing systems. The experimental setup is similar to our analysis of fairness in economic online scheduling in [1]. We want to evaluate *P-DLGM* and *DLGM* using this previous setting since this will allow us to compare the results of both analyses. We want to check our economic setting here without "tailoring" a specific setting towards the advantage of *P-DLGM*. For the ease of the exposition we describe our setting in the following.

**Workload Traces.** For our simulations we took four workload traces from the Parallel Workload Archive [6] (cf. Table 1). All these traces are taken from homogeneous clusters. The DAS2-FS4 cluster is part of a Dutch academic grid (http://www.cs.vu.nl/das2/). LPC is a French cluster that is part of the EGEE grid (http://www.eu-egee.org/). The WHALE and REQUIN traces are taken from two Canadian clusters (http://www.sharcnet.ca/). We chose these workloads due to the large number of jobs which will help us to mitigate stochastic outliers, the availability of technical parameters such as release dates and runtimes, and because of their relative recentness, as old workloads might contain outdated applications and utilization patterns. In all of the traces the CPUs were dedicated, meaning only one job is using each CPU at the same time.[1] Parallel jobs (using more than one CPU) are treated as a collection of serial jobs all with the same weight, release date and runtime. The addition "serialized" in the job column of Table 1 indicates the number of jobs after converting such parallel jobs to serial ones.

Table 1 contains descriptive statistics of the jobs in the traces. The homogeneity of the jobs within one trace as regards runtime is expressed by reporting the coefficients of variation (CV) of the runtimes, which normalize the standard deviation by the mean. The jobs in WHALE and REQUIN have long runtimes and are rather homogeneous, whereas the jobs in LPC-EGEE and DAS2-FS4 are short on average with DAS2-FS4 being highly heterogeneous.

To analyze the utilization patterns in these traces, we simulated them using a simple first-in-first-out scheduler. As the results in Figure 2 in Appendix B illustrate, the WHALE and the REQUIN cluster are highly utilized, a large number of jobs resides in the waiting queue most of the time. In contrast, the LPC-EGEE and the DAS2-FS4 clusters only have a small number of peaks in the waiting queue. The competition among jobs is small and CPUs are frequently

---

[1] Note that we take the actual job characteristics from the traces which have been measured by the system, not the user estimates.

idle. To measure the impact of preemption for the LPC-EGEE and the DAS2-FS4 clusters in more competitive settings, we increase the pressure in these two workloads and simulate these workloads if only 75% of the original CPUs are available.

**Waiting Cost Model.** Essentially, the users' waiting costs (weights) represent the users' valuations for the jobs. To the best of our knowledge, the only empirical investigation of economic scheduling mechanisms which uses a time-dependent user valuation model was performed by Chun and Culler [5]. Valuations were assumed to be bimodal with the majority of jobs having valuations following a normal distribution with a low mean, and some high valuation jobs with valuations coming from a second normal distribution with a higher mean.

In order to check the validity of our results for two different valuation models, we chose to simulate all settings for such a bimodal distribution with 80% of the job weights coming from a normal distribution with mean 30 and standard deviation 15, and 20% of the job weights coming from a normal distribution with mean 150 and standard deviation 15.[2] Consequently, on average, high-valuation jobs were assumed to be five times more important than low-valuation jobs. We additionally ran the simulation settings drawing job weights from a uniform distribution over [1, 100], i.e. there are 100 priority classes.

Due to space limitations, we will only include the results for the uniform distribution since the basic effects are more straightforward. However, we included the results for the bimodal distribution in Appendix C.

**Metrics.** Since we are investigating economic schedulers, we cannot base our evaluation on purely technical metrics, based on a single scalar, such as makespan or the sum of completion times. Instead, we have to develop metrics which capture the viewpoint of the users and measure the dependency between the "service" a job receives from the system and its reported valuation.

*Total weighted flow time* describes the overall system performance and is defined as $\sum_j w_j(C_j - r_j)$. In contrast to the previous section, for our empirical analysis we choose to measure the total weighted flow time instead of the total weighted completion time. First, minimizing completion time is equivalent to minimizing flow time up to an additive constant of $-\sum_j w_j r_j$.[3] Second, since we run traces which cover more than one year of workloads on a per second basis, this additive constant will be very large and hence might dominate this ratio. Thus, focussing on the flow time instead of the completion time will help us to determine the actual difference in system performance for *DLGM* and *P-DLGM*.

*Utility per priority value* describes the utility a job a receives in relation to its WSPT ratio.[4] Total weighted flow time only describes the overall system performance. In contrast, this measure will give us more insights into the impact of

---

[2] Note that we cut negative valuations.

[3] The optimal schedules are identical for both metrics. However, schedules that approximate each metric can differ even if the same approximation ratio is guaranteed.

[4] Note that for jobs playing the best myopic strategy of truthful reporting the tentative utility equals the ex post utility, as shown in Theorem 7(a) in [11].

performing preemptions on the single jobs' utility. Which jobs suffer from pre-emptions, which gain, or do all jobs gain by performing preemptions regardless of their priority? To capture the utility per WSPT ratio (which is a continuous random variable), we discretize this value range as follows: We sort all jobs regarding their initial WSPT priorities $w_j/p_j$. We then divide this sorted list into 100 slices, i.e. the percentile of jobs with the lowest WSPT ratios, the second percentile and so forth. We will then report the average utility for each percentile to compare *DLGM* and *P-DLGM*.

*Bounded slowdown per valuation* also reflects the perspective of a single job. The bounded slowdown of job $j$ is defined as

$$BSD_j = \begin{cases} \frac{C_j - r_j}{t_j} & \text{if } t_j \geq 60 \\ \frac{C_j - r_j}{60} & \text{else} \end{cases} \tag{5}$$

This canonical metric is widely used in the Computer Systems Evaluation literature (e.g. [10, 15]). We take the bounded slowdown instead of the slowdown because short jobs can easily experience a large slowdown, which does not necessarily reflect a bad service. Intuitively, job $j$ seeks to minimize $BSD_j$. Naturally, in economic schedulers jobs with higher valuations (and smaller run times) should get smaller (bounded) slowdowns. The rationale for looking at this metric is that this will give us hints towards the mechanisms' performance if we consider other job utility functions as the one introduced above, e.g. if the importance of the jobs' waiting costs increases compared to the job payments. Additionally, the utility function in our setting has many indifference points (a delay of job $j$ for a one time unit can be compensated with $w_j$). It seems reasonable to assume that agents have strict preference over these "indifference" points and would like to finish earlier rather than to be compensated.

## 5.2   Experimental Results

Table 2 shows the ratio of the total weighted flow time generated by *P-DLGM* to the total weighted flow time produced by *DLGM* for both the uniform and the bimodal weight distribution. *P-DLGM* always outperforms *DLGM* with respect to this overall performance metric. Consequently, *P-DLGM* not only improves upon *DLGM* in the worst case as shown in the previous section but also in the average case. Intuitively, the benefit of performing preemptions will increase (i.e. the ratio will decrease) as the pressure in the system increases, that is as more jobs compete for the resources. As our results hold for both the uniform and the bimodal weight distribution, we hypothesize that the overall benefit of performing preemptions is robust to the assumption about a specific weight distribution.

However, the results for the total weighted flow time cannot give us any insight into the impact of performing preemptions on the performance of the individual jobs. Which jobs benefit and which jobs suffer from this feature? Recall that *P-DLGM* uses dynamic priorities, and so the priority of every job is strictly increasing over time. Additionally, the payments in both mechanisms essentially

**Table 2.** Ratio of the total weighted flow time of *DLGM* to *P-DLGM* for the uniform and the bimodal weight distributions

| Trace | Uniform dist. | Bimodal dist. |
|---|---|---|
| WHALE | 1.09 | 1.08 |
| REQUIN | 1.06 | 1.05 |
| LPC-EGEE-75% | 1.07 | 1.07 |
| DAS2-FS4-75% | 1.22 | 1.20 |

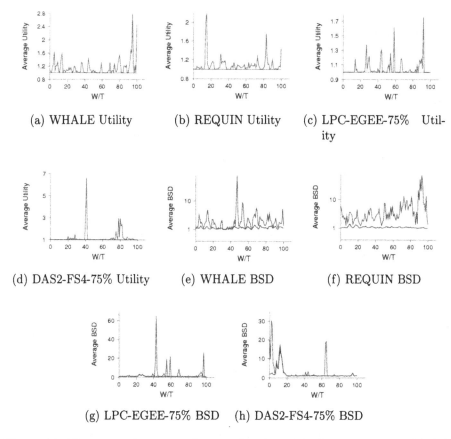

(a) WHALE Utility    (b) REQUIN Utility    (c) LPC-EGEE-75% Utility

(d) DAS2-FS4-75% Utility    (e) WHALE BSD    (f) REQUIN BSD

(g) LPC-EGEE-75% BSD    (h) DAS2-FS4-75% BSD

**Fig. 1.** (a)–(d): ratio of the average (negative) utility of *DLGM* to *P-DLGM*; (e)–(h): average bounded slowdown of *DLGM* and *P-DLGM*. W/T indicates the discretized WSPT percentiles.

increase if the priorities of other jobs in the queue are higher. This might cause larger payments (and thus smaller utilities) in *P-DLGM* than those of *DLGM*. Figures 1(a), 1(b), 1(c) and 1(d) show the ratio of the average utility per WSPT priority percentile (see explanation in Subsection 5.1) generated by *DLGM* to the average utility produced by *P-DLGM* (based on the uniform weight distribution). Since both are always negative, the bigger this ratio, the better *P-DLGM* performs in comparison to *DLGM* for a given priority range. In our simulations, we see that this ratio is almost always bigger than 1 for all four workload traces and priority ranges. This shows that *P-DLGM* almost always outperforms *DLGM* and that essentially all jobs benefit from performing preemptions, regardless of their WSPT priority.

But how does the ability of preempting jobs impact the jobs' service level, as captured by the bounded slowdown? As pointed out above, this will be important when considering other job utility functions where the waiting costs are more important. As Figures 1(e), 1(f), 1(g) and 1(h) show, *P-DLGM* strikingly outperforms *DLGM* regarding the bounded slowdown. On average, *P-DLGM* yields a lower bounded slowdown (better service) than *DLGM* across all priority ranges. Moreover, the bounded slowdown of *P-DLGM* is almost always close to 1 (the optimum), besides a small peak in the DAS-FS4 workload. This result can be explained by the use of the (dynamic) WSPT ratios, which divide the job weight by the runtime. This generally boosts the priority of small jobs compared to long jobs. Thus, in contrast to the static *DLGM*, the WSPT ratios in conjunction with preemptions give us the ability to suspend long jobs in favor of short jobs. Hence, *P-DLGM* tends to result in much smaller slowdowns for short jobs but only slightly larger slowdowns for long jobs, since the slowdown is normalized by the job runtime. From an overall perspective, the average slowdown will thus be much smaller for *P-DLGM* than for *DLGM*.

The results for the bimodal weight distribution closely resemble our results for the uniform distribution, cf. Figure 3 in Appendix C. As pointed out above, this suggests that the overall benefit of performing preemptions is robust to the assumption about a specific weight distribution.

# 6   Related Work

Online mechanisms can be distinguished into mechanisms which allocate *shares* of one or more divisible goods such as bandwidth or computing power (e.g. [4, 19]) and, similar to our approach, mechanisms which allocate *indivisible machines*. As such, strategic behavior of job agents is considered by [8] for the allocation of bandwidth. The paper elaborates online variants of the prominent VCG mechanism to induce the job agents to truthfully reveal their valuations and release dates. [13] studied "Set-Nash" equilibria mechanisms and also showed that no ex post dominant-strategy implementation can obtain a constant fraction of the optimum. [18] is most similar to the spirit of our paper in that it addresses the issue of preemption in economic online settings. The objective of the mechanism is to schedule strategic jobs with deadlines onto *one single machine* so as to induce these job agents to truthful reports of their characteristics and to maximize the overall value returned to the job agents. In [1], we identified several fairness criteria. We showed that so called economic busy schedulers can only satisfy these criteria if migration is allowed. We performed extensive numerical experiments with real-world workloads and varying degrees of realistic migration cost. The experiments showed that the performance of a fair (according to our criteria) scheduling algorithm is robust to even significant realistic migration cost.

Additionally many recent results studied the limitations of the dominant strategy approach on various scheduling settings (e.g. [3, 16]). This suggests that other notions of implementation should be studied. In this paper we study "myopic" best response where job agents do not have information about the future.

In [5], the authors also find that economic scheduling algorithms improve the system performance from the users's viewpoint. They conclude that introducing a limited preemption model (in which a job is preempted at most once) does not significantly improve the overall performance. The paper does not give sufficient details about the simulation setting, e.g. the level of competition in the artificially generated workloads. More importantly, it only considers overall performance as opposed to the intimate connection of the individual performance and the valuation of single jobs as well as the predictability of the service level.

## 7   Conclusion and Future Work

In this paper, we investigated the benefit of performing preemptions in economic settings where users have time-dependent valuations. By focusing on Heydenreich et al.'s *DLGM* mechanism, we have shown that both the worst-case as well as the average case economic performance of online mechanisms can be significantly improved by introducing preemptions. Virtualization technologies provide off-the-shelf support for virtual machine migration, thus making the use of preemption and migration more accessible. Our results suggest that designers of distributed systems should make full use of this feature to build in more flexible and efficient allocation and pricing mechanisms.

A natural extension to preemption is migration, i.e. the moving of jobs *across* machines during runtime instead of only the suspension and continuation on one single machine. Migration will allow for still more efficient mechanisms and may also help in introducing stronger game-theoretic solution concepts (e.g. in dominant strategies) in some settings. Additionally it will be interesting to consider settings in which the machines are paid for executing the jobs. We are currently building a simulation suite to perform in-depth analyses of potential mechanisms in realistic settings. Moreover, we are integrating a real grid market into MOSIX, a cluster and grid management system that supports preemptive migration [2].

## References

1. Amar, L., Mu'alem, A., Stößer, J.: On the importance of migration for fairness in online grid markets (submitted for publication)
2. Barak, A., Shiloh, A., Amar, L.: An organizational grid of federated mosix clusters. In: CCGrid 2005 (2005)
3. Christodoulou, G., Koutsoupias, E., Vidali, A.: A lower bound for scheduling mechanisms. In: SODA 2007 (2007)

4. Chun, B., Culler, D.: Market-based Proportional Resource Sharing for Clusters.Technical report, Computer Science Division, University of California (2000)
5. Chun, B.N., Culler, D.E.: User-centric performance analysis of market-based cluster batch schedulers. In: CCGrid 2002 (2002)
6. Feitelson, D.: Parallel workloads archive (2008),
   http://www.cs.huji.ac.il/labs/parallel/workload/
7. Figueiredo, R.J., Dinda, P.A., Fortes, J.A.B.: A case for grid computing on virtual machines. In: ICDCS 2003 (2003)
8. Friedman, E., Parkes, D.: Pricing WiFi at Starbucks: issues in online mechanism design. In: EC 2003 (2003)
9. Graham, R.L., Lawler, E.L., Lenstra, J.K., Kan, A.H.G.R.: Optimization and approximation in deterministic sequencing and scheduling theory: a survey. Annals of Discrete Mathematics 5, 287–326 (1979)
10. Harchol-Balter, M., Downey, A.B.: Exploiting process lifetime distributions for dynamic load balancing. ACM Trans. Comput. Syst. 15(3), 253–285 (1997)
11. Heydenreich, B., Müller, R., Uetz, M.: Decentralization and mechanism design for online machine scheduling. In: SWAT 2006 (2006)
12. Lavi, R., Mu'alem, A., Nisan, N.: Towards a characterization of truthful combinatorial auctions. In: FOCS 2003 (2003)
13. Lavi, R., Nisan, N.: Online ascending auctions for gradually expiring items. In: SODA 2005 (2005)
14. Megow, N., Schulz, A.: On-line scheduling to minimize average completion time revisited. Operations Research Letters 32(5), 485–490 (2004)
15. Mu'alem, A., Feitelson, D.: Utilization, predictability, workloads, and user runtime estimates in scheduling the IBM SP 2 with backfilling. IEEE TPDS 12(6), 529–543 (2001)
16. MuŠalem, A., Schapira, M.: Setting lower bounds on truthfulness. In: SODA 2007 (2007)
17. Nisan, N., Roughgarden, T., Tardos, E., Vazirani, V.V.: Algorithmic Game Theory. Cambridge University Press, New York (2007)
18. Porter, R.: Mechanism design for online real-time scheduling. In: EC 2004 (2004)
19. Sanghavi, S., Hajek, B.: Optimal allocation of a divisible good to strategic buyers. In: IEEE CDC (2004)
20. Smith, W.E.: Various Optimizers for Single-Stage Production. Naval Resource Logistics Quarterly 3, 59–66 (1956)

# A    Proof of Theorem 3

*Proof.* If job $j$ plays a myopic best response strategy $(r_j, p_j, w_j)$, at time $r_j$ it selects the machine $i$ that minimizes

$$-\hat{u}_j(i) = w_j \hat{C}_j(i) + \hat{\pi}_j(i) \tag{1}$$

$$= w_j(r_j + p_j + \sum_{\substack{k \in H_j(r_j) \\ k \to i \\ k < j \\ C_k > r_j}} p_k(r_j)) + p_j \sum_{\substack{k \in L_j(r_j) \\ k \to i \\ k < j \\ C_k > r_j}} w_k. \tag{2}$$

Let $i_j$ be this machine. As a result of the payment scheme, $-\hat{u}_j(i_j)$ exactly corresponds to the increase of the objective value $\sum_{k \in J} w_k C_k$ which is due to the addition of $j$. Furthermore, any change in $u_j(i_j)$ which results from the assignment of some job $k$ to machine $i_j$ after $r_j$, is absorbed by the payment scheme and $u_k(i_j)$. Thus the objective value can be expressed as $Z = \sum_{j \in J} -\hat{u}_j(i_j)$.

Since jobs are assumed to act rationally when choosing the machine $i$ at which to queue, we obtain $-\hat{u}_j(i_j) \leq \frac{1}{m} \sum_{i=1}^{m} -\hat{u}_j(i)$, and therefore $Z \leq \sum_{j \in J} \frac{1}{m} \sum_{i=1}^{m} -\hat{u}_j(i)$.

Hence

$$\frac{1}{m} \sum_{i=1}^{m} -\hat{u}_j(i) = w_j(r_j + p_j) + w_j \sum_{i=1}^{m} \sum_{\substack{k \in H_j(r_j) \\ k \to i \\ k < j \\ C_k > r_j}} \frac{p_k(r_j)}{m} + p_j \sum_{i=1}^{m} \sum_{\substack{k \in L_j(r_j) \\ k \to i \\ k < j \\ C_k > r_j}} \frac{w_k}{m}, \tag{3}$$

which can be shortened to

$$\frac{1}{m} \sum_{i=1}^{m} -\hat{u}_j(i) = w_j(r_j + p_j) + w_j \sum_{\substack{k \in H_j(r_j) \\ k < j \\ C_k > r_j}} \frac{p_k(r_j)}{m} + p_j \sum_{\substack{k \in L_j(r_j) \\ k < j \\ C_k > r_j}} \frac{w_k}{m}. \tag{4}$$

By including all jobs instead of only the jobs $k$ for which $C_k > r_j$, and by considering the total runtime of jobs $k \in H_j(r_j)$, $k < j$, we can upper bound this by

$$\frac{1}{m} \sum_{i=1}^{m} -\hat{u}_j(i) \leq w_j(r_j + p_j) + w_j \sum_{\substack{k \in H_j(r_j) \\ k < j}} \frac{p_k(r_j)}{m} + p_j \sum_{\substack{k \in L_j(r_j) \\ k < j}} \frac{w_k}{m} \tag{5}$$

$$\leq w_j(r_j + p_j) + w_j \sum_{\substack{k \in H_j(r_j) \\ k < j}} \frac{p_k}{m} + p_j \sum_{\substack{k \in L_j(r_j) \\ k < j}} \frac{w_k}{m}. \tag{6}$$

Following [11], the summation of the last term over all jobs in $J$ can be rewritten as

$$\sum_{j \in J} p_j \sum_{\substack{k \in L_j(r_j) \\ k < j}} \frac{w_k}{m} = \sum_{\substack{(j,k): \\ j \in H_k(r_j) \\ k < j}} p_j \frac{w_k}{m} = \sum_{\substack{(j,k): \\ k \in H_j(r_j) \\ j < k}} p_k \frac{w_j}{m} = \sum_{j \in J} w_j \sum_{\substack{k \in H_j(r_j) \\ k > j}} \frac{p_k}{m}. \tag{7}$$

Therefore,

$$Z \leq \sum_{j \in J} w_j(r_j + p_j) + \sum_{j \in J} w_j \sum_{\substack{k \in H_j(r_j) \\ k < j}} \frac{p_k}{m} + \sum_{j \in J} w_j \sum_{\substack{k \in H_j(r_j) \\ k > j}} \frac{p_k}{m} \qquad (8)$$

$$= \sum_{j \in J} w_j(r_j + p_j) + \sum_{j \in J} w_j \sum_{k \in H_j(r_j)} \frac{p_k}{m} - \sum_{j \in J} w_j \frac{p_j}{m} \qquad (9)$$

$$\leq \sum_{j \in J} w_j(r_j + p_j) + \sum_{j \in J} w_j \sum_{k \in H_j(r_j)} \frac{p_k}{m}. \qquad (10)$$

Let $Z_{pmtn}^{OPT}$ be the objective value which an omniscient offline mechanism can achieve for $P|r_j, pmtn| \sum w_j C_j$.

Obviously, $\sum_{j \in J} w_j(r_j + p_j) \leq Z_{pmtn}^{OPT}$.

Furthermore, consider the problem $1|| \sum w_j C_j$ for a single machine with speed $m$ times the speed of any of the identical parallel machines and with the same jobs all arriving at time zero. Without release dates, we get that $H_j(t) = H_j := \{k \in J \mid \tilde{w}_k/\tilde{p}_k > \tilde{w}_j/\tilde{p}_j\} \cup \{k \leq j \mid \tilde{w}_k/\tilde{p}_k = \tilde{w}_j/\tilde{p}_j\}$ for all $t$ since $\tilde{p}_j(t) \leq \tilde{p}_j$, i.e. the ordering of jobs does not change over time. Since $1|| \sum w_j C_j$ is a relaxation of $P|r_j, pmtn| \sum w_j C_j$ and $\sum_{j \in J} w_j \sum_{k \in H_j} \frac{p_k}{m}$ is the objective value of the optimal solution to $1|| \sum w_j C_j$, we obtain $\sum_{j \in J} w_j \sum_{k \in H_j(r_j)} \frac{p_k}{m} \leq Z_{pmtn}^{OPT}$ [14], and thus $Z \leq 2Z_{pmtn}^{OPT}$.

This proof is close in spirit to the proof to Theorem 10 in [11]. The basic differences are that we use dynamic WSPT ratios in contrast to the static priorities used in [11] and that we use different reductions to upper bound the competitive ratio in the last step of the proof.

# B  Workloads

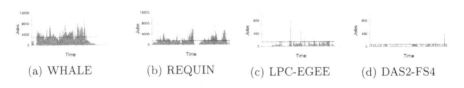

(a) WHALE          (b) REQUIN          (c) LPC-EGEE          (d) DAS2-FS4

**Fig. 2.** Utilization patterns of the workload traces with a FIFO scheduler (Waiting Jobs, Running Jobs)

# C    Bimodal Weight Distribution

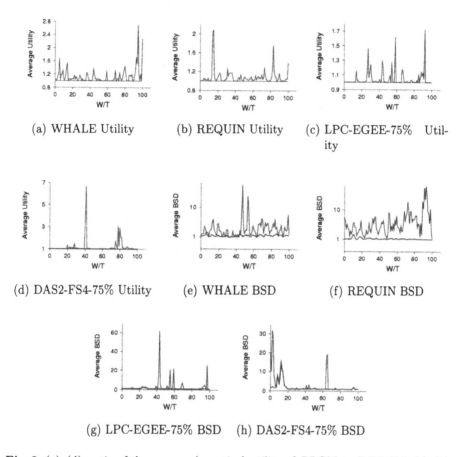

(a) WHALE Utility

(b) REQUIN Utility

(c) LPC-EGEE-75% Utility

(d) DAS2-FS4-75% Utility

(e) WHALE BSD

(f) REQUIN BSD

(g) LPC-EGEE-75% BSD

(h) DAS2-FS4-75% BSD

**Fig. 3.** (a)–(d): ratio of the average (negative) utility of $DLGM$ to $P\text{-}DLGM$; (e)–(h): average bounded slowdown of $DLGM$ and $P\text{-}DLGM$. Both evaluations are based on the bimodal weight distribution.

# Market Mechanisms for Trading Grid Resources

Costas Courcoubetis[1], Manos Dramitinos[1], Thierry Rayna[2],
Sergios Soursos[1], and George D. Stamoulis[1]

[1] Network Economics and Services Group (N.E.S.), Department of Informatics,
Athens University of Economics and Business (AUEB),
76 Patision Street, Athens, GR 10434, Greece
{courcou,mdramit,sns,gstamoul}@aueb.gr
[2] Internet Centre, Imperial College London, South Kensington Campus,
180 Queen's Gate, London SW7 2AZ, United Kingdom
t.rayna@imperial.ac.uk

**Abstract.** There has been recently an increasing interest in Grid services and economic-aware Grid systems both in the industry and the academia. In this paper we specify a market for hardware providers and consumers interested in leasing Grid resources for a time period. Our approach comprises a stock-market like mechanism that enables the trading of computational power on the basis of a spot and a futures market. The spot market comprises a pair of bid and ask queues. This grid market is more complicated than the standard spot/futures markets of storable commodities, because the computational service traded in our case comprises of resources that are perishable, and has both quantity and duration specified in terms of a time interval. This is an important feature of our market mechanism, complicating considerably the trading algorithms that we develop and assess in this paper.

**Keywords:** Market mechanism, grid market, bid and ask, spot, futures.

## 1 Introduction

Motivated by the electrical power grids and the time-sharing computational systems of the past, there has been an increasing interest in Grid services over the past years. In order to materialize the virtualization and wide-scale sharing of computational resources, a variety of related business models regarding utility computing and software on demand have been developed, while economic-aware Grid systems have become increasingly popular both in the industry and the academia [1]. A wide variety of related market systems have been proposed; these are based on fixed prices, bartering, negotiations or auction models for leasing "Grid contracts". A detailed overview and presentation of these economic-aware grid systems and architectures can be found in [2] and [3]. However, despite the various economic mechanisms that have been proposed as candidates to be adopted in a Grid market, very few efforts have been made to fully specify the design of a market that is tailored to the Grid products and services. Indeed most proposals neglect taking into account the fact that both the resource type and the time dimension are of significant importance for the perishable Grid resources.

J. Altmann, D. Neumann, and T. Fahringer (Eds.): GECON 2008, LNCS 5206, pp. 58–72, 2008.

In this paper, we specify a marketplace comprising all functionality for the leasing of computational service for a time period. It can serve as the core of the Grid economy. Customers (and hardware providers) interact through the marketplace, possibly by means of brokers, in order to lease (respectively offer) Grid resources. In Sect. 2 we outline a stock-market like mechanism and a corresponding system architecture that enables the trading of computational power on a spot market basis [4], as well as for selling futures contracts [5]. The underlying principle for this mechanism is that of a standard spot and futures market: All parties announce the maximum price they are willing to buy for and the minimum price they are willing to sell for. The spot bids (resp. asks) are put in the spot queue for bids (resp. asks). The futures are listed in the directory service of the futures market. All the compatible trades, i.e. when a bid is matched with a set of asks, are immediately executed. Note that matters are more complicated for our system's spot market than in standard spot markets of storable commodities, because in our case a the computational service is traded. This service is non-storable, because its specification includes both the quantity of resources and the relevant time interval. These matters are clarified in Sect. 3, 4 and 5, where we also introduce and assess an economically sound algorithm for matching bids and asks. Some additional important issues regarding matching that are left for future work, including the outline of a more sophisticated matching algorithm, are presented in Sect. 6.

## 2   The Marketplace and Its Architecture

So far, we have outlined the core functionality of the marketplace, i.e. the Grid Market, which is the main focus of this paper. It is worth noting that in order to be feasible for a *realistic* Grid marketplace to fully support the market mechanisms, a set of additional subsystems must be implemented as well. These subsystems are common among all existing (e.g. e-commerce) marketplaces, are not Grid-specific and both complement and support the core functionality of the Grid marketplace. Their detailed description is beyond the scope of this paper, which focuses on the presentation of a simple, fast and applicable, yet economically sound, Grid marketplace mechanism and the set of algorithms it comprises. However, we outline the marketplace system architecture (also depicted as Fig. 1) and highlight the subsystems functionality below for completeness reasons.

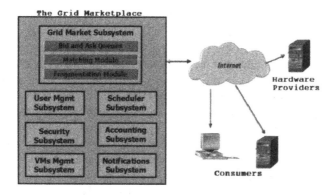

**Fig. 1.** The marketplace system architecture

*User Management Subsystem:* This subsystem is responsible for admitting users and providers into the marketplace. It uniquely authenticates and admits users/providers into the system, stores/checks their respective credentials and also interacts with the accounting/logistics and notifications subsystem.

*Resource Management Subsystem:* This subsystem is responsible for the management of the computational elements of the Grid marketplace and for the binding of the resources offered with a certain economic mechanism.

*Security Subsystem:* This subsystem enforces the marketplace's rules in the market transactions. It performs a wide variety of checks. For instance, it checks that the resources offered by the providers are indeed idle. It also interfaces with the Accounting and Logistics subsystems described below.

*Accounting/Logistics Subsystems:* Perform accounting and logistics management.

*Directory Services Subsystem:* This subsystem allows the organization and the advertisement of the leasing of resources. It is complemented with a search.

*Notifications Subsystem:* This subsystem is responsible for sending notifications to users. There are plenty of cases where this is desirable, such as: inform a bidder whether his bids are winning or not, or send reports to the virtual machines providers about their resource usage status and the respective revenue attained.

*Scheduler Subsystem:* This subsystem allows the execution of tasks at certain epochs, possibly periodically.

## 3 The Grid Market

First, we need to define the service that is to be traded in the grid market. Obviously, this must be suitable for the types of Grid applications currently existing or emerging. Hardware providers offer for leasing virtual machines (VMs) of different types that can be traded by means of different mechanisms [6], [7], [8]. It is expected that these resources be offered for a minimum desirable price and for certain time duration within a specific time interval, depending on the providers' supply constraints. Note that a virtual machine does not just correspond to a certain computational speed, but rather to an entire configuration of the hardware. This configuration is henceforth and throughout the remainder of this paper referred to as VM or unit of computation; these terms are used interchangeably.

An additional assumption of our model throughout the paper is that time is discretized in time slots. For simplicity of presentation reasons, the duration of this time slot in all the examples presented in the remainder of the paper is taken to be 1 hour, though in practice it would be set to a different value.

Customers are interested in accommodating their needs for computational power from the Grid market. They can achieve this by leasing some of the virtual machines that the providers make available in the Grid market. Depending on the nature of the tasks consumers may wish to execute, their demand can be expressed in a multitude of ways. A general type of "contract" is specified by means of a certain rate of computation for a specific time interval. For instance, this could be the case for a

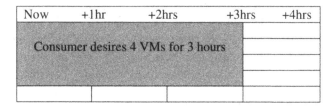

**Fig. 2.** A consumer's demand for 4 VMs for 3 hours is depicted by means of a rectangle

company's web server that leases Grid resources when it is critically loaded. This type of consumer need can be also graphically depicted by means of a rectangle (see Fig. 2): The height of the rectangle denotes the number of virtual machines required at any time of the interval, while width of rectangle denotes the amount of time for which these machines are needed.

Another type of contract could be specified by means of computational volume, i.e. a total number of VMs must be made available up to a maximum deadline constraint, so that a certain computationally intensive task is executed in time. As opposed to the previous case, only the total quantity of computational power is of interest, while the rate of computation provided at the various time epochs is not. This could be the case for a weather prediction program or a stock market data mining application that must be executed up to a deadline, i.e. the announcement of the weather forecast and the prediction of stock market prices before the markets open respectively. Note that the consumer needs in this case no longer correspond to rectangles, but rather to areas of rectangles, possibly with a maximum width (i.e. deadline) constraint. An extension of the Grid market mechanisms for this type of contracts is provided later in the penultimate section of this paper.

## 3.1 Bids

A bid in our system prescribes the resources required, which are specified by means of: a) the type and quantity of resources required, b) the starting time of the interval for using the resources, and c) the time duration of using the resources. It also specifies d) the price, expressed in €/min/unit and e) the time limit for which the bid applies. The latter is the maximum time at which the bid is considered to be valid. If this time is reached without the bid being matched, the bid must be removed.

The bid definition could also be complemented by a definition of whether or not the bid is atomic, i.e., it should be fully served by resources of a single provider. Atomicity may be the result of technological constraints on the possibility to switch execution environments. If such constraints are absent, economic theory suggests that the market should refrain from supporting atomic bids, due to the market power that large providers would obtain, which is not compatible with a bid and ask mechanism. In fact, even if the market would only support atomic bids, then it is likely that consumers would post-sale combine the resources of multiple such bids to obtain a more extended service Therefore, it is henceforth assumed that bids are non-atomic; more on this issue will be discussed later.

There are two types of bids in our system, namely future and spot bids. Future bids are the bids for which the starting and ending times are fixed instants in the future.

For instance, a future bid is the following: "User X bids for 5 processing power units (i.e. VMs) of type A to be used for 5 hrs, starting at time 13:00, with bid price 0.5 €/min/unit". Note that in practice the time contains also the Date, but this is omitted for brevity reasons throughout this paper. Note also that different providers may offer the resources required or even a subset thereof; e.g. Provider Y1 offers 2 units from 13:00 to 14:00, while Provider Y2 offers 1 unit from 14:00 to 18:00 and Provider Y3 offers 4 units from 15:00 to 18:00. As opposed to future bids, spot bids demand to utilize resources as soon as they are available. Such bids are distinguished from futures by setting the starting time at a special value (e.g. 0) and by the fact that their start and end time are continuously moving as time passes and the bid is not matched (up to the maximum time allowed by the expiry of the bid). Therefore, spot bids are more flexible than future bids, since they allow users to express demand for service of a certain duration over a larger time interval, as opposed to futures. Note that the actual time of the service of the consumer in this case is a priori unknown, since this depends on when these bids will be matched by asks. For instance, a spot bid is the following: "User X bids for 5 VMs of type A to be used for 5 hrs, starting at time 0, with bid price 0.5 €/min/unit, and time limit 20:00". In this example the bid could end up be executed the latest starting at 20:00.

## 3.2 Asks

An ask in our system prescribes the resources offered, which are specified by means of: a) the type and quantity of resources offered, b) the starting time and the end time of the interval when the resources are made available, and c) the total time duration of using the resources. It also specifies d) the price, expressed in €/min/unit and e) the time limit for which the ask is valid and can be used for matching bids. The latter is the maximum time at which the ask is considered to be valid, i.e., the provider of the ask will remove the ask or any remainder of it from the system after the above time. That is, this is the expiry time of the offer, and can be earlier than the maximum time deadline for which the resources offered in the ask can be made available to users.

Similarly with bids, there are also two types of asks, namely future and spot asks. Future asks are those for which the starting and ending times are fixed instants in the future. For asks, the ending time equals the starting time plus the duration, while the time limit also has the same value by default. For instance, a future ask is the following: "Provider Y offers for leasing 2 VMs of type A to be used for 8 hrs, starting at time 15:00, with ask price 0.2 €/min/unit". On the contrary, spot asks offer resources that can be utilized as soon as there is demand for them. Such asks are distinguished from future asks by setting the starting time at a special value (e.g. 0) and because they are more flexible than future asks, since they offer service of a certain duration over a larger time interval. For instance, a spot ask is the following: "Provider Y offers 2 VMs of type A to be used for 3 hrs, starting at time 0 and until 22:00, with ask price 0.2 €/min/unit, and time limit 19:00". The semantics is that up to two machines can be used each for up to three time slots (hours), not necessarily consecutive, during the next time slots; this ask will be removed from the system when the time is 19:00 if it has not been matched until then.

## 3.3  Bid and Ask Queues

Trading is performed by means of a continuous double auction mechanism. This is an extension of the standard spot market mechanism so as to provide for the trading of computation service that can be fully specified only when the associated time is also defined. Similarly to the standard mechanism, the spot bids and asks submitted by traders are placed in the *bid queue* and the *ask queue* respectively. Each queue is ordered according to the price and time of issuance, with the *bid* queue being sorted in *decreasing* order of price, and the *ask* queue being sorted in *increasing* order of price. In the case of the futures market, the bids and asks are listed in a directory service that enables searching and matching.

If two or more orders at the same price appear in a spot queue, then they are entered by time with older orders appearing ahead of newer orders. Since price is discretized in our model, then an equivalent representation of this queue is an ordered (per price) list of queues, one per price asked/bidded, where the asks/bids are sorted by time. The prices displayed to traders when they log into the market are the highest bid price in the bid queue and the lowest ask price in the ask queue. If no price is displayed it is because the corresponding queue is empty.

Orders remain in the queues until they are removed by the system due to expiration, or until they are accepted by other traders (a matching occurred) and result in trades. Expirations are determined according to the terms of the order. In particular, a spot bid expires at its time limit, and the same applies for spot asks.

## 3.4  Matching

The matching module is invoked when a new bid or ask is submitted. The rationale behind the matching module is that bids are completely satisfied, i.e. there are never remainder bids (parts of a bid that may be satisfied in the future). For simplicity reasons and in order to reduce the potential communication overhead that occurs for customers being served simultaneously by multiple providers, we assume that each bid is served by one provider at any time instance, while multiple providers can only be involved in different times during the servicing of the bid. This assumption will be henceforth referred to as *vertical atomicity*. This assumption is adopted for one more reason: the possibility of serving an application at a certain time with resources belonging to multiple providers depends on the parallelizability of the application, which would then have to be input to the market mechanism and taken into account thereby. Thus, we assume that the matching algorithm considers as candidate matches of a bid only asks whose height is greater than or equal to that of the bid.

Furthermore, we assume that the matching algorithm considers as candidate matches of a bid only asks whose price (per unit) does not exceed that of the bid. Therefore, we omit examining higher price asks and try combine them with lower price asks, even if such combinations could in fact serve the bid with the bidder attaining positive net benefit from the overall charge of the service. This is justified from an economic point of view, since serving customers using higher price asks than the price of the bid would be misleading and distorting for the information signals regarding the actual market price.

Note also that the bid and the ask should be matching in both time and quantity, i.e. all the bid constraints should be satisfied using the existing state of the ask queue. If the bid price and the ask price are different, then the price used is the one of the oldest order. Although this idea is similar to that of a double auction, matters are considerably more complicated because we are dealing with perishable resources with a time dimension. Finally, the matching module must also periodically check for expired bids and asks, which should be removed. In Sect. 4 we present in detail the matching procedure that is to be executed when a new bid/ask is submitted, while in Sect. 5 and Sect. 6 we specify two matching algorithms that could be adopted.

## 4  Matching and Remainder Asks

The rationale of the matching procedure is to provide the required coverage of the bid with the cheapest matching asks (asks overlapping in time whose price is at most as high as that of the bid) by means of a matching algorithm. If a bid is matched *fully* then reservation of resources, accounting and computation of remainder asks that replace the original asks in the ask queue are performed and the bid is withdrawn from the bid queue and subsequently serviced. Though a bid is always fully matched (fully satisfied), this is not the case for asks. Therefore, in general a fraction of an ask may be used to (partly) match and serve a bid, thus generating a remainder ask.

Specifying the remainders in the futures (forward) market is much simpler than the spot market. Since both future bids and asks are fixed in time, the remainder is a valid ask and can remain in the futures market. This remainder in general corresponds to a non-rectangular shape, in the sense that the amount of VMs offered in not the same for the entire time interval spanned. Such a remainder ask can also be equivalently represented as a collection of at most three rectangular shapes. We henceforth adopt this representation, to clarify the presentation of the algorithms to follow. A related example is depicted in Fig. 3.

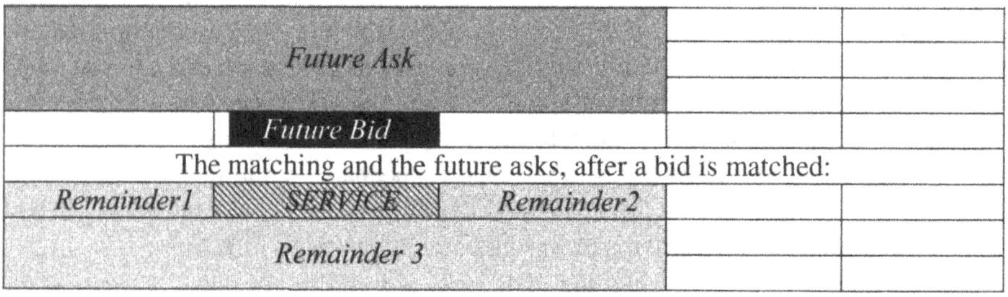

**Fig. 3.** Matching and remainder asks in the futures market

Things are more complicated for the spot asks, since some of the remainders generated may not be able to offer resource immediately, as opposed to others. The matching procedure and the respective remainders, which are considered as individual rectangles by our matching algorithm, are depicted in Fig. 4 and Fig. 5.

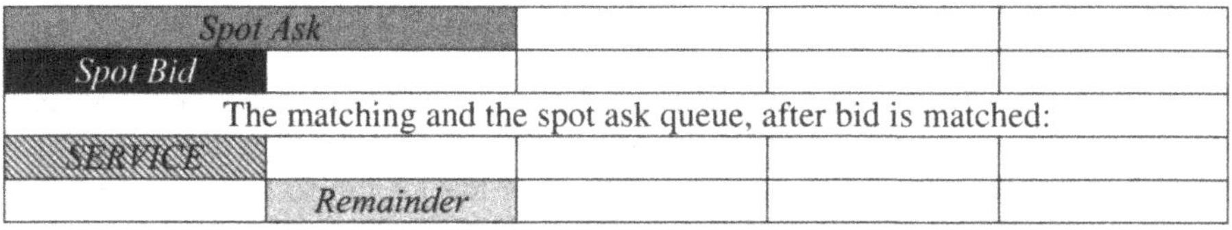

| Spot Ask | | | | |
|---|---|---|---|---|
| Spot Bid | | | | |
| The matching and the spot ask queue, after bid is matched: | | | | |
| SERVICE | | | | |
| | Remainder | | | |

**Fig. 4.** Matching and remainder of a spot bid with an ask offering same number of VMs

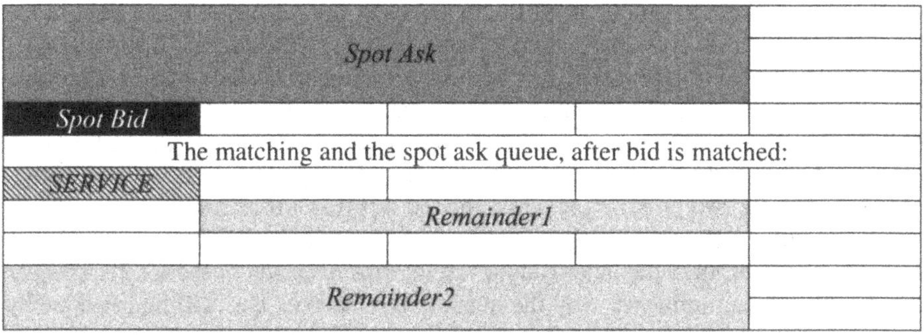

| | Spot Ask | | | |
|---|---|---|---|---|
| | | | | |
| Spot Bid | | | | |
| The matching and the spot ask queue, after bid is matched: | | | | |
| SERVICE | | | | |
| | Remainder1 | | | |
| | | | | |
| Remainder2 | | | | |

**Fig. 5.** Matching and remainder of a spot bid with an ask offering different number of VMs

An interesting issue here is that a matching of a spot bid with a much larger spot ask creates remainders that offer resources "as soon as possible" but not immediately, namely *Remainder* of Fig. 4 and *Remainder1* of Fig. 5. There are three options on the treatment of these remainders: a) transfer them to a "waiting queue" and reinsert them into the spot queue when the system time is such that they can indeed offer resources immediately, or b) cancel them and notify the provider, or c) treat all the remainders of a spot ask as valid spot asks which remain in the spot ask queue and are considered for matching, but tagged with additional constraints on when they can be used. Option a) is not economically sound because the market should be kept simple and refrain from making any "brokering" decisions on users' behalf. Indeed, the automated re-insertion of an ask after some time where the market conditions and prices may be completely different than those at the moment, would be confusing for providers who would face uncertainty regarding their strategy. Options b) and c) are both economically sound, with the first being the simplest one, yet resulting in overhead for the hardware providers. On the contrary, option c) does not suffer from this problem, yet it complicates significantly both the representation of asks since now a task description must also include the time slots where the machines of the ask are not free to be used by other bids, and the matching algorithm. In this paper, we investigate both approaches. In particular, option b) is the fundamental assumption for the matching algorithm of Sect. 5. Option c) and its implications on matching are investigated in the penultimate section of this paper, where the outline of a more sophisticated matching algorithm is also presented.

# 5  The Matching Algorithm

We begin the presentation by focusing on the forward market. For simplicity reasons, it suffices to adopt a one-pass of the queues matching algorithm. The matching algorithm in the futures market is much simpler than that of the spot queue, since the timespan of all bids and asks is fully specified, i.e. their start and end times are decided upon their submission and cannot be changed subsequently, as opposed to spot bids/asks. A meaningful matching procedure for the futures market is to try to match a bid with the cheapest matching asks.

The algorithm for the spot market has to make the same decision but in light of the feature that spot asks may start contributing resources to the matching at some later time, due to the flexibility associated with the provision of their resources. Note that we refrain from adopting a combinatorial approach due to the high computational complexity. The algorithm presented in the remainder of this section is in line with the sorting and treatment of the ask queue in terms of price and time of arrival (in case of equal price for two or more asks), despite the fact that it uses some temporary data structures with a different sorting. Its fundamental property is that if an ask is of lower price than another, then the latter cannot "steal" time of match of the former cheaper ask, i.e. an ask can influence only the quantity of resources that will be provided by higher price asks, as opposed to that of lower asks. This property is very important, since it ensures that the matching algorithm does not violate the rationale of the bid and ask spot market. Also, as mentioned in the previous section, it relies on the assumption that all the spot asks of the queue can offer their resources immediately. This implies that if a spot ask can offer service at some time $t$, then it can also provide service at any time $t'$ prior to $t$.

The matching algorithm of this section examines how to cover a particular bid, and produces as the matching solution an ordered list of asks matching the bid in terms of price; the list is ordered with respect to the deadlines of the asks (i.e. latest time to start providing resources). This list would then be passed to the scheduler, who could serve the bid accordingly. However, the algorithm matches the bid with resources taken as much as possible from cheapest asks in the list, which are considered first. That is, the ordering of the list yields the order in time according to which the bid will be served by the various matching asks (or parts thereof).

This code is run from scratch every time a new matching is to be performed, either because a new bid arrived, or because a new ask arrived. Note that when we encounter an ask that could provide some service because its price does not exceed that of the bid we need to decide a) where to place it in the order of asks to serve this bid, b) how much of it to use. The solution we adopt is a) to order the matching asks according to the time constraints b) use as much as possible of cheapest asks. In particular, for any matching ask we use the part of it that does not render any of those asks invalid[1] by any part in time. Indeed if we use less of the specific ask considered than this part, we leave a part of service that could be provided unfulfilled. Yet, if we use a larger portion of it, then we would actually replace service that could be provided by cheaper asks. This would increase the customer's charge and violate the ordering and treatment of asks of the queue with respect to prices. An example of this matching algorithm is provided below:

---

[1] I.e. it does not cause any time deadline violation due to the "shifting" in time of the service start of the respective ask.

Assume that a spot bid is received, requesting 1 VM for 3 hours for a price of 4€/VM/hr. Assume that there are the following matching asks in the queue, which for simplicity are taken as offering each as many resources as those required by the bid: a) *Ask1*: Offer 1 VM for 1 hour, time deadline: now + 0,5 hour p: 1€/VM/hr. b) *Ask2*: Offer 1 VM for 1 hour, time deadline: now + 1 min p: 2€/VM/hr. c) *Ask3*: Offer 1 VM for 2 hours, time deadline: now + 6 hours p: 3.8€/VM/hr. Note that both for this example and throughout the paper, "now" denotes the start of the next time slot, due to the fact that in our model time is not continuous but discretized in slots.

The algorithm would initially partly match the bid with the **cheapest** ask of the queue, namely *Ask1*. Therefore, the outcome of the execution of the algorithm after examining the first ask in the queue is as follows:

| Now | 0.5hr | 1hr | 1.5hr | 2hr | 2.5hr | 3hr |
|-----|-------|-----|-------|-----|-------|-----|
| *Ask1* | | | | | | |

**Fig. 6.** The algorithm initially partly matches the bid with the cheapest ask

The algorithm would subsequently examine the second cheapest ask, namely *Ask2*. *Ask2* is inserted prior to *Ask1*, due to its shorter deadline. This means that *Ask1* would be shifted in time and then *Ask1* would violate its time constraint by 0.5hr.

| Now | 0.5hr | 1hr | 1.5hr | 2hr | 2.5hr | 3hr |
|-----|-------|-----|-------|-----|-------|-----|
| *Ask2* | | *Ask1* | | | | |
| ←*Violation*→ | | | | | | |

**Fig. 7.** Ask1 is shifted in time due to the selection of Ask2 as part of the matching solution

This time violation means that only 0.5 hr of service will be provided by *Ask2*, since an ask cannot influence the quantity of resources that will be utilized by any lower price ask, namely *Ask1* in this example. Since we can have in total 1.5 hour of service, our algorithm opts to get as much as possible from the cheapest provider. This means that *Ask2* will provide only 0.5 hr of service, as depicted below:

| Now | 0.5hr | 1hr | 1.5hr | 2hr | 2.5hr | 3hr |
|-----|-------|-----|-------|-----|-------|-----|
| *Ask2* | *Ask1* | | | | | |

**Fig. 8.** A fraction of Ask2 is used for the matching since Ask1 must be fully used

Subsequently Ask3 is examined and it provides the remaining 1.5 hr of service. Therefore, this bid will be served as follows:

| Now | 0.5hr | 1hr | 1.5hr | 2hr | 2.5hr | 3hr |
|-----|-------|-----|-------|-----|-------|-----|
| *Ask2* | *Ask1* | | *Ask3* | | | |

**Fig. 9.** The solution of the matching algorithm

It is easy to prove that the aforementioned algorithm clearly favors low price asks. By construction, if an ask is of lower price than another, then the latter cannot "steal" time of match of the former cheaper ask, although it can influence its position in the order of providing service to the bids. Therefore, this matching procedure provides nice incentives for providers to submit low price asks. Also, this procedure attempts to match a bid with a low-cost coverage of matching asks.

Yet, this algorithm fails either to always discover matching of a bid with the asks in the queue whenever such a matching is feasible, or guarantee that when it finds a match that this is the lowest-cost match of the bid. This algorithm does not guarantee these properties because its objective is to match the bid completely without violating the queue order. In fact, we have also developed an algorithm that always produces one matching whenever there does exist one. However, the latter is not economically sound because it violates the queue order principle of the bid and ask mechanism and can only serve as a benchmark in order to assess the ratio of matches that the present algorithm misses. To illustrate these shortcomings of the present algorithm, it suffices to modify *Ask2* as follows: Offer 1 VM for 6 hours, time deadline: now + 1 min p: 2€/VM/hr. It is now obvious that the lowest-cost matching for the bid is to match it for its entire duration with *Ask2*; this is depicted as Fig. 10. However, the matching algorithm still returns the same solution, which is depicted as Fig. 11.

| Now | 0.5hr | 1hr | 1.5hr | 2hr | 2.5hr | 3hr |
|-----|-------|-----|-------|-----|-------|-----|
| | | | *Ask2* | | | |

**Fig. 10.** The cheapest matching solution for the bid submitted

| Now | 0.5hr | 1hr | 1.5hr | 2hr | 2.5hr | 3hr |
|-----|-------|-----|-------|-----|-------|-----|
| *Ask2* | | *Ask1* | | | *Ask3* | |

**Fig. 11.** The matching solution computed by the algorithm

Note that the solution that the matching procedure provides is in fact more expensive, due to the much higher cost of *Ask3*. It is also worth noting that if *Ask3* were absent from the queue, the algorithm would not find the matching with *Ask2* and the bidder would not be served, although this is actually feasible.

Last but not least, we remind the reader that this algorithm relies on the assumption that all spot asks can offer their resources immediately; (remainder) spot asks which could offer resources from some time in the future have been removed from the queue and their providers have been notified accordingly. In addition to the overhead for the hardware providers, the fact that this algorithm works with a subset of the spot asks that could be used for matching bids, further limits the number of matches computed. This is in contrast with the algorithm outlined in the next section, which also favors low price asks and also treats all the remainders of a spot ask as one non-rectangular spot ask which remains in the spot ask queue and is considered for matching.

# 6 Extensions and Future Work

As opposed to the algorithm of the precious section, we proceed to outline an algorithm, which considers spot asks whose resources are not necessarily available from the current system time (such asks are the *Remainder* of Fig. 4 and *Remainder1* of Fig. 5) as candidate matches. In order to allow such asks in the spot queue, we need to generalize the definition of spot asks (see Sect. 3) so as to be the asks that prescribe that a certain quantity of resources (e.g. 1 VM) for a certain duration (e.g. 2 hours) is made available as soon as possible within certain time intervals (e.g. from 13:00 till 20:00 today, except the intervals [14:00-15:00] and [16:00-17:00] where this VM has already being previously reserved to service some bid) and the ask is valid and present in the queue up to a maximum time deadline, e.g. 18:00 today. Note that this ask is still a spot ask since the starting and ending times are not fixed instants in the future, as opposed to futures.

Note also that this spot ask is different at different times, due to the fact that prior reservations that keep the resources busy are fixed in time. Therefore, the matching of a bid with a set of such asks that are also changing in time is more complicated, in the sense that the algorithm should first specify the current state of the ask. In particular, solving this scheduling problem is a well-known NP-complete problem. Due to the problem's high complexity, we outline an algorithm which is fast enough to be adopted in a realistic market, performs well in terms of the matches computed and does not violate the fundamental rationale of the spot ask queue, i.e. prioritization of cheap asks. Nevertheless, this algorithm is a heuristic approach that does not claim to solve the scheduling problem, i.e. it cannot always compute a set of matching asks for a bid if there is indeed one. Its formal definition and assessment are beyond the scope of this paper and are left for future work. However, the rationale of the algorithm is presented below.

The algorithm initially computes the candidate matches for the ask (i.e. asks of the demanded quantity of VMs) that can offer service from time *Now* (denoting the start of the next time slot) and for a service duration equal to that specified in the bid. This is performed by means of creating a matrix. Such an example matrix is depicted as Fig. 12. Each column of the matrix corresponds to a slot of the time interval where service will be provided. Each row corresponds to a provider that can offer service within this time interval, with the cheapest being on the top row. The cells where each provider can offer service are marked, as well as the total availability of each provider's (i.e. number of slots where they can offer the desired amount of VMs). For instance, Provider2 in Fig. 12 can offer three hours of computation anywhere within the 4-hour time interval, i.e. provider's availability is 3. If there is a slot where it is not possible to provide service for any provider, then the algorithm fails and proceeds to find a match for the time interval [Now + 1 slot, Now + 1 slot + service duration]. The algorithm then detects the slots where there is only one provider offering service; these providers are matched for those slots and their total availability for service is subsequently reduced. Then the algorithm attempts to fill the slots where there are multiple candidate providers, regardless of their total availability: For these slots, the algorithm attempts to do a probabilistic matching. In particular, the algorithm starts with the cheapest ask and according to the provider's availability randomly fills some slots, so that the provider's availability becomes zero. I.e. the cheapest ask is fully

| Now | +1hr | +2hr | +3hr | +4hr | Availability |
|---|---|---|---|---|---|
| Unavailable | Provider1 | Provider1 | Provider1 | | 2 |
| Provider2 | Provider2 | Provider2 | Provider2 | | 3 |
| Provider3 | Provider3 | Unavailable | Provider3 | | 3 |

**Fig. 12.** The matrix used from Algorithm 2 to match a spot bid demanding 4 hours of service

utilized. It then proceeds with the next cheapest ask and does the same. Note however that after the second step, there might be slots allocated to two candidate providers. For these slots, each provider is assigned a probability of moving from this slot, depending on his total availability. A dice is thrown and a provider is moved to an empty slot according to a transition probability, which is larger for slots where the number of providers that could serve this slot is small. The algorithm terminates when all the slots are assigned to some provider and thus a match is found. In case there are slots where there is no provider serving it, while there are not any slots with more than one provider, the algorithm has failed to compute a match. Due to the matching algorithm's probabilistic nature, it can be repeated for a maximum prespecified number of times until it computes a match. If it fails, then it attempts to compute a match at a next time window, i.e. at the second time for the time interval [Now + 1 slot, Now + 1 slot + service duration]. This is performed until a match is indeed found or the algorithm fails for the entire duration where the bid is valid.

Note that for some services, e.g. non-parallel distributed applications, such as a company's web server, it might be meaningful to enforce *horizontal atomicity* instead of *vertical atomicity*. This means that the user should be assigned a provider's VM for the entire duration of service demanded. However, multiple providers may offer the total number of VMs requested. If this is indeed the case, the matching algorithm is greatly simplified. The reason is that under this assumption, candidate asks are only the asks of providers that can offer VMs for the entire duration of service demanded by the bid. Therefore, the algorithm sorts the asks providing a VM for the entire duration within each time interval, starting from [Now, Now + service duration]. If the number of matching asks in this interval is at least that demanded, then the cheapest VMs are selected and provided as match. If the number of matching asks is less, there is no possible match and the algorithm proceeds to compute a match at a next time window, i.e. at the second time for the time interval [Now + 1 slot, Now + 1 slot + service duration]. This is performed until a match is indeed found or the algorithm fails for the entire duration where the bid is valid. It is trivial to prove that this algorithm never fails to detect a match if any and that it also always computes the cheapest matching ask that can be provided as soon as possible to the user.

Throughout the paper we have assumed that customers are interested in rate of computation in a certain time interval. Replacing the "rectangles" of this market with a total quantity of computation greatly simplifies the matching algorithms presented earlier applicable for this market as well. Thus, instead of trying to match a bid with a rectangle constructed by a set of asks with proper height, the matching algorithm simply picks the cheapest asks that can provide the desired computation within the specified deadline.

As already mentioned it is possible that a bid be satisfied by the asks submitted by multiple providers. This clearly increases the switching costs of users and reduces the value of the allocations of the market. Therefore, this problem should be mitigated by means of a special algorithm. Such an algorithm could prescribe that units allocated to different users should be "swapped" if possible, thus resulting in a less fragmented with respect to number of providers per user, outcome. It is worth emphasizing that though units of allocation can be swapped between consumers, prices and quantities are not. A preliminary idea for such an algorithm is to swap units between two users, if and only if for some performance index (e.g. total number of different asks matched) the post-swap value is better for one user while being non-worse for the other. The formal definition of such an algorithm, as well as conducting simulations for the evaluation of the algorithms presented in this paper, is left for future work.

## 7  Conclusions

In this paper, we have specified a market where hardware providers can interact with users interested in leasing Grid resources for a price and a time period. Our approach comprises a stock-market like mechanism that enables the trading of computational power on the basis of a spot and a futures market. The spot market comprises a pair of bid and ask queues. This grid market is more complicated than the standard spot/futures markets of storable commodities, because the computational service traded in our case comprises of resources that are perishable, and has both quantity and duration specified in terms of a time interval. This is an important feature of our market mechanism that has been taken into account by both the market mechanism and the related matching algorithms that operate on the spot bid/ask queues and futures market. Finally, we have briefly addressed the issue of post-sale optimization in order to mitigate the switching cost of consumers being served by multiple providers over time. The formal definition of such an algorithm is left for future work. Another direction for future research is to formally specify and evaluate the algorithm that provides matchings according to which service can start with a delay, due to the fact that remainder asks that do not provide readily available resources are employed.

**Acknowledgments.** This work has been supported in part by the European Commission within the Framework Programm FP7, ICT, through the project GridEcon. The authors would like to thank all consortium members for useful discussions on the subject of this paper.

## References

1. Buyya, R., Abramson, D., Venugopal, S.: The Grid Economy. Proceedings of the IEEE 93(3), 698–714 (2005)
2. The Gridecon Project Consortium: Deliverable D2.1. Economic Modelling Requirement Report (2008), http://www.gridecon.eu/html/deliverables.shtml
3. Buyya, R., Abramson, D., Giddy, J., Stockinger, H.: Economic Models for Resource Management and Scheduling in Grid Computing. The Journal of Concurrency and Computation Practice and Experience (CCPE) (2002)

4. Denton, M.J., Rassenti, S.J., Smith, V.L.: Spot market mechanism design and competitivity issues in electric power. In: Proceedings of the Thirty First HICS
5. Lien, D., Quirk, J.: Measuring the Benefits from Futures Markets: Conceptual Issues. International Journal of Business and Economics 1(1), 53–58 (2002)
6. http://www.amazon.com/gp/browse.html?node=201590011
7. http://www.sun.com/service/sungrid/index.jsp
8. http://h20338.www2.hp.com/enterprise/cache/ 250417-0-0-225-121.html

# Rational Bidding Using Reinforcement Learning
## An Application in Automated Resource Allocation

Nikolay Borissov[1], Arun Anandasivam[1],
Niklas Wirström[2], and Dirk Neumann[3]

[1] University of Karlsruhe, Information Management and Systems,
Englerstr. 14, 76131 Karlsruhe
{borissov,anandasivam}@iism.uni-karlsruhe.de
[2] Swedish Institute of Computer Science, Box 1263, SE-164 29 Kista, Sweden
niwi@sics.se
[3] University of Freiburg, Platz der Alten Synagoge, 79085 Freiburg, Germany
dirk.neumann@vwl.uni-freiburg.de

**Abstract.** The application of autonomous agents by the provisioning and usage of computational resources is an attractive research field. Various methods and technologies in the area of artificial intelligence, statistics and economics are playing together to achieve i) autonomic resource provisioning and usage of computational resources, to invent ii) competitive bidding strategies for widely used market mechanisms and to iii) incentivize consumers and providers to use such market-based systems.

The contributions of the paper are threefold. First, we present a framework for supporting consumers and providers in technical and economic preference elicitation and the generation of bids. Secondly, we introduce a consumer-side reinforcement learning bidding strategy which enables rational behavior by the generation and selection of bids. Thirdly, we evaluate and compare this bidding strategy against a truth-telling bidding strategy for two kinds of market mechanisms – one centralized and one decentralized.

**Keywords:** Bid Generation, Reinforcement learning, Service Provisioning and Usage, Grid Computing.

## 1 Self-organized Resource Provisioning and Usage

Grid Computing is becoming more and more popular both as a research field, and in the industry. Prominent examples are Sun Microsystems' *Network.com*, Salesforce's *force.com*, *Amazon's Elastic Compute Cloud* (EC2) and its *Simple Storage Service* (S3) as well as *SimpleDB Service*. The companies often offer a fixed pay-per-use price for static resource configurations, which can lead to inefficient utilization, profit and usability, as it does not reflect the dynamics of the market supply and demand. Efficient provisioning and usage of computational resources as well as pricing in a thriving environment like Grid Computing is not manually manageable. Such processes should be automated with no or minimal

J. Altmann, D. Neumann, and T. Fahringer (Eds.): GECON 2008, LNCS 5206, pp. 73–88, 2008.

human interaction. Hence, market mechanism and strategic behavior play an important role for the design of the environment. Self-organization and automatic adaptation to the changing market conditions are key prerequisites for efficient allocation of computational resources [1].

To efficiently allocate consumers' jobs to providers' resources is a complex task where participants' decisions on resource provisioning and usage are executed online. Moreover, the wide heterogeneity of computational resources, complicates the process of finding an appropriate set of resources for given consumer's preferences. Since demand and supply of computational resources fluctuates in the course of time, information about current and future resource utilization and prices are often not known a-priori to the participants. In this case consumer and provider agents try to maximize their utilities by generating bids based on their valuations and historic experiences [2]. This enables strategic behavior both on provider and consumer side.

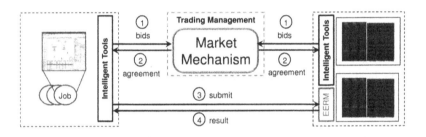

**Fig. 1.** Self-organized service offering and requesting

This paper is written in the context of the SORMA[1] project, with the focus on components and methodologies that constitutes the SORMA *Intelligent Tools*. Figure 1 depicts the approach taken by SORMA for automated provisioning and usage of computational resources. As illustrated, consumers and providers use the intelligent tools to generate and submit bids to the *Trading Management* component which executes a collection of different market mechanism. When an agreement has been made, the two parties are informed of this. The process of submitting and executing the job is exercised by the intelligent tools on the consumer side and the *Economically Enhanced Resource Management* (EERM) on the provider side.

This paper is structured as follows: Section 2 describes components and methodologies of the *Intelligent Tools* supporting the automated bidding process. Section 3 introduces the Truth-Telling strategy, and proposes a novel consumer-side reinforcement learning bidding strategy – the Q-Strategy. In Section 4 we evaluate this strategy against the Truth-Telling strategy using two different market mechanisms and show the convergence of the proposed Q-Strategy. Section 5 discusses related work and Section 6 concludes this paper.

---

[1] SORMA: Self-Organizing ICT Resource Management, www.sorma-project.org

## 2    Automated Bidding

Within this section we investigate the processes of automated bidding on provider and consumer sides and describe the tools supporting these. In SORMA, a set of *Intelligent Tools* are provided, which purpose is to assist consumers and providers by the description of their technical and economic preferences as well as by the automated generation of bids and offers.

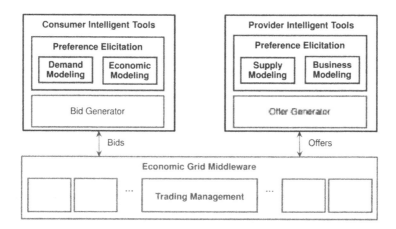

**Fig. 2.** Intelligent Tools for provider and consumer

Figure 2 shows the intelligent tools for the provider and consumer. In order to derive and describe their preferences, a consumer uses the *Demand Modeling* and *Economic Modeling* tools. The *Demand Modeling* component supports the consumer by the specification of the technical requirements on resources, such as CPU, Memory and Storage of her application. For this it offers a GUI for entering the technical requirements which are formatted in a predefined resource description language such as the *Job Submission and Description Language* [3]. *Economic modeling* allows consumers to describe their economic preferences that will determine their bidding strategies e.g. specifying the valuation of the required resources, validity of a bid and the preferred bidding strategy. The *Bid Generator* is the "intelligent" component that autonomously generates and places the consumer's bids on the market. For this purpose it considers the afore specified consumer preferences and the current state of the market, such as actual prices. The bid generator is implemented through agents using common and novel bidding strategies and learning algorithms. The bids are submitted to the *Trading Management* component, which implements mechanisms for technical and economic matching. Similar to demand modeling, *Supply Modeling* aids the provider to describe the technical specification of the offered resources. Within the *Business Modeling* component, providers have to describe the desired business models, which determine what bidding strategy to be used for the generation of their offers. For example one part of such a description is the pricing policy that specifies if the consumer has to pay for booked time-slots or for the actual usage. As the example indicates, the models specified by means of this component depend on the implemented market mechanism. Analogously to the bid generator, the *Offer Generator* is the component implementing the bidding strategies for the generation of the offers. The offers are assembled from the technical resource descriptions and the business model of the respective provider. The offer generation component also submits offers to the *Trading Management*. The market mechanisms are implemented within the *Trading Management* component, which is a part of the SORMA *Economic Grid Middleware*. In the following sections we will focus on the components of the *Intelligent Tools* and present them in more detail.

## 2.1   Preference Elicitation

In order to request computational resources for its application or job, a consumer has to make some estimations regarding preferred technical resource description, QoS and a price. On the other side, a provider has to make a price estimation for its offered resources. These consumer and provider preferences for a specific application can be either static or dynamic. Static information is collected once, and can be manually provided by the consumer or provider each time a resource has to be acquired or offered. These static information may also be stored in databases enabling intelligent tools to use this information for predicting requirements of applications and services with similar properties. However, the requirements of a given application are often subject to change as technology evolves e.g. consumers' desired quality of streamed video might increase as their Internet bandwidth increases. It is thus desirable to dynamically adapt the resource requirements. In [4] the authors specify a model for *Job Valuation Estimation* using evolutionary techniques. The presented approach is based on the assumption that a consumer who wants to buy a set of resources does not generally know her exact valuation for them, but has only a rough estimate of her true valuation. Thus, she decides whether to accept the offer, or to continue her search and look for alternative offers.

Going through following iterative process steps, the bidding agent can approximate the results and successively refine its estimate:

1. *Initialization:* The market participant (consumer, provider) or bidding agent initially assumes a valuation of $v_0^A$ for an application $A$ based on its resource specification $x^A$. It is assumed that the current price for each resource is published by the market mechanism in a price vector $p_0 \in \Re_+^n$, and an initial weight $\Theta_0^A \in N$ set by the user: $v_0^A(\Theta_0^A, p_0, x^A) = \Theta_0^A p_o^T x^A$ For each run of the application j:
2. *Bidding:* the bidding agent bids on the market according to its estimate $v_j^A(\Theta_j^A, p_j, x^A)$ and selected bidding strategy.
3. *Refinement:* There are two possible outcomes of the bidding process:
   - *Successful:* The bidding agent obtains the necessary resources and reports this information to the participant. The participant then indicates

whether he is satisfied with the outcome or not, and the bidding agent refines its estimate.

- *Unsuccessful:* The bidding agent was not able to obtain the necessary resources. If the participant indicates that the price was indeed too high, the bidding agent does not update its estimate. If the user indicates that he would have preferred to pay that price rather than not getting the resources ($\Theta^A_{j+1} = 0$), the bidding agent updates its estimate of $v^A$ with the current price.

The bidding agent will iteratively try to converge its estimate to the participant's true valuation and at the same time to assists her in identifying a bid rather than forcing the participant to directly reveal its valuation.

## 2.2   Demand Modeling

The *Demand Modeling* component supports consumers and providers on editing their estimated preferences – technical requirements on resources, such as CPU, Memory and Storage, QoS and price. The component implements a GUI for entering the consumer or provider preferences and generates a XML output in form of predefined resource description language such as *Job Submission and Description Language* [3].

The main parts of this component are:

- *User Interface* to allow the input of technical resource specifications on consumer and supplier side
- *Matchmaking library* implementing methods and algorithms for technical matching of resource requests to offers and
- *Service Description Language* that is able to express service specifications traded on the SORMA marketplace

The service description language contains a high-level specification of the service to be run on the requested resource. To allow different levels of abstraction and granularity, the resource needs to be technically specified in terms of its grounding hardware and the required software environment. Together with the technical specification comes the specification of several non-functional technical resource properties as for example the quality of service. Beyond that, further sections like economic parameters, job-specific parameters or possible inter-job dependencies complete the resource specification.

## 2.3   Bid and Offer Generator

In the SORMA Grid Market scenario each consumer and provider is configuring and using the intelligent tools i.e bidding agents in order to use or provide resources with the objective to maximize its own utility, and thus it acts rationally.

The bid and offer generator component is implemented within SORMA's *Bidding Agent Framework*, which core classes and relations are illustrated in Figure 3. The framework is defined and discussed in more detail in [5].

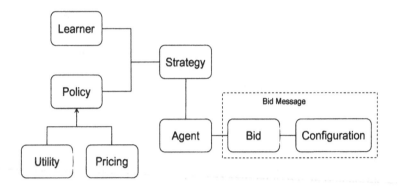

**Fig. 3.** Framework for Automated Bidding

According to the framework, a bidding *strategy* implements the bidding behavior of the bidding agent, e.g. how, when and what to bid. For this purpose it adopts learning algorithms to learn from earlier actions and predict future rewards by selecting a particular price for a given resource description.

Furthermore a strategy profile can be configured with policies, which are defined in a rule description language and executed within a rule engine. *Policies* in our case are *utility* and *pricing* functions, which are defined externally to the implementation and thus enable a flexible modification. Through the utility function, the participant specifies the overall objectives as a mathematical function that is to be maximized by its bidding agent. For a job $j$, the pricing policy enables a static specification of a valuation $v_j$ or price calculation function, which is used by the bidding strategy to calculate the bid $\tilde{v}_j \leq v_j$, which is reported to the SORMA Grid Market.

For example, in the case of allocating computational resources for a job execution, a common utility function in the scheduling literature minimizes the weighted completion time $w * C$ of a job, where the weight $w$ represents the importance of a job expressed in some unit. In the economic literature the unit is often a price or so called valuation. The authors of [6] propose a utility function $u_{i,j} = -w_j * C_{i,j} - \pi_{i,j}$, which forces the minimization of the weighted completion time and payments in their particular machine scheduling mechanism, where the weight $w_j$ is the waiting costs of the job $j$, $C_{i,j}$ the reported completion time of machine $i$ and $\pi_{i,j}$ the amount to be paid to be scheduled on that machine.

The core classes *Bid* and *Configuration* define together the format of the overall bid message [5]. The bid message contains in the consumer case, the consumer's technical and economic preferences and in the provider case, the provider's technical and economic description.

## 3   Bidding Strategy

To implement a strategic behavior on the consumer side, we implemented consumer agents using two rational bidding strategies, a *Truth-Telling* and a *Reinforcement Learning* bidding strategy. The reinforcement learning bidding strategy is implemented through the Q-Learning algorithm with epsilon-greedy selection strategy (see Section 3.2).

## 3.1   Truth-Telling

In the model of [6], agents do not remember the outcomes of earlier market interactions but are somewhat "myopic" in the sense that they only consider the current situation. As shown for the model in [6], without knowledge about the future, at time $\tilde{r}_j$ it is a utility maximizing strategy $s_j$ for agent $j \in J$ to report its true type $t_j$ to the system and to choose the machine $i$ which maximizes $\hat{u}_j(i|s_{-j}, \tilde{t}_j, t_j)$.

The *Truth-Telling* bidding strategy places a bid price, which equal to the provider's or consumer's valuation for a certain resource. Although it is a simple strategy, truth-telling is essential in case of incentive-compatible mechanisms, where this strategy guarantees to obtain the optimal pay-offs for consumers no matter what strategies are adopted by the others. In budget-balanced double-auction mechanisms, this strategy is not dominant [7].

## 3.2   Q-Strategy

Our aim is to develop rational agents with learning capabilities which may strategically misreport about their true valuation based on previous experiences. We refer to these strategies as "rational response strategies".

---

**Algorithm 1.** Q-Strategy: Bid Generation Rule

---

**Require:** *economicpreferencesofthejob*
 1: **if** $\epsilon < Stochastic.random(0,1)$ **then**
 2:    //*Explore* :
 3:    $scale \in (0,1)$
 4:    $price = Stochastic.random(scale * job.getValuation(), job.getValuation())$
 5: **else**
 6:    //*Exploit* :
 7:    $state = State.getState(job)$
 8:    $action = qLearner.bestAction(state)$
 9:    **if** $action! = nil$ **then**
10:      $price = action.getBidPrice()$
11:    **else**
12:      $price = job.getValuation()$
13:    **end if**
14: **end if**

---

The Q-Strategy consists of two algorithms (see Algorithm 1 and 2). The first algorithm describes the case where an agent generates a bid (or offer) for a given configuration of resources it wants to buy (or sell). The second algorithm applies to the case where an agent receives a number of offers for a given configuration of resources, and has to select one of them to buy.

Both algorithms are based on a reinforcement learning approach – Q-Learning [8] with a $\epsilon$-greedy selection policy [9, 10]. Using this policy, the agent explores the environment with a probability of $\epsilon$, by selecting an action randomly, and exploits its obtained knowledge with probability of $1 - \epsilon$, by selecting an action that has been beneficial in the past. We use the following notation:

- Each job $j$ has a type $t_j = \{r_j, d_j, v_j\}$, where $r_j$ represents the instance of time when the job was "created", $d_j$ the requested duration and $v_j$ its valuation.
- $S$ is a finite discrete set of states, where each state $s$ is defined by a tuple $\{d, v\}$, such that an agent is in state $s = \{d_j, v_j\}$ if it is to bid for a job with duration $d_j$ and valuation $v_j$.
- $A$ is a repertoire of possible actions, where, in the context of this paper each action $a$ represents the assignment of a specific price to a bid.
- $Q(s, a)$ denotes the expected value of being in state $s$ and taking action $a$.
- $\rho$ is a mapping from stimuli observed, caused by an action, to the set of real numbers. Here, we use $\rho = -v_j C_j - \pi_j$, where $C_j$ is the time-span between creation and completion of job $j$, and $\pi_j$ is the price paid for it.

In other words, the objective is to learn the function $Q(s, a)$, so that, given any job with a specific duration and valuation, a price $\tilde{v} \leq v$ can be selected so that the utility is maximized. However, due to the sizes of the state and action spaces, and the fact that the environment in which the agent operates is continuously changing, only a rough estimate of the $Q$-function is feasible.

As stated earlier, learning is made through exploration of the environment. After finishing a job, the $Q$-function, is updated with the new information according to the *Q-Learning update rule*:

$$Q(s_t, a_t) := Q(s_t, a_t) + \alpha_t(s_t, a_t)[\rho_t + \gamma \max_a Q(s_{t+1}, a) - Q(s_t, a_t)] \quad (1)$$

Here, $s_t$ is the state defined by the duration and valuation of the job that the agent bids for at time $t$, $a_t$ is the action selected at time $t$, $\rho_t$ is the received utility of the job. The learning rate $\alpha_t \in [0, 1]$ determines how much weight we give to newly observed rewards. A high value of $\alpha_t$ results in that high importance is given to new information, while a low value leads to that the $Q$-function is updated using small steps. $\alpha_t = 0$ means no learning at all. The discounting factor $\gamma$ defines how much expected future rewards affect current decisions. Low $\gamma \rightarrow 0$ imply higher attention to immediate rewards. With higher ($\gamma \rightarrow 1$) implies orientation on future rewards, where agents may be willing to trade short-term loss for long-term gain.

In Algorithm 1, during exploration, the bid is randomly generated within the interval $p^s \in [s * v_j, v_j]$ with $s \in (0, 1)$. During exploitation, the bid is retrieved from the Q-Table, the "best" bid that in the history achieved the highest average payoff.

In Algorithm 2, during exploration, the strategy selects the "best offer" (maximizing its utility) of a resource provider, for which there is no stored information in the Q-Table. During exploitation it selects the best offer, which maximizes its utility.

---

**Algorithm 2.** Q-Strategy: Offer Selection Rule

---

**Require:** $economic preferences of the job; provider offers$
1: **if** $\epsilon < Stochastic.random(0, 1)$ **then**
2:    $//Explore:$
3:    $offer = bestOfferForProviderNotStoredInQTable(job, offers)$;
4: **else**
5:    $//Exploit:$
6:    $offer = myopicBestResponse(state, offers)$;
7: **end if**

---

## 4   Evaluation

Auction and strategy selection are closely connected in the sense that a given choice of strategy should affect the choice of auction, and vice versa. For example some bidding strategies perform well in a Continuous Double Auction (CDA), but not in a Dutch auction. This also implies that the choice of auction to participate in depends on the available strategies. Other factors to take into account in auction selection are the market rules, transaction costs, and the current and average prices in the different auctions.

In this section, we evaluate the Truth-Telling and Q-Learning strategies for two different types of market mechanisms for allocation of computational resources. The first market mechanism is a decentralized on-line machine scheduling mechanism, called Decentralized Local Greedy Mechanism (DLGM) [6]. The second one is a centralized continuous double auction (CDA) [11]. The market mechanisms are implemented within the *SORMA Trading Management* component. The simulation is run on a light version of this component.

As a measure we use the average utility per job received by the consumers. In the Truth-Telling scenario, this is the same as measuring the common wealth for this particular strategy, since all players have the same strategy. In the case of the Q-Learning strategy, however, this is not equivalent, since the behavior of the players diverge as the players observe different information.

In the case of the decentralized DLGM mechanism,, each time a job arrives on the consumer side, her bidding agent generates a bid in form of a job type $t_j = \{r_j, d_j, v_j\}$ (see Section 3) and report this to all providers. Based on this bid, each provider reports back a tentative completion time and tentative price for each of its machines. When sufficiently many provider offers have been collected, the consumer can decide, typically simplistically, which offer to choose. The providers in the DLGM market do not behave strategically and do not request compensation for the use of their resources. The payments are divided only among the consumer agents for compensating the displaced jobs.

In the centralized CDA, consumers and providers submit bids and offers consisting of only a price per time unit, and are matched based on this information. Providers act strategically, trying to achieve as much money as possible for their resources. To calculate the price of their bids, they use a ZIP (Zero Intelligence Plus) agent [12].

In the following section we describe the evaluation settings and simulation results.

## 4.1  Evaluation Setting

For each market – CDA and DLGM, and each strategy – Q-Learning and Truth-Telling, we simulated four different scenarios described by settings 1 through 4 in Table 1. In each scenario there are 50 consumers and 50 providers (each controlling a single machine). In each of the first three settings, the rate of which jobs comes in on the consumer side is determined by a Poisson process. To increase the competition in the market, we successively increased the mean $\lambda$ of the Poisson process from $\lambda=.1$ (setting 1) to $\lambda=.5$ (setting 3). The amount of jobs for these settings is a direct consequence of these values. For these settings, the duration of each job is drawn from the normal distribution with a mean value of 5 hours and a variance $s^2$ of 3.

The fourth setting is based on the logs of a real workload at the LPC (Laboratoire de Physique Corpusculaire) cluster which is a part of the EGEE Grid environment, and located in Clermont-Ferrand, France [13]. The log contains 244,821 jobs that was sent to the nodes during a period of 10 months starting from August 2004 through May 2005. We have, however, only extracted jobs with a duration between one and 24 hours. The LPC log was chosen because it contains a large variety of jobs with different run-times, numbers of used CPUs, and varying submit and start times.

**Table 1.** Simulation settings

| Setting | Arrival Rate | Duration | # Jobs | # Consumers | # Providers |
|---|---|---|---|---|---|
| 1 | $Poisson(0.1)$ | $\max(1, N(5,3))$ | 751 | 50 | 50 |
| 2 | $Poisson(0.3)$ | $\max(1, N(5,3))$ | 1502 | 50 | 50 |
| 3 | $Poisson(0.5)$ | $\max(1, N(5,3))$ | 3004 | 50 | 50 |
| 4 | As in LPC-Log | As in LPC-Log | 105,578 | 50 | 50 |

## 4.2  Simulation Results

The results of the simulations are summarized in Table 2. Each line in the table represents the evaluation of one strategy for one setting. The first two columns represent the setting used (corresponding to those of Table 1) and the strategy evaluated. The next two columns represent the average utility $\mu$ per job achieved as well as the standard deviation $\sigma$ of job budget and actual payment in the DLGM market, and the last two columns represent the results for the CDA in the same way.

The results show that the *Truth-Telling* strategy achieves the highest utility for all four settings.

The *Q-Strategy* reproduces a "rational behavior" by the generation of the bids. More specifically, we assume that rational agents have an incentive to

**Table 2.** Simulation results

| Setting | Strategy | $DLGM\mu$ | $DLGM_\sigma$ | $CDA_\mu$ | $CDA_\sigma$ |
|---|---|---|---|---|---|
| 1 | Truth-Telling | $-110,48$ | $272,37$ | $-7,92*10^4$ | 95,33 |
| 1 | Q-Strategy | $-174,74$ | $257,54$ | $-10,33*10^4$ | 93,56 |
| 2 | Truth-Telling | $-212,66$ | $285,16$ | $-11,95*10^4$ | 94,13 |
| 2 | Q-Strategy | $-392,42$ | $265,96$ | $-14,63*10^4$ | 93,30 |
| 3 | Truth-Telling | $-403,58$ | $286,43$ | $-7,89*10^4$ | 86,74 |
| 3 | Q-Strategy | $-901,18$ | $265,24$ | $-23,22*10^4$ | 90,77 |
| 4 | Truth-Telling | $-1104$ | $647,27$ | $-9,91*10^4$ | 391,97 |
| 4 | Q-Strategy | $-1172$ | $580,68$ | $-11,04*10^4$ | 313,69 |

understate their true price in relation to their valuation. Due to the fact that they understate their true price the achieved utility is lower than by the *Truth-Telling* strategy. The simulation results showed that bidding truthfully in both mechanisms can only increase your utility. Understating the truthful valuation in lower bid results in a poorer "job priority" $p_j/d_j$ by DLGM and this job can be displaced by other jobs which have higher priority. By the CDA mechanism, the price depends on the current demand and supply, bidding a lower price instead of the truth valuation increases the risk of no allocation by the mechanism.

Like in the DLGM market mechanism, the Truth-Telling strategy in the CDA market mechanism achieves higher average utility than the Q-Strategy. However, by the specified CDA market mechanism, the matching is based only on the price without considering the "priority" of a job as with DLGM, and thus achieves very low utility compared to DLGM. The origin of this can be searched in the CDA mechanism itself. First, each agent - provider and consumer - receives all the bids of the other agents as public information and based on this they adapt their bid/offer through the implemented bidding strategy. The CDA-provider agents are also acting strategically and adapting their offered price based on the received public information. Thus, the matching is based on the price resulting from the demand and supply and not on the "job priority" as with DLGM. Secondly, the CDA-provider machine agents do not maintain a priority queue of the submitted job bids and by an allocation the job is immediately submitted and executed on the provider machine. A provider submits an offer as soon as he becomes idle. Thus each time the agents are competing by adapting their job bids based on the used strategy.

Furthermore we investigated the price convergence of the Q-Strategy itself using the real workload data of setting 4 (105.578 jobs). Figure 4 shows six graphs, which represent the time development of the bid for particular classes of jobs, for six selected consumers and six selected jobs. The selection of the consumers and their jobs is based on statistical analysis of the output data, where we selected classes of jobs of different consumers, that have a statistically high number of generated bids. The minimum number of generated bids per job-class is 1, the maximal 49 and the average 12.

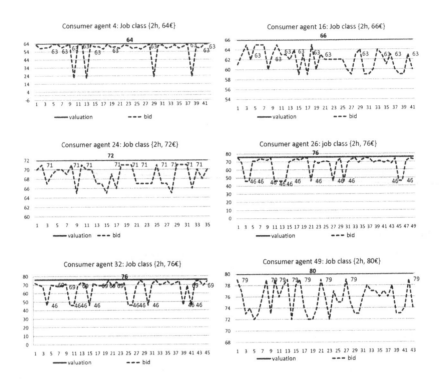

**Fig. 4.** Convergence of the bids using Q-Strategy

Each graph shows a valuation of a particular job class, the development of the bid over the time and the convergence trend of the bid. An interesting result is that for some cases of jobs with lower "job priority" – $p_j/d_j$, the bid does not converge to the truth-valuation and for jobs with higher priority, bids of the Q-Strategy converge to the truth-valuation of the specific job type.

## 5    Related Work

Preference elicitation deals with extraction of user's preferences for different combinations of resource configurations and prices. The aim of this methodology is to find the best choice of configuration, without explicitly presenting all possible choices. Two important approaches for job preference estimation are discussed in the literature – *Conjoint Analysis* and *Analytical Hierarchy Process* [4, 14, 15]. Conjoint analysis estimates the user's value for a certain attribute level by performing regression analysis on the user's feedback to the presented attribute profiles. In contrast to the conjoint analysis method which aims at determining the value of a certain attribute, the analytical hierarchy process tries to determine the relative importance of a certain attribute among a set of attributes [16]. The analytical hierarchy process suffers from the large number of pair-wise comparisons which the user has to perform to generate the matrix from which the relative weights are computed. With n attributes, the user essentially has to do n-1 comparisons.

The field of autonomous bidding is explored by many researchers. [17] gives an overview of the various agents and their strategies used in the trading agent competition (TAC). The literature described trading agents in stock markets [18], supply chain management [19] and in various market mechanisms [20, 21]. Since agents are self-interested, they aim to implement a strategic behavior in order to maximize their utility. In this context the mechanism design and auction literature investigated various bidding strategies for market-based scheduling [7, 22, 23, 24].

Phelps elaborated co-evolution algorithms to learn the strategy space for autonomous bidding by the allocation of resources in market mechanisms. In his thesis he classified bidding strategies into non-adaptive strategies such as *Truth Telling, Equilibrium-Price* and *Zero Intelligence*, and adaptive strategies – *Zero-Intelligence Plus, Kaplan's Sniping Strategy, Gjerstad-Dickhaut* and *Reinforcement-learning*[9].

The non-adaptive Zero Intelligence ZI [25] agent ignores the state of the market when forming a bid or offer and generates and submits random values drawn from a uniform distribution, where Zero Intelligence Plus ZIP [12] agents maintain a profit margin, a ratio of the trader's profit to its valuation, that determines their bid or offer at any time during the trading process. Furthermore this profit margin adapts to the market conditions using a learning mechanism, so that the agent can submit bids or offers that remain competitive. GD-agents store history information about the submitted bids and use a belief function for the price estimation. FL-agents [21] use fuzzy logic to generate a bid or offer based on a base price, which is a median of previous prices. Risk-Based agents [20] perform prediction of expected utility loss resulting from missing out on a transaction. Kaplan agents [26] define strategic conditions ("juicy offer", "small spread" and "timeout") under which a bid is generated and submitted. [27] introduced a stochastic $P$-strategy which takes the dynamics and uncertainties of the auction process. A comparison between some bidding strategy is evaluated by [28, 29, 30]. Beside auction strategies, [24] discusses utility functions and strategic negotiations in Grid environments.

The AI literature introduces three main approaches for learning – supervised, unsupervised, and reward-based learning. These methods are distinguished by what kind of feedback the critic provides to the learner. In supervised learning, the critic provides the correct output. In unsupervised learning, no feedback is provided at all. In reward-based learning, the critic provides a quality assessment (the 'reward') of the learner's output. A wide summary of common learning algorithms and decision rules are presented by [11, 29, 31, 32, 33, 34, 35].

# 6   Conclusions and Outlook

In this paper we have described consumer and provider components supporting the automated bidding process. We introduced the Q-Strategy as novel consumer bidding strategy, which implements a rational strategic behavior, and evaluated it against the *Truth-Telling* bidding strategy in two different market mechanism.

The Truth-Telling strategy "slightly" outperforms the Q-Strategy in both markets, but nevertheless it offers properties implementing a rational bidding behavior and learning capability. We show that it tends to converge to optimal action values. A common drawback of reinforcement learning algorithms is that they need some time to learn the environment and start to converge to an optimal action. To evaluate the properties of the Q-Strategy we need further research and simulations with different simulation settings and in various mechanisms. Future work will include its evaluation and analysis in further market mechanisms e.g. proportional-share [36, 37, 37] and pay-as-bid [38] as well as a comparison against state-of-the art bidding strategies like *ZIP*, *GD* and *Kaplan* agents.

Moreover, we looked at strategic behavior on consumer side, where truth telling is supposed to be an optimal bidding strategy in the sense of maximizing the consumer's utility. In the next step we are going to introduce strategic behavior on the provider side by extending the DLGM mechanism with payments for the resource usage. In this case the truth telling strategy could be not optimal.

# References

1. Byde, A., Salle, M., Bartolini, C.: Market-based resource allocation for utility data centers. HP Lab, Bristol, Technical Report HPL-2003-188 (September 2003)
2. Smith, W., Foster, I., Taylor, V.: Predicting application run times using historical information. In: Feitelson, D.G., Rudolph, L. (eds.) IPPS-WS 1998, SPDP-WS 1998, and JSSPP 1998. LNCS, vol. 1459. Springer, Heidelberg (1998)
3. Anjomshoaa, A., Brisard, F., Drescher, M., Fellows, D., Ly, A., McGough, S., Pulsipher, D., Savva, A.: Job Submission Description Language (JSDL) Specification, Version 1.0. Job Submission Description Language WG (JSDL-WG) (2005)
4. Stoesser, J., Neumann, D.: A model of preference elicitation for distributed market-based resource allocation. Working paper, University of Karlsruhe (TH) (2008)
5. Borissov, N., Blau, B., Neumann, D.: Semi-automated provisioning and usage of configurable services. In: 16th European Conference on Information Systems (ECIS 2008), Galway, Ireland (2008)
6. Heydenreich, B., Müller, R., Uetz, M.: Decentralization and Mechanism Design for Online Machine Scheduling. METEOR, Maastricht research school of Economics of TEchnology and ORganizations (2006)
7. Phelps, S.: Evolutionary mechanism design. Ph.D. Thesis (July 2007)
8. Watkins, C., Dayan, P.: Q-learning. Machine Learning 8(3), 279–292 (1992)
9. Kaelbling, L., Littman, M., Moore, A.: Reinforcement learning: A survey. Arxiv preprint cs.AI/9605103 (1996)
10. Whiteson, S., Stone, P.: On-line evolutionary computation for reinforcement learning in stochastic domains. In: Proceedings of the 8th annual conference on Genetic and evolutionary computation, pp. 1577–1584 (2006)
11. Tesauro, G., Das, R.: High-performance bidding agents for the continuous double auction. In: Proceedings of the 3rd ACM conference on Electronic Commerce, pp. 206–209 (2001)
12. Cliff, D.: Minimal-intelligence agents for bargaining behaviors in market-based environments. TechnicalReport, Hewlett Packard Labs (1997)

13. Medernach, E., des Cezeaux, C.: Workload analysis of a cluster in a grid environment. In: Feitelson, D.G., Frachtenberg, E., Rudolph, L., Schwiegelshohn, U. (eds.) JSSPP 2005. LNCS, vol. 3834. Springer, Heidelberg (2005)
14. Luce, R., Tukey, J.: Simultaneous conjoint measurement: A new type of fundamental measurement. Journal of Mathematical Psychology 1(1), 1–27 (1964)
15. Green, P., Rao, V.: Conjoint Measurement for Quantifying Judgmental Data. Journal of Marketing Research 8(3), 355–363 (1971)
16. Saaty, T.: Axiomatic foundation of the analytic hierarchy process. Management Science 32(7), 841–855 (1986)
17. Wellman, M., Greenwald, A., Stone, P.: Autonomous Bidding Agents: Strategies and Lessons from the Trading Agent Competition. MIT Press, Cambridge (2007)
18. Sherstov, A., Stone, P.: Three automated stock-trading agents: Acomparative study. In: Agent-mediated Electronic Commerce VI: Theories for and Engineering of Distributed Mechanisms and Systems: AAMAS 2004 Workshop, AMEC 2004, New York, NY, USA, July 19, 2004, Revised Selected Papers (2006)
19. Stone, P.: Multiagent learning is not the answer. it is the question. Artificial Intelligence (to appear, 2007)
20. Vytelingum, P., Dash, R., David, E., Jennings, N.: A risk-based bidding strategy for continuous double auctions. In: Proc. 16th European Conference on Artificial Intelligence, pp. 79–83 (2004)
21. He, M., Leung, H., Jennings, N.: A fuzzy-logic based bidding strategy for autonomous agents in continuous double auctions. IEEE Transactions on Knowledge and Data Engineering 15(6), 1345–1363 (2003)
22. Reeves, D., Wellman, M., MacKie-Mason, J., Osepayshvili, A.: Exploring bidding strategies for market-based scheduling. Decision Support Systems 39(1), 67–85 (2005)
23. Li, J., Yahyapour, R.: Learning-based negotiation strategies for grid scheduling. In: Proceedings of the Sixth IEEE International Symposium on Cluster Computing and the Grid (CCGRID 2006), vol. 00, pp. 576–583 (2006)
24. Li, J., Yahyapour, R.: A strategic negotiation model for grid scheduling. Journal International Transactions on Systems Science and Applications, 411–420 (2006)
25. Gode, D., Sunder, S.: Allocative efficiency of markets with zero-intelligence traders: Market as a partial substitute for individual rationality. The Journal of Political Economy 101(1), 119–137 (1993)
26. Kaplan, S., Weisbach, M.: The success of acquisitions: Evidence from divestitures. The Journal of Finance 47(1), 107–138 (1992)
27. Park, S., Durfee, E., Birmingham, W.: An adaptive agent bidding strategy based on stochastic modeling. In: Proceedings of the third annual conference on Autonomous Agents, pp. 147–153 (1999)
28. Das, R., Hanson, J., Kephart, J., Tesauro, G.: Agent-human interactions in the continuous double auction. In: Proceedings of the International Joint Conference on Artificial Intelligence, vol. 26 (2001)
29. Sherstov, A., Stone, P.: Three automated stock-trading agents: A comparative study. In: Faratin, P., Rodriguez-Aguilar, J. (eds.) AMEC 2004. LNCS (LNAI), vol. 3435, pp. 173–187. Springer, Heidelberg (2006)
30. Kearns, M., Ortiz, L.: The penn-lehman automated trading project. Intelligent Systems, IEEE [see also IEEE Intelligent Systems and Their Applications] 18(6), 22–31 (2003)
31. Stone, P.: Learning and multiagent reasoning for autonomous agents. In: The 20th International Joint Conference on Artificial Intelligence, pp. 13–30 (January 2007)

32. van den Herik, H.J., Hennes, D., Kaisers, M., Tuyls, K., Verbeeck, K.: Multi-agent learning dynamics: A survey. In: Klusch, M., Hindriks, K.V., Papazoglou, M.P., Sterling, L. (eds.) CIA 2007. LNCS (LNAI), vol. 4676, pp. 36–56. Springer, Heidelberg (2007)
33. Erev, I., Roth, A.: Predicting how people play games: Reinforcement learning in experimental games with unique, mixed strategy equilibria. The American Economic Review 88(4), 848–881 (1998)
34. Shoham, Y., Powers, R., Grenager, T.: If multi-agent learning is the answer, what is the question? Artificial Intelligence 171(7), 365–377 (2007)
35. Panait, L., Luke, S.: Cooperative multi-agent learning: The state of the art. Autonomous Agents and Multi-Agent Systems 11(3), 387–434 (2005)
36. Lai, K., Rasmusson, L., Adar, E., Zhang, L., Huberman, B.: Tycoon: An implementation of a distributed, market-based resource allocation system. Multiagent and Grid Systems 1(3), 169–182 (2005)
37. Stoica, I., Abdel-Wahab, H., Jeffay, K., Baruah, S., Gehrke, J., Plaxton, C.: A proportional share resource allocation algorithm for real-time, time-shared systems. In: Proceedings of the 17th IEEE Real-Time Systems Symposium, pp. 288–299 (1996)
38. Sanghavi, S., Hajek, B.: Optimal allocation of a divisible good to strategic buyers. In: 43rd IEEE Conference on Decision and Control-CDC (2004)

# Grid and Taxation: The Server as Permanent Establishment in International Grids

Davide Maria Parrilli

Interdisciplinary Centre for Law and Technology (ICRI),
K.U. Leuven, IBBT, Sint-Michielsstraat 6, 3000 Leuven, Belgium
davide.parrilli@law.kuleuven.be

**Abstract.** Tax issues can be a great barrier to the development of international Grids and can be perceived as an obstacle for ICT companies. Provided this fact, the scope of this paper is to analyse the concept of server (to the ends of income taxation) in case of international Grid infrastructures, in the light of the findings of the Organisation for Economic Cooperation and Development (Model Tax Convention and Commentaries) and of the practices so far developed in some countries and, in particular, to assess whether any server can be considered to be a permanent establishment of the company acting as Grid provider, with all its consequences in terms of tax liability.

**Keywords:** taxation; server; permanent establishment.

## 1 Introduction: An Overview of the Problem

The relations between Grid technology[1] and taxation still form part of a new, challenging and basically unexplored field and do raise the concerns of the executives of companies that are willing to set up and manage a Grid infrastructure. The problem is more compelling in case of international Grids split among different countries provided the lack of clear and unequivocal regulations at international level. The institutions that so far attempted to provide e-commerce with some sort of 'tax instructions', in fact, based their reasoning on scenarios and models that are very simple and do not match the actual technological and business reality. This is particularly true, as it will be showed in the following pages, as regards the notion of permanent establishment (PE) proposed by the Organisation for Economic Cooperation and Development (thereinafter, OECD) in connection with the server used by the taxpayer to carry on its business. If, to a certain extent, a server, located in a country different from the place where the undertaking (taxpayer) is located, is deemed to be a permanent establishment of such a company, and therefore the competent authorities can tax the profits generated there, what if the same taxpayer

---

[1] The analysis carried out in this article is based on the research that the author is doing for the FP6 European project BEinGRID (http://www.beingrid.eu).

J. Altmann, D. Neumann, and T. Fahringer (Eds.): GECON 2008, LNCS 5206, pp. 89–102, 2008.
© Springer-Verlag Berlin Heidelberg 2008

performs its activities through a Grid infrastructure with servers placed in different jurisdictions?[2]

We see, in other words, that Grid technology raises new problems or requires new solutions to more 'traditional' ICT[3] issues. The scope of this paper is precisely to address the concept and nature of server in an international Grid[4] and to provide for new ICT-oriented solutions, in the light of the principles set forth by the OECD. As a matter of method, in fact, it is absolutely necessary to take into account the guidelines issued by the above organization for the very fact that they constitute the basis for the majority of the international treaties for the avoidance of double taxation and for their interpretation. Apart from the OECD sources, namely the Tax Model Convention[5] and its Commentaries[6], the attention will be paid to the solutions adopted, from a comparative point of view, in some countries where the issue analysed in this paper has been perceived as being particularly important and urgent.

Grid technology is widely employed in many commercial and industrial sectors thanks to its potential in terms of costs and benefits. It is useful to show the relevance of the analysis carried out in these pages with a scenario that is likely to happen in reality. Company 'A' is a financial institution with offices and activities worldwide. In order to face their needs and to optimize the internal management, the executives of the undertaking decide to (i) 'gridify' their applications and to (ii) spin off the ICT department into a separate legal entity, company 'B', controlled by A. B will be in charge of the entire ICT infrastructure of the group and will trade with A and its subsidiaries at market conditions (i.e. in the light of the arm's length principle[7]). Provided that A, before the spin off, decided to set up a certain number of servers (or, in a more complex scenario, Grid infrastructures) located in different countries, B has

---

[2] The literature points out, in general terms, that "one important question related to the Internet, which perhaps reflects most obviously the tension between advances in technology and current tax rules, arises from the fact that an e-commerce business can provide goods or services to Internet users located in a country without necessarily having any significant physical presence in that country." Smith, G.J.H.: Internet Law and Regulation. Sweet & Maxwell, London (2002), p. 601.

[3] As regards the relations between ICT and taxation, it has been said that technology "makes the traditional initial starting points of taxation – residence and source of income principle – increasingly mutable." Albregtse, D.A.: The Server as a Permanent Establishment and the Revised Commentary on Article 5 of the OECD Model Tax Treaty: Are the E-Commerce Corporate Income Tax Problems Solved? Intertax vol. 30, no. 10 (2002), p. 356.

[4] With the expression 'international Grid' we mean a complex infrastructure composed of elements (e.g. servers, nodes, Grids) located in different countries. See *infra*, note no. 7. In general terms, the research carried out in these pages takes as background the assumption of the literature that "Grid computing enables or facilitates the conduct of virtual organisations – geographically and institutionally distributed projects – and such organisations have become essential for tackling many projects in commerce and research." Berman, F., Fox, G.C., Hey, A.J.G.: Grid Computing. Making the Global Infrastructure a Reality. John Wiley & Sons Ltd., Hoboken (2003), p. xiv.

[5] Articles of the Model Convention with Respect to Taxes on Income and on Capital [as they read on 28 January 2003].

[6] In particular, Commentary on Article 5 Concerning the Definition of Permanent Establishment.

[7] See *infra*, note no. 37.

the task to manage and use such devices to provide the services requested by A (for instance, to calculate equity and credit derivatives, etc.).

In the model taken into account here, B owns a certain number of servers or Grids[8], for instance located in USA, Germany, Italy and the UK. The executives of B nevertheless think that the unification of these infrastructures would enhance the level of the services they provide and would allow to process more data in a shorter period of time. Such unification, then, raises some fiscal problems, and in particular the managers of B should wonder whether the tax authorities of the four abovementioned countries could tax the portion of profits generated by every component of the international Grid. This issue, if not carefully assessed, can be a potential and costly barrier to the implementation of transnational Grids. In the following lines it will be attempted to find a general solution to the problem which can be applied at wide level and is consistent with the actual technological era, taking into account the current notion of server for international tax purposes.

## 2 Server as a Permanent Establishment: A Critical Approach to the OECD Perspective

In order to find a solution to the above question, regarding the nature and treatment of the different components of an international Grid, it is firstly necessary to assess what a single server is from the tax point of view. The question is both pivotal under the theoretical and practical perspective, for the very fact that the determination of the legal qualification of the server[9] will grant the power to tax the profits generated by it (see *infra*). Provided that "so many bilateral treaties are based on the OECD model"[10] Convention, we will base our analysis on the sources published by this organization, namely the abovementioned Model Convention and its Commentaries, which clearly show the attempt to harmonise tax concepts and regulations at international level.

As basic assumption, we have to point out that, for logical reasons of rationalization and simplicity, a single element of an international Grid, i.e. (in the example below) any server and any single Grid that constitutes the bigger, transnational, infrastructure, has to be seen, to the ends of taxation, as a single server. The opposite solution would create further uncertainty and confusion and, at the same time and from a practical perspective, if the Grid is located in only one country, it is not really relevant, to the ends of taxation, to assess whether it can be conceived as a single server or as a bundle of different servers.[11] In other words, we adopt here, to the ends

---

[8] The two models taken into consideration, in other words, are: (i) servers or computing sites, placed in different countries, that form an international Grid; (ii) Grids located in different jurisdictions that compose a bigger international Grid.

[9] "A company may install servers in different geographic places, while the use or non-use of one or more of the installed servers depends on the fiscal consequences." Albregtse: op. cit., p. 359.

[10] Westin, R.A.: International Taxation of Electronic Commerce. Kluwer Law International, Alphen aan den Rijn (2007), p. 405.

[11] In this case, in fact, there is no potential conflict between tax authorities as regards the power to tax the profits generated by the Grid. The same consideration applies concerning the applicability of value added tax (VAT) or other similar consumption taxes.

of taxation, a legal-oriented definition of server which corresponds only to a certain extent to the technical notion and which is wider than the latter.

Things are different and obviously more complex if a plurality of jurisdictions is involved. The principle stated by the OECD, in fact, is that a server[12] is deemed to be, if some requisites are met, a permanent establishment of the taxpayer, thus the profits generated by it are taxable in the country where the server is located, in the light of the rule set forth by article 7(1) of the Model Convention.[13] Pursuant to the Commentaries (article 5, paragraph 42.2), then, "the server...is a piece of equipment having a physical location and such location may thus constitute a "fixed place of business" of the enterprise that operates that server." The OECD draws a distinction between server and website: the former, as showed in the previous lines, can be a permanent establishment of the taxpayer, while the latter cannot be a permanent establishment in any case because, basically, it "does not in itself constitute tangible property."[14]

More specifically, as provided for by Article 5 of the Model Convention, a server is a permanent establishment if it is fixed[15] and if the business of the undertaking is "wholly or partly carried on at a location where the enterprise has equipped such a server at its disposal"[16] and, on the other side, it is pivotal to state that "no permanent

---

[12] "The server is a physical object. If it is substantial it may qualify as PE-constituting 'machinery or equipment'. Substantial in this respect would be all computers that are not portable or otherwise easy to carry away by hand. Thus, portable equipment does not qualify as a 'place of business'. However, even if the server is not considered to be a PE-constituting place of business, the room or office in which the server is located would qualify for this purpose." Skaar, A.A.: Erosion of the Concept of Permanent Establishment: Electronic Commerce. Intertax, vol. 28, no. 5 (2000), p. 189.

[13] "The profits of an enterprise of a Contracting State shall be taxable only in that State unless the enterprise carries on business in the other Contracting State through a permanent establishment situated therein. If the enterprise carries on business as aforesaid, the profits of the enterprise may be taxed in the other State but only so much of them as is attributable to that permanent establishment." The Commentary on Article 7 of the Model Convention, paragraph 1, states that "the first question is whether the enterprise has a permanent establishment in their country; if the answer is in the affirmative the second question is what, if any, are the profits on which that permanent establishment should pay tax." It would go beyond the scopes of this paper to provide the reader with a definition of 'profits' to the ends of international taxation but we want nevertheless to highlight the following provisions of Article 7 of the Model Convention: pursuant to paragraph 2, in fact, "in determining the profits of a permanent establishment, there shall be allowed as deductions expenses which are incurred for the purposes of the permanent establishment, including executive and general administrative expenses so incurred, whether in the State in which the permanent establishment is situated or elsewhere." Paragraph 5, then, sets forth the principle that "no profits shall be attributed to a permanent establishment by reason of the mere purchase by that permanent establishment of goods or merchandise for the enterprise."

[14] Commentary on Article 5 of the Model Convention, paragraph 42.2.

[15] Pursuant to paragraph 42.4 of the Commentary on Article 5 of the Model Convention, "in the case of a server, what is relevant is not the possibility of the server being moved, but whether it is in fact moved."

[16] According to paragraph 42.5 of the Commentary on Article 5 of the Model Convention, which points out that "the question of whether the business of an enterprise is wholly or partly carried on through such equipment needs to be examined on a case-by-case basis, having regard to whether it can be said that, because of such equipment, the enterprise has facilities at its disposal where business functions of the enterprise are performed."

establishment may be considered to exist where the...operations carried on through computer equipment at a given location in a country are restricted to...preparatory or auxiliary activities."[17] Examples of such preparatory or auxiliary activities are the provision of a communication link between suppliers and customers, advertisement of goods and services, relay of information through a mirror server (e.g. for security and efficiency purposes), gathering market data, the supply of information.[18]

Provided our assumption that a single element of an international and complex Grid infrastructure can be, at least in principle, conceived as a permanent establishment of an undertaking, in the above example it will result that company B has four different permanent establishments in various countries, and this means that four national tax authorities in principle have the power to tax the profits generated by the individual components of the international Grid. It is nevertheless necessary to point out two aspects. Firstly, this conclusion has been assessed in the light of the principles stated by the OECD, but it is necessary to evaluate whether or not the bilateral tax treaties (entered into between the concerned countries) and their national tax authorities follow the positions of the OECD. In the next paragraphs we will show that such opinions do not represent a general consensus at global level.

On the other side, then, it is fundamental to consider the nature of the activities carried on by the elements of the international Grid, in particular whether or not they are preparatory or ancillary to the main business of the company.[19] In our example it is probably difficult to safely state that this requisite is not met, for the very fact that the calculation of prices and risk constitutes one of the core activities of a financial institution. Such analysis, nevertheless, must be carried out on a case-by-case basis, and in many situations it will be possible to assess that the actions performed by the components of the international Grids do not "form in themselves an essential and significant part of the business activity of the enterprise as a whole."[20]

It is doubtful whether or not the notion of permanent establishment provided for by the OECD is really applicable to ICT-related equipments like a server. It is necessary to consider, in fact, that such a concept has been drafted with a focus on traditional

---

[17] Pursuant to paragraph 42.7 of the Commentary on Article 5 of the Model Convention.

[18] For completeness, it is suitable to point out that, pursuant to paragraph 42.8 of the Commentary on Article 5 of the Model Convention, "where, however, such functions form in themselves an essential and significant part of the business activity of the enterprise as a whole, or where other core functions of the enterprise are carried on through the computer equipment, these would go beyond the activities [of preparatory and auxiliary nature] and if the equipment constituted a fixed place of business of the enterprise...there would be a permanent establishment." As pointed out in the literature, "it is the functions performed on the server that may result in the server constituting a permanent establishment, and whether the server is at the disposal" of the company. Doernberg, R.L., Hinnekens, L., Hellerstein, W., Li, J.: Electronic Commerce and Multijurisdictional Taxation. Kluwer Law International, The Hague (2001), p. 208.

[19] Provided that "it is often difficult to distinguish between activities, which have a preparatory or auxiliary character, and those, which do not." Albregtse: op. cit., p. 361. The same Author points out that "to make a distinction between preparatory and auxiliary activities and commercial activities (as core functions of a particular enterprise) the character of the specific activities must be investigated in light of the core business aim of the enterprise" (p. 362).

[20] Commentary on Article 5 of the Model Convention, paragraph 42.8.

productions of goods and services, as showed by the list provided for by article 5(2) of the Model Convention, pursuant to which the idea of permanent establishment comprises especially the following: a place of management; a branch or an office of the company; a factory; a workshop; a mine, an oil and gas well, a quarry or any other place of extraction of natural resources. It is evident, therefore, that the concept of permanent establishment relies on the existence of a real, physical place through which acts of production, management, extraction of resources etc. are carried out. These activities, in other words, are real and measurable (even if such a measurement can be cumbersome in case of services provided by a place of management or office) and this is not the case in point for a server.[21]

Apart from this, the assumptions of the OECD are based on very simple e-commerce scenarios which involve the use of only one server and which do not really match the actual technological advancements. In the following lines we will support our opinion with the positions expressed by some national tax authorities.

## 3  Server as Permanent Establishment: A Comparative Perspective and Further Critical Approach to the OECD Position

The idea proposed by the OECD that a server, to a certain extent, is deemed to be a permanent establishment of a company[22] has not been accepted by all its member States. One of most notable exceptions is represented by the UK which made an official reservation to the interpretation contained in the Commentaries. As pointed out by the Revenue and Customs authorities, in fact, "the development of e-commerce places a strain on the traditional definition of a permanent establishment in cases where the computer equipment is positioned in one territory whilst the enterprise has no personnel active in the business in that territory. The UK does not concur with other OECD Member States on whether a server of itself can constitute a fixed place of business permanent establishment."[23] Therefore, UK tax authorities "take the view that a server either alone or together with web sites could not as such constitute a PE of a business that is conducting e-commerce through a web site on the server… regardless of whether the server is owned, rented or otherwise at the disposal of the business."[24] It is correct to apply this statement not only to traditional e-commerce

---

[21] In the literature it has been pointed out that "the concept of permanent establishment, designed for a world of trade based in tangible products with traceable physical locations, does not work in a world of electronic commerce where information is transmitted in intangible form." Pastukhov, O.: International Taxation of Income Derived from Electronic Commerce: Current Problems and Possible Solutions. B.U. J. Sci. & Tech., vol. 12:2 (2006), p. 319.

[22] In other words, "a server, by which the primary activities of an enterprise are fulfilled and which server is fully at the disposal of that enterprise, may be regarded as a PE." Albregtse: op. cit., p. 362.

[23] INTM266100 – Non-residents trading in the UK: Treaty permanent establishment, available at http://www.hmrc.gov.uk/manuals/intmanual/INTM266100.htm (last accessed: 31/3/2008).

[24] See *supra*, note no. 23.

scenarios (e-tailing) but to any situation in which the business activity implies the use of servers, so that the position of the tax department in the UK can be summarised as to exclude in general terms servers from the notion of permanent establishment.[25]

The approach taken in the UK is, to a certain extent, similar to the one adopted in France. In principle, in fact, servers are not deemed to be permanent establishments of the taxpayer, according to French national authorities, provided that no human activity associated with the server's operations is performed.[26] With this regard the French approach is remarkably different from the perspective of the OECD, which stated, in its Commentaries, that "a permanent establishment may nevertheless exist if the business of the enterprise is carried on mainly through automatic equipment, the activities of the personnel being restricted to setting up, operating, controlling and maintaining such equipment"[27], as it is expected to happen with servers. It is pivotal to point out, then, that a permanent establishment may be formed if the server carries out a complete and autonomous cycle of business transactions. The French position, thus, can be summarised in the following statement: "the server needs to perform virtually all aspects of a business transaction before a permanent establishment is constituted."[28]

The opinion followed by the French authorities, thus, lies in the middle between the ideas expressed by the OECD, aimed to include servers into the notion of permanent establishment, and the attitude of UK tax department, according to which a server cannot be deemed to be a permanent establishment of the company. Apart from

---

[25] See, in the literature, Westin: op. cit., p. 568. It has been pointed out that "the UK's view, like that of the Electronic Commerce Directive, as set out on 11 April 2002, is that a website of itself is not a permanent establishment, and that a server is insufficient of itself to constitute a permanent establishment of a business that is conducting ecommerce through a website on the server." Gringras, C.: The Laws of the Internet. Butterworths LexisNexis, London (2003), p. 406. The European Directive on electronic commerce (Directive 2000/31/EC of the European Parliament and of the Council of 8 June 2000 on certain legal aspects of information society services, in particular electronic commerce, in the Internal Market, OJ L 178, 17.7.2000, p. 1-16), then, apparently excludes for non-tax purposes websites and servers from the notion of place of establishment, and the same considerations can be applied to taxation. Pursuant to recital 19 of the Directive, in fact, "the place at which a service provider is established should be determined in conformity with the case-law of the Court of Justice according to which the concept of establishment involves the actual pursuit of an economic activity through a fixed establishment for an indefinite period; this requirement is also fulfilled where a company is constituted for a given period; the place of establishment of a company providing services via an Internet website is not the place at which the technology supporting its website is located or the place at which its website is accessible but the place where it pursues its economic activity; in cases where a provider has several places of establishment it is important to determine from which place of establishment the service concerned is provided; in cases where it is difficult to determine from which of several places of establishment a given service is provided, this is the place where the provider has the centre of his activities relating to this particular service."

[26] See Ministerial reply 56961, Official Gazette of 22 January 2001, as reported in Mbwa-Mboma, M.N.: France, OECD Take Different Views of Unstaffed Servers as Permanent Establishments, WTD, 102--5 (2002).

[27] Commentary on Article 5 of the Model Convention, paragraph 10.

[28] Cockfield, A.J.: The Rise of the OECD as Informal 'World Tax Organization' Through National Responses to E-Commerce Tax Challenges. YJoLT 8 (2006), p. 151.

any theoretical consideration, from the practical point of view it may be difficult to apply the French criteria for the very need to provide an evidence of the fact that the server carries out all aspects of a business transaction and that some form of human activity is performed in connection with the server itself.

Other countries either follow the approach of the OECD[29] or have developed specific guidance. Spain and Portugal, for instance, "do not consider that physical presence is a requirement for a permanent establishment to exist in the context of e-commerce, and therefore, they also consider that, in some circumstances, an enterprise carrying on business in a State through a web site could be treated as having a permanent establishment in that State."[30] Such an approach, which is not widely followed at international level, can be reasonably criticised, but nevertheless it shows that the virtualisation of business activities has to be taken into account by lawmakers and tax authorities, and the notion of web site in the field of e-commerce should be necessarily re-drafted in the light of the current technological and business developments.

It is interesting, before assessing some conclusions regarding the relations between servers and permanent establishments and applying such findings to international Grids, to shortly define the position of the US authorities. Provided that "current tax concepts, such as the US trade or business, permanent establishment, and source of income concepts, were developed in a different technological era",[31] the US federal tax department shows an attitude which can be defined as very realistic. A discussion paper issued in 1996 by the Treasury, in fact, assessing whether or not telecommunications or computer equipments could constitute a fixed place of business of the foreign person in the US, points out that "for a business which sells information instead of goods, a computer server might be considered the equivalence of a warehouse", and thus would not be a permanent establishment of a foreign company. In principle, then, "examination and interpretation of the permanent establishment concept in the context of electronic commerce may well result in an extension of the policies and the resulting exceptions to electronic commerce."

On the other side, in a case involving servers of American companies located in a foreign jurisdiction, it has been reported that "the U.S. tax authorities have entered into an undisclosed settlement agreement with Indian tax authorities whereby both parties accept that a U.S. taxpayer's server within India constitutes a permanent establishment."[32] Such an approach is manifestly fully consistent with the assessment of the OECD in its Commentaries to the Model Convention.

This short comparative overview shows the need of harmonisation at international level, provided that, if technology is basically universal, its impact on taxation should be as much as possible similar among jurisdictions. The nature of modern

---

[29] At European level, for instance, national tax authorities of Austria, Switzerland and Germany follow the principles stated in the OECD Commentaries.

[30] OECD: Clarification on the Application of the Permanent Establishment Definition in E-Commerce: Changes to the Commentary on the Model Tax Convention on Article 5. (2000), available at http://www.oecd.org/dataoecd/46/32/1923380.pdf (last accessed: 31/3/2008).

[31] Department of the Treasury: Selected Tax Policy Implications of Global Electronic Commerce. (1996), available at http://www.treas.gov/offices/tax-policy/library/internet.pdf (last accessed: 31/3/2008).

[32] Cockfield: op. cit., p. 159.

Internet-based automations and the fact that their speed corresponds to its potential mobility should support the consideration that traditional concepts, developed, as it has been pointed out above, with focus on material devices or measurable services, cannot be *per se* applied to virtualised items or businesses. For this reason, it is definitely advisable to adopt an approach that tends to exclude servers from the notion of permanent establishment and thus from taxation in the place where they are located. This exigency is even more compelling in case of international Grids.

## 4 International Grid and Permanent Establishment: Assessment of the Issue

The OECD, when drafting and reviewing the Model Convention and the Commentaries[33], was absolutely unaware of the potential represented by Grid computing and of its novelty. The approach taken was focused purely on simple e-commerce scenarios which involve the use of one server, and we have to assess whether the findings applicable to single, stand-alone, components[34] are valid also for more complex structures like an international Grid. Such a question has great practical importance and is likely to influence the business strategies of ICT companies, provided that the solutions proposed by the OECD and the lack of harmonisation creates the possibility to locate the elements of the Grid infrastructure where it is more convenient from the tax point of view. At the same time, nevertheless, taxation of the profits generated by such components is a great barrier to the creation of multinational Grid structures.

The practical problems of implementing and enforcing the findings of the OECD, according to which a server can be in principle a permanent establishment of a

---

[33] Many paragraphs of the Commentary on Article 5 of the Model Convention have been added in 2003.

[34] In fact, "the OECD consideration is focused on the server as a single location for the business activities of [the company]. That business model in many cases is somewhat dated. It is more likely that [the company] will conduct its business on multiple servers each of which may perform a particular function. Furthermore, multiple servers may perform the same function with customer load directed to the server which can respond the quickest which may be a function of demand and location. Operation through multiple servers raises several permanent establishment issues". According to a possible interpretation of the Commentary to Article 5 (paragraph 27.1), "multiple servers at the same geographical location might constitute a permanent establishment, but multiple servers at different locations within [a] country (or some location within [a] country and some outside [that] country...) could not be cumulated into a single permanent establishment." Doernberg, Hinnekens, Hellerstein, Li: op. cit., p. 212. We do not completely agree with this reasoning, provided that the abovementioned paragraph 27.1 states that in case a company maintains several fixed places of business (which are separated each other locally and organisationally), "each place of business has to be viewed separately and in isolation for deciding the question whether or not a permanent establishment exists. Places of business are not "separated organisationally" where they each perform in a Contracting State complementary functions such as receiving and storing goods in one place, distributing those goods through another etc. An enterprise cannot fragment a cohesive operating business into several small operations in order to argue that each is merely engaged in a preparatory or auxiliary activity."

company, are self-evident and have been carefully analysed by the literature.[35] Nevertheless, it would not be satisfying to criticise the opinions expressed by the OECD in its Commentaries purely on the ground of practical problems, as it is necessary to provide also a theoretical framework aimed to support the opinion that servers should be excluded from the notion of permanent establishment. In the following lines we will define two scenarios as regards international Grid. The first model will take into account the solutions proposed by the OECD while the second one will represent a different, ICT-oriented, proposal.

The idea that a server is deemed to be a permanent establishment of an undertaking implies that, in principle, in the abovementioned example a company managing a Grid infrastructure in USA, Germany, Italy and the UK bears the risk to pay taxes in all four countries for the profits generated there by the Grid components, provided that the tax authorities concerned follow the findings of the OECD (and, as we said above, this is not the case in point).[36] The biggest issue, from the practical point of view, is the allocation of the portion of profits between the jurisdictions that host elements of the international Grid, and this can be cumbersome for both tax authorities and taxpayers.[37] In case of litigation, then, the taxpayer could base his defence on the assumption that the activities carried out by the components of the international Grids are of preparatory or auxiliary nature, provided that only the international Grid as a whole performs the core business job of the company. The Commentary on Article 5 provides for an example which can be analogically applied to an international Grid: in case of e-tailing, in fact, "the enterprise is not in the business of operating servers and the mere fact that it may do so at a given location is

---

[35] "Even when a permanent establishment location of an Internet-based business is determined, attribution of income to the permanent establishment is extremely difficult, because it is unclear where and when the income-generating event occurs. The use of linked servers located across many jurisdictions that switch signals from one server to the other to balance network traffic makes it difficult to identify which servers are used at any particular time and for which activities. Furthermore, even if it were possible to associate a particular domain name with a certain person and computer, all three could still be located in different countries." Pastukhov: op. cit., p. 321. See *infra*, note no. 37.

[36] The recent trend followed by Italian tax authorities (decision of the *Agenzia delle Entrate* no. 119/E of 28 May 2007), for instance, is to recognise a server as a permanent establishment of a company, provided that the undertaking owns the server (or that the apparatus is at exclusive disposal of the firm), the server has been installed for an indefinite period of time in Italy and that such a device is used to carry on the core activity of the business.

[37] In fact, "the separate but related question arises of what part of the total profits of the company are to be properly attributed to the permanent establishment (over which the country in which the permanent establishment exists will have primary taxing rights)." Smith: op. cit., p. 603. In principle, "the profits to be attributed to a permanent establishment are those which that permanent establishment would have made if, instead of dealing with its head office, it had been dealing with an entirely separate enterprise under conditions and at prices prevailing in the ordinary market. This corresponds to the "arms' length principle" discussed in the Commentary on Article 9. Normally, the profits so determined would be the same profits that one would expect to be determined by the ordinary process of good business accountancy. The arm's length principle also extends to the allocation of profits which the permanent establishment may derive from transactions with other permanent establishments of the enterprise" (Commentary on Article 7 of the Model Convention, paragraph 11).

not enough to conclude that activities performed at that location are more than preparatory or auxiliary."[38]

In the above example, B could assert that they operate a Grid infrastructure but only with the aim of providing services to banks and other financial institutions. The issue is not clarified if we read the solution proposed by the OECD for e-tailing: "if, however, the typical functions related to a sale are performed at that location (for example, the conclusion of the contract with the customer, the processing of the payment and the delivery of the products are performed automatically through the equipment located there), these activities cannot be considered to be merely preparatory or auxiliary."[39] The taxpayer, in case of hypothetical litigation, would stress out that the acts performed by the components of the international Grid do not meet these requisites, and thus it would be necessary to conduct a case-by-case analysis. On the other side, a Court would have probably much less problems in recognising the presence of a permanent establishment if the same activities carried on by the elements of the Grid would be performed, in an highly unrealistic scenario, by a network of offices located in different countries where real accountants are employed to perform the same job than the one done by the Grid.

The criterion that seems suitable to adopt in judging whether or not a server (or other component) of an international Grid has to be considered as a permanent establishment of the company is the link between such an element and the territory where it is placed. In other words, we have to follow the rationale behind the traditional notion of permanent establishment and apply it to new scenarios. If, in fact, a factory or office is deemed to be a permanent establishment of an enterprise because such a factory or office plays a role (in terms, for instance, of employment) in the life and economy of a certain region, this is not the case in point for servers and, in general, ICT components of an international Grid.

It would be possible to counter-argue that also a vending machine is deemed to be a permanent establishment even if it does not need any personnel and the impact on a local economy is usually very limited. In this case, nevertheless, the machine serves only local customers, and this is enough to say that there is a link between the vending apparatus and the place where it is located.

In the light of these considerations, it is possible to propose a different model in which the profits of the company that manages the international Grid are not taxed in the countries where the components of the Grid are located, for the very fact that they do not have any real and effective link with the place of settlement. This policy, already followed, as said above, by the tax department in the UK is a potential enabler for the implementation of international Grids and it assures simplicity and less costs (including litigation) for taxpayers. The reader should be aware, at the same time, of the possible consequences, i.e. no taxation at all for ICT companies that manage Grid infrastructures (or, in more general terms, servers). If the profits will not be taxed where the enterprise has a permanent establishment, they should be levied in the country of incorporation of the company or where it has its main headquarter.[40] In the

---

[38] Commentary on Article 5 of the Model Convention, paragraph 42.9.

[39] See *supra*, note no. 30.

[40] See, in the literature, Bivona, B.: La Stabile Organizzazione e le Nuove Frontiere della Tassazione. Fisconelmondo.it (2007), available at http://www.fisconelmondo.it/news-article.storyid-835.htm (last accessed: 1/4/2008).

case of ICT undertakings, nevertheless, they can easily decide to incorporate or place the main office in a so-called tax heaven[41] and, therefore, their profits could be tax-exempted[42] at all.

This can anyway happen also with the actual framework drafted by the OECD, provided that not all the tax authorities at global level follow its approach. In practice, a careful tax planning as regards place of incorporation and countries were the elements of the international Grid are placed can dramatically reduce[43] the tax burden of an ICT company that is willing to 'gridify' its solutions.

## 5 Conclusions

The implementation of Grid technology is a challenge for lawyers and the fact that the relation between tax law and Grid is absolutely pioneering makes it even more interesting and fascinating. We can summarise the analysis carried on in the previous lines by saying that the actual OECD position, expressed in the Commentary on Article 5, as regards the link between servers and permanent establishment is a barrier for ICT companies that are willing to set up international Grids. In particular, if such approach is followed by national tax authorities (as it is in many cases) it implies practical problems like, for instance, the calculation of the portion of profit generated by every component. In other words, undertakings have to face an increase of costs and the risk of litigation with tax departments.

This danger is not really mitigated if we assume that the activities performed by every element of the international Grid are preparatory or auxiliary in connection with the overall performance of the Grid. Apart from technical considerations, it would be probably very cumbersome for the taxpayer to give the evidence[44] of it, and in any case the proceedings will be costly and risky for the Grid company. The overall conclusion is that the most consistent and correct solution consists of the exclusion of servers from the notion of permanent establishment, or, more radically, that the

---

[41] Apart from this, "from a fiscal point of view, settling servers in tax heavens is most lucrative." Albregtse: op. cit., p. 364.

[42] In a more general scenario, in fact, "companies trading over the Internet, in contrast to traditional kinds of companies, may find that an offshore structure does have its advantages. …Whether it is best to site a business in a tax heaven, in the UK or another taxing jurisdiction with a good tax treaty network very much depends on the nature of the business. In addition, in determining the most appropriate location from which to conduct an Internet business, the effect on VAT payments should also be considered." Gringras: op. cit., p. 408--9.

[43] As regards traditional e-commerce scenarios (but the same applies in case of international Grids) it has been said that "it is in all interests that taxation does not create a barrier to the growth of e-commerce while, at the same time, each nation's tax base is appropriately secured (in order that public services be adequately funded), a fair sharing of the tax base from e-commerce between countries is maintained and any double taxation or unintentional non taxation is avoided." Smith: op. cit., p. 579.

[44] We agree with the following statement in the literature: "because of the plethora of activities on the electronic highways, the great velocity of activities undertaken, combined with the application of encryption techniques, problems are arising with respect to the traceability of the activities and of the participants involved. Finally the privacy legislation creates restraint with respect to the traceability of the Internet activities and the participants involved." Albregtse: op. cit., p. 364.

permanent establishment concept "in general is no longer useful in the era of information."[45]

ICT firms do nevertheless have to face the actual reality and the fact that the OECD findings are widely followed by national tax authorities. They have the possibility in any case to choose the locations of the components of their international Grid and to take advantage of the tax competition between jurisdictions. The UK and Estonia, for instance, are in a good position to attract foreign companies, the former because it does not consider servers to be permanent establishments, the latter for the very fact that the profits reinvested in the country are not taxed.

From a broader perspective, then, policymakers should re-think the concept of permanent establishment and adapt it to the actual technological development, in order to find ICT-oriented solutions that nevertheless respect the principle of non-discrimination between traditional and e-business. At the same time, new solutions have to be found in order to avoid that companies, as explained above, exploit the 'volatility' and potential of technology to elude any sort of income taxation.

# References

1. Albregtse, D.A.: The Server as a Permanent Establishment and the Revised Commentary on Article 5 of the OECD Model Tax Treaty: Are the E-Commerce Corporate Income Tax Problems Solved? Intertax 30(10), 356–364 (2002)
2. BEinGRID FP6 European project, http://www.beingrid.eu
3. Berman, F., Fox, G.C., Hey, A.J.G.: Grid Computing. Making the Global Infrastructure a Reality. John Wiley & Sons Ltd, Hoboken (2003)
4. Bivona, B.: La Stabile Organizzazione e le Nuove Frontiere della Tassazione. Fisconelmondo.it (last accessed: 1/4/2007) (2008), http://www.fisconelmondo.it/news-article.storyid-835.htm
5. Cockfield, A.J.: The Rise of the OECD as Informal 'World Tax Organization' Through National Responses to E-Commerce Tax Challenges. YJoLT 8, 136–187 (2006)
6. Department of the Treasury: Selected Tax Policy Implications of Global Electronic Commerce (1996) (last accessed: 31/03/2008), http://www.treas.gov/offices/tax-policy/library/internet.pdf
7. Doernberg, R.L., Hinnekens, L., Hellerstein, W., Li, J.: Electronic Commerce and Multijurisdictional Taxation. Kluwer Law International, The Hague (2001)
8. Gringras, C.: The Laws of the Internet. Butterworths LexisNexis, London (2003)
9. INTM266100 – Non-residents trading in the UK: Treaty permanent establishment (last accessed: 31/03/2008),
   http://www.hmrc.gov.uk/manuals/intmanual/INTM266100.htm
10. Mbwa-Mboma, M.N.: France, OECD Take Different Views of Unstaffed Servers as Permanent Establishments, WTD, 102–5 (2002)
11. OECD: Clarification on the Application of the Permanent Establishment Definition in E-Commerce: Changes to the Commentary on the Model Tax Convention on Article 5 (2000) (last accessed: 31/03/2008), http://www.oecd.org/dataoecd/46/32/1923380.pdf

---

[45] Loc. cit.

12. Pastukhov, O.: International Taxation of Income Derived from Electronic Commerce: Current Problems and Possible Solutions. B.U. J. Sci. & Tech. 12(2), 310–339 (2006)
13. Skaar, A.A.: Erosion of the Concept of Permanent Establishment: Electronic Commerce. Intertax 28(5), 188–194 (2000)
14. Smith, G.J.H.: Internet Law and Regulation. Sweet & Maxwell, London (2002)
15. Westin, R.A.: International Taxation of Electronic Commerce. Kluwer Law International, Alphen aan den Rijn (2007)

# The Pricing Strategy Analysis for the "Software-as-a-Service" Business Model

Dan Ma[1,*] and Abraham Seidmann[2]

[1] School of Information Systems, Singapore Management University, Singapore
School of Information Systems, Singapore Management University,
80 Stamford Road, Singapore 178902
madan@smu.edu.sg
Tel.: +65 6828 0926
[2] University of Rochester, United States

**Abstract.** The Software-as-a-Service (SaaS) model is a novel way of delivering software applications. In this paper, we present an analytical model to study the competition between the SaaS and the traditional COTS (Commercial off-the-shelf) software. The main research goal is to analyze the pricing strategy of the SaaS in a competitive setting. The model captures the most salient differences between the SaaS and COTS, including their distinct pricing structures, user initial setup costs, system customization levels, and delivery channels. We find that the two could coexist in a competitive market in the long run, and more importantly, we show how the SaaS could gradually take over the whole market even when its quality is inferior. Surprisingly, our analysis shows that the SaaS should raise (reduce) its prices when its software quality declines (increases) over time (in the relative sense).

**Keywords:** the SaaS business model; pricing strategy; competition; the COTS software.

## 1 Introduction

The Internet has enabled a new business model for software providers: the Software-As-A-Service (SaaS) model. The providers could bundle software applications, an IT infrastructure, and all necessary support services and deliver them to users across a network when users have a demand for them. Meanwhile, the providers should store the software system and users' data in a central location and are in charge of daily software maintenance, data backups, software upgrades, and security management. Hence, users obtain and pay for the final computing utility on demand. Such a business arrangement is totally different from the conventional delivery model for software applications. Traditionally, most software has been delivered as commercial off-the-shelf (COTS) products.[1] The provider sells the software application to users

---

* Corresponding author.

[1] A COTS product is a commercial software application that "is designed to be easily installed and to interoperate with existing system components" (see http://whatis.techtarget.com). Almost all software bought by the average computer user fits into the COTS category, such as operating systems, office product suites, word processing, and e-mail programs.

J. Altmann, D. Neumann, and T. Fahringer (Eds.): GECON 2008, LNCS 5206, pp. 103–112, 2008.
© Springer-Verlag Berlin Heidelberg 2008

and helps to install it on users' sites. The users possess the full ownership of the software, and must provide IT infrastructure, hardware, and support services in order to enable continuous use of the software.

The SaaS is experiencing fast growth. The AMR Research reports that the on-demand software market is growing more than 20% a year, compared with single-digit growth in traditional software (Lacy 2006). It is expected to reach $10 billion in annual revenue by 2009, up from $1.5 billion in 2006 (Pallatto 2006). To many users, the SaaS constitutes an attractive alternative to the traditional COTS solution. The recent study by *InformationWeek* indicates that 29% of the 250 business technology pros surveyed were using at least one licensed application hosted by a provider and accessed over the Internet, and 35% were planning to buy software that way, or were considering it. More interestingly, interest is found not just among small companies. Instead, 55% of the respondents have annual revenue of more than $100 million, and a third have more than $1 billion in revenue (InformationWeek 2007). Large organizations, such as Amazon.com, Cisco, Sprint, Morgan Stanley, Nokia, and Target, are also attracted by the SaaS and choose to obtain their software on demand, although they can easily set up the internal system without subjecting to any budget constraint. It is clear that the SaaS providers are stealing market share from the traditional providers of COTS software, and putting significant competitive pressure on them (Economist, 2007).

However, the long-term success of the SaaS in such a competitive setting remains uncertain. Data security and reliability as well as application control are always among users' top concerns (Bednarz 2006) which prevent them from opting for this new business model. In addition, the multi-tenancy design by the SaaS, under which providers are hosting a single instance of the software on a single server and maintaining the customer data on a single database (Hickins 2007), brings users the concern of lack of customization. For example, SourceRad, which provides clinical practices with "*integrated office scheduling, web-based viewing, online archiving, disaster recovery, and transcription, all in an affordable, hassle free hosted platform,*" (Author visit with SourceRad team, July 2007), operates a "one-to-many" service model, with no customization. As a result, users must exert additional effort to make its standard software application fit smoothly with their existing IT systems.

Although some researchers have already investigated the SaaS, such as Susarla et al. (2003) and Cheng and Koehler (2002), they focus on the monopoly setting and exclude the existence of COTS software providers as well as their market influence. In this study, I look at a marketplace in which the SaaS and COTS software solutions both are available. Our analysis focuses on the competition between the two. The model characterizes three salient differences between the SaaS and COTS. First, they deliver different products: a customized software application (from the COTS) versus a bundle of standard software and services (from the SaaS). Second, they adopt distinct pricing modes: an outright purchase (the COTS) versus a "per transaction" fee structure (the SaaS). Third, they employ different delivery methods: software installed on a user's in-house server (the COTS) versus an interface delivered over the Internet remotely (the SaaS).

We identify several interesting features of such a competition. First of all, we show that pricing its products strategically would allow the SaaS coexist with the COTS in the long run. The market will be segmented in such a way that firms with low transaction volume opt for the SaaS model because of the cheapness and scalability, and firms with high transaction volume prefer the COTS model to enjoy software that fits their specific business needs well. Moreover, we find that if users are concerned about potential changes in their future business environment, the SaaS providers should *increase* their prices. By doing this, they give up the competition with the COTS provider for high-volume users and instead focus on attracting small and medium firms. In contrast, if users expect the unfit costs of using standard software to decrease due to the advance of web technologies, the SaaS providers should *reduce* their prices to compete aggressively with COTS providers for those large corporate users. These counter-intuitive yet important findings help to suggest useful competitive pricing strategies to providers of on-demand software.

The rest of the paper is organized as follows. In Section 2, we describe the model. The analysis of the competition is given by Section 3. Section 4 summarizes our major findings, discusses their practical implications, and concludes the paper.

## 2  The Model

There are three parties in the market: software users, the COTS provider, and the SaaS provider.

Software users have different IT needs, which are measured by the expected volume of software use. Users who use the software application more frequently (in expectation) are considered with larger IT needs. To capture this heterogeneity, we assume users are uniformly distributed on a unit-length line normalized from 0 to 1. The location of a user on this line represents its expected transaction volume (in terms of the number of transactions). In addition, we assume that each user's actual transaction volume is stochastic. The user only knows the demand distribution, but not the exact number of transactions needed. In light of this, the actual demand for software use for each user $i$ is modeled as a random variable uniformly distributed on $[d_i - \theta, d_i + \theta]$, where the parameter $d_i$ represents his expected number of transactions and $\theta$ measures the volatility of the actual transaction volume. Note that $d_i$ itself is a random number distributed from 0 to 1.

The COTS provider sells the packaged software application to users and charges a one-time upfront fee. The source code of the application will be modified to fit the user's specific business needs, and thus the COTS in-house system is well customized. The provider bears an operating cost $C$ to serve one user and receives a one-time payment $P$ from the user. The user needs to install hardware and infrastructures, hire IT staff, and organize an internal IT group to provide software maintenance, data backups, and security and capacity management. Such service costs associated with each use of the software are denoted by $c$ (i.e., the service costs per transaction). Each transaction creates a value of $u$ to the user.

The SaaS provider sells the bundle of software and services on demand. The cost structure faced by the SaaS provider has two components: a setup cost $S$ per user (the fixed part) and a service cost $c$ per transaction (the variable part). Users pay as they go, incurring a payment $p_a$ per transaction to the provider. The software is installed on a central location which is controlled by the provider. All users can access and run it remotely via the Internet. To any individual user, the application is not well-customized, and each transaction gives the user a total value of $u$-$t$. The parameter $t$ measures the user's disutility from not using its ideal product and is called users' unfit costs in this paper. In many cases, it also represents the cost of extra effort to make the outside application work with the user's existing IT components smoothly.

Competition goes as follows. The two software providers are competing on prices. They set their respective prices simultaneously to maximize profit by considering the other's responses. Given the prices, users choose one provider or just stay out of the market by comparing the costs and benefits of using each provider.

## 3  Competition Analysis

In what follows, we analyze three different competition scenarios and then compare the pricing strategies under each. Section 3.1 first studies the providers' prices in a static competition. It will be used as a benchmark case. Then we discuss the essence of competition in a longer time window with possible dynamic changes in unfit costs, which could increase or decrease for some practical reasons. Section 3.2 and 3.3 study each of the two changes respectively and compare the findings to the benchmark case.

### 3.1  Pricing Strategy in the Static Competition (The Benchmark Case)

Consider user $i$ with expected transaction volume $d_i$. Denote its actually transaction volume by $D_i$. If the user opts for COTS which charges a one-time payment $P$, it needs first to decide and install proper IT service capacity level $q_i$ internally, which is obtained by maximizing the user's expected utility:

$$\underset{q_i}{Max} \quad E[u\min\{D_i,q_i\}-P-cq_i]=uq_i[1-F(q_i)]+uF(q_i)E[D_i/D_i<q_i]-P-cq_i$$

where $F(.)$ is the cumulative density function of the transaction volume for user $i$.

With probability $1-F(q_i)$, the actual transaction volume will be larger than the user's pre-installed service capacity. The user loses excess demand. With probability $F(q_i)$, the actual transaction volume will be smaller than the user's service capacity. The user incurs the costs of carrying excess capacity. Solving the optimization problem gives a closed form solution $q_i^* = d_i + \theta\left(1-\dfrac{2c}{u}\right)$. Hence, the expected utility for a COTS user is $d_i(u-c)-P-\dfrac{c(u-c)}{u}\theta.^2$ On the other hand, if the user opts for the SaaS, it gains an expected utility of $(u-p_a-t)d_i$.

---

[2] To understand this expression: the first term is the expected value from using the software; the second term is the user's one-time payment to the provider; and the last term represents the user's loss due to transaction uncertainty. Detailed derivations are available upon requests.

It is easy to see that in equilibrium the market is segmented in such a way that users with low transaction volume choose the SaaS and users with high transaction volume choose the COTS software, and the indifferent user has the expected transaction volume of $d^* = \dfrac{P}{P_a - c + t} + \dfrac{c(u-c)\theta}{u(p_a + t - c)}$. Hence, the COTS provider serves users in $[d^*, 1]$, with a market share of $1 - d^*$, and the SaaS serves users in $[0, d^*]$, with a market share of $d^*$.

The two providers choose prices $P$ and $p_a$ to maximize respective profit as follows: $\underset{P}{Max}\ (P-C)(1-d^*)$ and $\underset{p_a}{Max}\ \dfrac{1}{2}(p_a - c)(d^*)^2 - Sd^*$.

The equilibrium price pair is characterized in Proposition 1.

**Proposition 1.** *In the static competition, the price equilibrium exists. There is a threshold value $t^*$ for the unfit cost parameter.*

*a) When $t^* \le \dfrac{u-c}{2}$, the equilibrium prices are given by equations (1) and (2).*

$$P = \frac{p_a + t - c}{2} + \frac{C}{2} - \frac{c(u-c)\theta}{2u} \tag{1}$$

$$p_a = \frac{B(t+c) + 2Su(t-c)}{B - 2Su}, \text{ where } B = Pu + c(u-c)\theta. \tag{2}$$

*b) When $t \ge t^*$, the equilibrium prices are $\left(P^*, p_a^*\right) = \left(\dfrac{C}{2} + \dfrac{(u-c)}{2} - \dfrac{(u-c)c}{2u}\theta, u - t\right).$*

Proposition 1 describes the software providers' pricing strategy in a static competition. It is noticeable that the unfit cost parameter plays an important role. Whether or not it exceeds the given threshold value $t^*$ defines distinct pricing strategy. When such threshold value $t^*$ is not reached yet, both providers' prices are increasing in the unfit cost but the SaaS' price is capped at $u - t$. When the unfit cost exceeds $t^*$, the SaaS charges $u - t$, the upper limit of the price which could attract users and leaves zero consumer surplus.[3]

In practice, however, unfit costs could change. Unfit costs could grow over time, given software or hardware changes on the users' side, or decrease over time due to technology improvements. For example, if the SaaS uses a browser interface that is dependent on nonstandard aspects of IE7 but business circumstances faced by users drive a demand for the latest IE or Firefox, or if the SaaS's interface involves a module built on top of a program that only works in a pre-Vista MS Windows environment but hardware replacement at the user's site leads to multiple PCs with the Vista OS, unfit costs may increase. On the other hand, if the SaaS provider continuously

---

[3] At this price upper limit $u$-$t$, the SaaS provider extracts all consumer surpluses. Any price higher this upper limit will drive users to be out of the market.

invests in improving its system integration features, users' unfit costs may be decreasing over time. For instance, Salesforce.com developed and launched AppExchange in January 2006. AppExchange is an online marketplace for on-demand business software. Currently it includes over 150 applications, and Adobe, Skype, and Factiva are among the various partners. AppExchange allows Salesforce.com and other on-demand software providers to integrate their applications and therefore promises software users seamless extension of their existing systems (Cowley 2005; Kuchinskas 2006). In this case, users expect to have reduced unfit costs because a uniform platform eases collaboration across applications. Considering such changing natures of the market, we need a two-stage model to capture the essence of competition in a longer time window with possible dynamic changes in unfit costs. In the first stage, the vendors choose their prices ($p_a, P$) simultaneously, which are assumed unchangeable in the time line we are studying. The SaaS imposes unfit costs $t_1$ in the first stage. Users could have certain expectations about a future change in unfit costs: users may expect unfit costs to increase if they anticipate changes in demand or hardware upgrades, or to decrease if they anticipate technological advances that favor the shared software business model. In the second stage, such a change is realized. Users will then consider switching. We make two simplifying assumptions for model tractability. First, users and software providers weight utilities and profits obtained from both stages equally. Second, the initial setup costs of the SaaS to serve a new client are negligible. These two assumptions help to ease the analytical exposition without changing the results qualitatively.

## 3.2 The Two-Stage Model with Increased Unfit Costs

Consider the scenario that the initial unfit cost is $t_1$ while users expect such cost to increase to $t_H$ later. Figure 1 depicts this two-stage competition. In the first stage, with an unfit cost $t_1$, users in $[0, d_1]$ choose the SaaS, and users in $[d_1, 1]$ opt for the COTS software. The user $d_1$ should be indifferent between the two choices. In the second stage, with an increased unfit cost $t_H > t_1$, SaaS users in $[d_S, d_1]$ switch to the COTS system for a better fit while the rest stay with their initial choices. The "marginal" switcher is given by $d_S = \dfrac{P}{p_a + t_H - c} + \dfrac{c(u-c)\theta}{u(p_a + t_H - c)}$.[4] On the other hand, the user $d_1$, since it is indifferent between the two providers in the first stage, gains the same total utility from both. If it chooses the SaaS and switches to the COTS later, its total utility is $\left\{(u - p_a - t_1)d_1\right\} + \left\{(u-c)d_1 - P - \dfrac{c(u-c)\theta}{u}\right\}$; if it chooses

---

[4] An existing SaaS user $i$ compares the utility from the SaaS, $(u - p_a - t_H)d_i$, with the utility from the COTS, $(u-c)d_i - P - \dfrac{c(u-c)\theta}{u}$, to decide whether to switch. Therefore, the marginal switcher is the one who gets same utility from both providers.

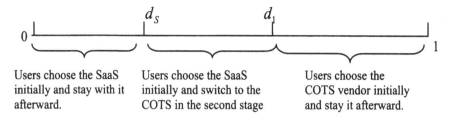

Fig. 1. Competition with Increased Unfit Costs

the COTS initially, it obtains $\left\{(u-c)d_1 - P - \dfrac{c(u-c)\theta}{u}\right\} + \left\{(u-c)d_1 - \dfrac{c(u-c)\theta}{u}\right\}$.

By equating these two utilities, we get:

$$d_1 = \frac{c(u-c)\theta}{u(p_a + t_1 - c)}. \tag{3}$$

The COTS provider gets $[d_1, 1]$ users in the first stage and $[d_s, d_1]$ users in the second stage. Its profit comes from users' one-time payment. The SaaS provider serves $[0, d_1]$ users in the first stage and $[0, d_s]$ users in the second stage. It gains profit from users' every use of the software. Their prices are determined as follows.

$$\underset{P}{Max}\ (P - C)[1 - d_s]. \tag{4}$$

$$\underset{p_a}{Max}\ (p_a - c)\left[\int_0^{d_1} x\,dx + \int_0^{d_s} x\,dx\right] = \frac{1}{2}(p_a - c)(d_1^2 + d_s^2). \tag{5}$$

Let $p_a\big|_{t_1, t_H}$ and $P\big|_{t_1, t_H}$ be the equilibrium prices in such a two-stage competition and let $d_1\big|_{t_1, t_H}$ be the indifferent user defined by equation (3). Let $p_a\big|_{t_1}$ and $P\big|_{t_1}$ be the equilibrium prices in the static competition with unfit costs $t_1$, i.e., the prices in the benchmark case, and $d_{t_1}^*$ be the indifferent user in that case.

***Proposition 2.*** *When users anticipate a future increase in unfit costs, $t_1 \to t_H$, both vendors will increase their prices; i.e., $p_a\big|_{t_1, t_H} > p_a\big|_{t_1}$, and $P\big|_{t_1, t_H} > P\big|_{t_1}$. More users will choose the COTS software initially, i.e., $d_1\big|_{t_1, t_H} < d_{t_1}^*$, and the SaaS will lose existing clients to the COTS provider once the cost increase occurs.*

Proposition 2 states three important findings. First, although increased unfit costs imply a decrease in the quality of the SaaS product ($u - t$), the on demand software provider should nevertheless increase its price: $p_a|_{t_1,t_H} > p_a|_{t_1}$. By charging a high price, the provider gives up competing for high-volume users with the COTS provider; it instead concentrates on exploiting low-volume users that are unable to afford the COTS anyway. Second, the COTS provider also raises its price, which is intuitive because its product becomes more attractive. Interestingly, we find that the COTS provider's pricing function ($P = \dfrac{p_a + t_H - c}{2} + \dfrac{C}{2} - \dfrac{c(u-c)\theta}{2u}$, equation (1)) is the same as that in a static competition with $t = t_H$. This means that the COTS provider should adopt a simple pricing strategy. Software is priced as if it were in a one-stage competition with invariant unfit costs. Finally, we conclude that a belief that unfit costs will increase benefits in-house solution providers but hurts the SaaS providers.

## 3.3 The Two-Stage Model with Decreased Unfit Costs

Figure 2 shows the two-stage competition when $t$ decreases. In the first stage, with unfit costs $t_1$, users in $[0, d_1]$ choose the SaaS, and users in $[d_1, 1]$ buy the COTS. The indifferent user is at $d_1$. In the second stage, the unfit cost decreases to $t_L < t_1$, which could be the result of web technology improvements, adoption of software standards and protocols, or creation of a uniform software platform. In such cases, existing COTS users compare their utility from switching to the SaaS, $(u - p_a - t_L)d_i$, and staying with the COTS, $(u-c)d_i - \dfrac{c(u-c)\theta}{u}$. The "marginal" switcher, $d_S$, is the one who gains the same utility from these two options:

$$d_S = \frac{c(u-c)\theta}{u(p_a + t_L - c)}.$$

The indifferent user $d_1$ can be found as follows. If this user chooses the COTS and then switches to the SaaS later, its expected total utility is $\left\{(u-c)d_1 - P - \dfrac{c(u-c)\theta}{u}\right\} + \left\{(u - p_a - t_L)d_1\right\}$; if it chooses the SaaS in the first stage, its total utility is $\left\{(u - p_a - t_1)d_1\right\} + \left\{(u - p_a - t_L)d_1\right\}$. By equating both, we get

$$d_1 = \frac{P}{p_a + t_1 - c} + \frac{c(u-c)\theta}{u(p_a + t_1 - c)}. \tag{6}$$

Note that the number of switchers (from the COTS to SaaS) is *not* affected by the COTS price because it is considered a sunk cost at the second stage.

The COTS and SaaS providers choose profit-maximizing prices respectively, as described by equations (4) and (5).

Let $p_a|_{t_1,t_L}$ and $P|_{t_1,t_L}$ be the prices of the SaaS and COTS products, and let $d_1|_{t_1,t_L}$ be the indifferent user defined by equation (6).

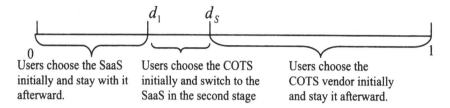

**Fig. 2.** Competition with decreased unfit costs

**Proposition 3.** *When users anticipate a decrease in unfit costs, $t_1 \to t_L$, both providers will reduce their prices; i.e., $p_a\big|_{t_1,t_L} < p_a\big|_{t_1}$, and $P\big|_{t_1,t_L} < P\big|_{t_1}$. More users will choose the SaaS initially; i.e., $d_1\big|_{t_1,t_L} > d_{t_1}^*$. Existing clients of the COTS provider have little incentive to switch to the on-demand software even if unfit costs decrease, but they may do so if transaction volatility is high.*

Three important findings are stated in Proposition 3. First, the SaaS provider's response to the expected decrease in unfit costs, which represents an increase in the quality of its product, is to reduce its price. The increased quality and reduced price together put the SaaS in a much better position in the competition with the COTS provider to gain high-volume users, who are much more profitable in the eyes of the SaaS.[5] Second, the COTS provider once again will stick to a simple pricing strategy. Its pricing function, $P = \dfrac{p_a + t_1 - c}{2} + \dfrac{C}{2} - \dfrac{c(u-c)\theta}{2u}$ (Equation (1)), is the same as that in a static competition with unfit costs $t = t_1$. It therefore can just ignore the expected future changes and price its software as if in a one-stage competition. Third, existing users of COTS software are unlikely to switch to the on-demand software. These users have two choices: stay with the COTS solution, with a utility of $(u-c)d_i - \dfrac{c(u-c)\theta}{u}$, or switch, with a utility of $(u - p_a - t_L)d_i$. Since $p_a > c$ always, the user switches only if its transaction volatility ($\theta$) is high. Hence, we conclude that once an in-house system has been installed, users have little incentive to switch to the SaaS unless they need to manage risks caused by volatile demand.

## 4 Discussion and Conclusion

In this paper we try to shed light on the pricing strategy of the SaaS providers in the competition with the traditional COTS software providers. We examine the equilibrium prices in both static and dynamic market conditions where users face stochastic demand. Our findings show that the SaaS on-demand model is superior when a user faces low transaction volume and/or high transaction volatility. It offers small firms

---

[5] The SaaS gets paid per transaction. So high-transaction-volume users are more profitable than low-transaction-volume users.

cost-saving access to software and becomes the natural choices of them, and meanwhile it competes with the COTS solution on firms with large transaction volume.

One common belief in designing the SaaS software is that increasing the product quality by reducing its unfit cost should support higher prices. Hence, some results from our two-period analysis may seem counter-intuitive at first glance. We establish that the SaaS provider's optimal response to users' anticipation of decreased unfit costs (which means an increase in product quality) is to *reduce* its price. The SaaS is more competitive in this situation and thus can go after the more profitable high-volume users. Since the SaaS provider is paid on a per transaction basis, users with high transaction volumes are considered more profitable. Although the provider gains smaller revenue per transaction (due to the reduction in its unit price), its market share expands to encompass part of the segment with larger transaction volume. On the other hand, when users anticipate a future increase in unfit costs (which means a decrease in the quality of the SaaS product), the on-demand software provider should *increase* its price. By charging a higher price, it gives up competing against the COTS provider for high-volume users. Instead, it separates the market and concentrates on exploiting low-volume users that are unable to afford the COTS anyway.

Although this work only focuses on analyzing the SaaS providers' pricing strategy in the competitive market, there are many possibilities for further SaaS studies. It would be interesting to examine the role of differential service level agreements (SLAs). When users have demand for different levels of service, the SLA constitutes a way to segment the market and improve the SaaS's profit. Another possible extension encompasses the design and management of a dual channel. Certain vendors (such as Oracle and IBM) have changed their business models to offer both COTS and SaaS products. Typically, they are selling a sophisticated version of their software products as a COTS product and are leasing simplified operating versions as the SaaS. Future research may investigate the proper pricing and functionality bundle per channel.

# References

1. Bednarz, A.: Manufacturers Eye on On-Demand Software. Network World, April 24 (2006)
2. Cheng, H.K., Koehler, G.J.: Optimal Pricing Policies of Web-enabled Application Services. working paper (2002)
3. Cowley, S.: Salesforce.com Makes Platform Move with AppExchange. InfoWorld (September 2005)
4. Hickins, M.: Oracle: On-demand is Now On The Grid. Enterprise (April 2007)
5. Kuchinskas, S.: Salesforce Finally Ships AppExchange. Ecommerce, January 17 (2006)
6. Lacy, S.: The On-Demand Software Scrum. Business Week, April 17 (2006)
7. Proponents of Software as a service say it will wipe out traditional software. The Economist, April 21 (2006)
8. Pallatto, J.: IBM Recruiting IS vs. Partners to SaaS. Channel Insider, Feburary 23 (2006)
9. Software as a Service (Research Report). InformationWeek (March 2007)
10. Susarla, A., Barua, A., Whinston, A.: Understanding the Service Component of Application Service Provision: An Empirical Analysis of Satisfaction with ASP Services. MIS Quarterly 27, 123–919 (2003)

# On the Assessment of the S-Sicilia Infrastructure: A Grid-Based Business System

Carmelo Ragusa[1], Francesco Longo[1], and Antonio Puliafito[2]

[1] Cometa Consortium research group at University of Messina,
98166, S. Agata, Messina
[2] Department of Mathematic, University of Messina,
98166, S. Agata, Messina
{cragusa,flongo,apuliafito}@unime.it

**Abstract.** The enablement of the Grid paradigm for commercial solutions is a fundamental issue for both research bodies and companies. Different technologies seem to be mature to serve the purpose, but still research and experimentation is needed. In fact, the introduction of the business aspect poses new challenges such as new business models, service composition, relationships management, etc. In this paper, we present the S-Sicilia project, a 2-year collaboration between Oracle and the COMETA consortium, aiming to setup a Grid-based business infrastructure to provide business services with guaranteed QoS for companies. The system does not aim to provide answers for all business related issues, but rather be a kind of benchmark where experimentation on real cases takes place.

**Keywords:** Grid, Business Grids, SLA, SOA, Web Services, B2B, B2C.

## 1 Introduction

Business Grid promises the wide adoption of economic valuable Grid services. Lot of effort is being spent by the research community as well as by companies that are interested in its adoption. The business component involves more stringent requirements in terms of security, confidentiality, trust, guarantees etc. Moreover, by its nature a business process requires most of the times interactions with other business processes and therefore the Business Grid has to provide service composition. Also, regulations of Business-to-Business (B2B) and Business-to-Consumer (B2C) interactions have to be performed through Service Level Agreements (SLAs) which need a management system that deals with those contracts. Researchers are now focusing on those business aspects, trying to address some of the new arising challenges namely business models, pricing models and market economies. Also, some of the current Grid middlewares (Globus [15], Gria [16], Unicore [17], gLite [9]) are including some of the mentioned aspects within their solutions.

In this paper we describe a real case study, the S-Sicilia project [2][3], which aims to create real services for SME companies with specific needs. The project does not pretend to address all aspects related to a Business Grid but, by solving particular requirements, be a sort of benchmark to reach a global business-based Grid adoption.

J. Altmann, D. Neumann, and T. Fahringer (Eds.): GECON 2008, LNCS 5206, pp. 113–124, 2008.
© Springer-Verlag Berlin Heidelberg 2008

The Grid infrastructure we started with is primary used for scientific applications with no QoS guarantees (i.e. gLite-based). We have created a business layer on top of this Grid infrastructure in order to provide business services with guaranteed quality. Service demand being in most cases unpredictable, the ability to scale the system with it can be a winning factor for SME companies, which normally have limited budget to spend compared to large enterprises.

In the next section we set the background of our work. In section 3 we describe the S-Sicilia project, the system architecture and a reference scenario. The assessment of the scenario is also discussed. Section 4 shows further scenarios that will be developed in the future. Finally, in Section 5 we give the conclusions and the next steps of our work.

## 2  Background

The business element adds complexity to the Grid approach. Although, some of the requirements in this context might coincide with the ones in scientific Grids, in business scenarios they are more strict. Research is focusing on all those aspects that will bring the Grid paradigm to the next level. In particular, a business oriented Grid infrastructure needs to address the following issues:

- **Distributed data management:** a solution providing support for integrating and updating data residing at multiple transactional resources. For example a distributed query and transaction facilities approach can serve the purpose;
- **Service composition:** services will tend to provide specific features addressing particular needs. Composition of such services across multiple domains is fundamental. Web services and Service Oriented Architecture (SOA) enable this important aspect;
- **Security:** the composition of services through different administrative domains gives rise to new security issues. A business Grid system must guarantee that the execution of a program on behalf of the vendor does not violate security policies, especially when the program has been supplied by the vendor or some delegated third party. New security policy languages allowing the definition of security driven service composition mechanisms are required;
- **Privacy:** user's data has to be protected through an efficient access management system;
- **SLA management:** a Business Grid enables the delivery of services as utilities and provides means for meeting SLA commitments for such services. Tools for service design to handle the definition of QoS contracts in SLAs have to be developed;
- **Accounting and billing:** currently, accounting and billing arrangements for outsourced services are based on raw machine resource consumption (CPU-time, storage capacity etc.). A Business Grid has to define a framework that allows accounting and billing in terms of the services that were completed, taking into consideration the QoS provided;
- **Business models:** new business models have to be developed to make business Grid services effective. Different approaches to business relationships and new business roles need to be experimented. This will create new source of revenue;

- **Trust:** relationships in economic environments might be long term based, but also very short and dynamic. Trust is definitely more solid and easier to achieve in the former than in the latter. Qualification information on suppliers to select business partners, clear and transparent contracts, security, monitoring of business operations can enable trust at all levels;
- **Risk assessment:** companies relying on business Grid services need to have tools to support their choices. Assess the risk of such choices can make a difference. The provision of specific tools is very important. Research of this aspect is therefore required;

Projects such as EGEE [18], NextGrid [28], Globus [15], Akogrimo [30], GRIA [16], GRASP [29], TrustCom [27] and AssessGrid [35] have all focused to address specific Grid business concepts, resulting in the development of new components, architectures or more generically guidelines. On the other hand the GridEcon project [25][26][36] aims to provide a generic framework addressing all aspects.

Gridipedia [19] defines itself as a Grid meeting point for individuals and organizations on the use of the Grid technology to address their business needs. The case studies section gives an overview of real cases that have successfully adopted the Grid technologies in different areas. Improvements in terms of resilience, performance, scalability and flexibility have been achieved within the financial, pharmaceutical and engineering sectors. Examples of commercial providers of business Grid are Digipede [20], DataSynapse [21], Sun Grid [22], Platform [23], EC2 [31]. The difference with research ones is that their solutions usually do not involve several providers and are based on single domains. Also, being commercial solutions they do not provide the inside and mechanisms of how services are implemented.

In the next section we introduce the S-Sicilia project. As said, our work is based on the gLite Grid middleware, which does not provide most of the functionalities mentioned. On the other hand, the aim of our system is not to address all Business related issues, but on delivering services with guaranteed quality. Aspects such as SLA management, accounting and billing, service composition and security are relevant.

## 3  Experimenting with Business Grids: The S-Sicilia Project

The S-Sicilia project, a 2-year collaboration between Oracle and the COMETA consortium [1], intends to setup a Grid-based business infrastructure able to provide services for industry. SMEs can benefit from Grid-based economy by reducing their costs to setup and run new services and hence increasing their competitiveness. On the other hand, large enterprises can take advantage from this new marketplace too. In fact, while normally large enterprises possess in-house data centers to serve normal work load, they could upload extra load to business Grids in case of peak demands.

An e-service is usually defined and managed through SLAs (Service Level Agreement), service contracts between a service provider and a service consumer. Those contracts specify  parties' commitments, obligations, violations, performance levels and price.

In our system SLAs are based on the WSLA schema [4]. Its main characteristic is the ease of creation of SLAs via an XML schema that can be modified accordingly to the necessity. The schema structure also matches the SLA management tasks implemented within the system. At the time of the project start, this was the most appropriate choice. However, WS-Agreement [32] has gained consensus over time resulting in a recommendation from the OGF and therefore a future step will be to migrate the framework from WSLA to WS-Agreement.

The system manages services by monitoring the relative contracts and taking any due action such as service re-configuration, service re-location or resources re-allocation. Decisions are taken according to the customer's SLA and compensations are given in case of contracts violations. This known mechanism should give the right level of guarantees for business customers.

Other aspects are also addressed by the system such as accounting and billing. In this business environment, customers are billed not for raw resources as in common scientific Grids but for the service used. In order to provide such level of abstraction, contracts are specified in business terms, using terminology closer to customers.

Although, as stated in the background section, other Grid middlewares are focusing on business aspects, the use of the gLite middleware is compulsory to us. Therefore, the S-Sicilia project extends gLite basic functionalities by adding a business management layer to offer business services. However, the system has been designed to do not rely on a particular middleware, but to be rather generic.

In the next sections we present the details about our solution, describing the system architecture and illustrating the first scenario we have setup. An initial assessment of this scenario is also discussed.

## 3.1  System Architecture

Our system is based on different technologies. In particular, we have used a SOA approach to create a set of services dealing with high level requirements, and a Grid infrastructure for the low level resources.

The system is logically divided into two layers: the first and higher layer deals with customers, processing their requests, providing possible offers and managing SLAs; the second and lower layer interfaces with the Grid infrastructure. A set of QoS mechanisms have been implemented at both layers, in order to provide functionalities that the Grid does not offer natively.

The higher layer is called SLA engine and handles the service lifecycle. In particular, it manages service definition, deployment, monitoring, compliance and termination. Customers' requests are received in the forms of SLAs and are processed accordingly. A check for availability is performed and consequently an offer is sent back to the customer who can accept or reject it. Accepted SLAs are monitored to check their compliance and in case of needs actions are taken. As mentioned, the SOA approach was used and in particular the SLA engine is composed of a set of interconnected services providing the contracts' lifecyle management functionalities as well as billing and payment processes. The tools used to build this layer are the ORACLE SOA suite [5] and the ORACLE DB 10G [6]. The Oracle SOA Suite is a complete set of service infrastructure components for building, deploying, and managing SOA applications. Services can be created, managed, and orchestrated into composite applications and business processes.

The SOA suite contains the following packages:

1.  The Oracle BPM (BPEL Process Manager), which offers a comprehensive and easy-to-use infrastructure for creating, deploying and managing BPEL business processes [7];
2.  The Oracle ESB (Enterprise Service Bus), which provides everything for seamless integration of data and enterprise applications within an organization and with trading partners [8];

Figure 1 shows the system that has been implemented. We have used the BPM to create a BPEL process that combines together the small services represented in the figure:

1.  **Accounting Service**: this service registers the user and grants the access to the infrastructure;
2.  **Negotiation Service**: this process is started by the user that requests an offer for a service. The *negotiation service* gets the SLA from the user and submits it to the *performance prediction service*. Based on the result from the *performance prediction service*, the strategy and the pricing model in use this service fills the SLA and sends the completed offer back to the user;
3.  **Performance Prediction Service**: it returns an estimate of the raw resources that can potentially satisfy the SLA, based on the history of similar SLAs stored within the DB;
4.  **Process Scheduler Service**: this service receives the user agreed SLA and stores it in the DB;
5.  **SE Uploader Service**: this service allows the user to upload its application files and stores the files paths, within the SE (the gLite Storage Element [9]), in the DB;
6.  **Monitoring Service**: this service monitors the SLA lifecycle. It checks if there are SLAs in a new state and sends them to the *QoS service*. It also detects if an SLA needs attention and informs the *QoS service*. Finally, it determines when an SLA finished and contacts the *billing service*. The operations performed by this service are also implemented by some procedures within the *Service Repository*;
7.  **QoS service**: this service performs a match operation of the user requests with the Grid resources. It also deals with SLAs that need attentions by taking due actions;
8.  **Billing Service**: this service gets the finished SLA, invokes the credit service and informs the user that his/her service has been completed;
9.  **Credit service**: this service invokes an external service, usually offered by a bank, which debits the user credit card or account;
10. **JDL maker service**: this service invokes a script that creates a JDL (i.e. gLite Job Description Language) file for the SLA and sends it to the gLite User Interface (UI);

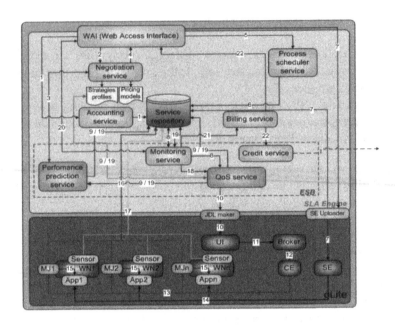

**Fig. 1.** S-Sicilia system architecture

One of the key element of the system is the *Service repository*, which is used by the SOA suite internal components, the SLA engine processes and the resource *sensors*. Users credentials, data and SLAs are stored in the *Service repository*. A native XML DataBase (DB) was needed, due to its higher performance in managing/storing XML data. Oracle DB 10g provides such feature. The *Service repository* structure was designed to accommodate generic applications, so that each time a new application has to be supported it can be easily integrated into the system. An application is composed by a main process which is supplied by the user, a set of services needed to run the application and a DB. Services have dependencies in terms of other services. Those dependencies are stored in the *Service Repository* as well. The main process as well as its services have to maintain some information needed to run such as addresses, ports, files, etc., which are also kept within the *Service repository*. Resources runtime consumption data is stored in specific tables to provide the current and past state of the system. Finally, an archive of the past SLAs is maintained. The *Service repository* contains also a  number of stored procedures implementing the logic to instantiate and manage applications and services. Some of those procedures are exposed to external entities that need to interact with the *Service repository*.

Finally, gLite is the Grid middleware used and it can be seen as an integrated set of components allowing resource sharing. It provides a framework for building grid applications exploiting the power of distributed computing and storage resources across the Internet.

In order to integrate the SLA engine with the gLite infrastructure, a set of resource *sensors* has been created. These have been implemented and deployed in the gLite

Worker Nodes[1] (WNs). Their task is to timely measure resource instant consumption and send those measurements to the *Service repository*. *Sensors* have been implemented as linux cron jobs and scripts measuring computing (CPU and RAM), storage and network resources.

## 3.2  Scenario: Web Applications Hosting Service

Web applications have gained popularity over the past years, due to benefits they bring such as rapid development, scalability, user mobility. Also the possibility to have an initial low investment has given the chance to small businesses to get online and therefore extend their range of actions. However, with low investment only small infrastructure can be built which somehow limits the company chances to grow. On the other hand if a higher investment is considered it may be too risky if the success is not fully accomplished. Giving the companies the possibility to ease their activities from managing their IT-system and potentially lowering their investment will be indeed welcomed.

This scenario concerns a hosting solution for a hardware vendor's web application. Customers connect to the vendor's website and make their orders. Normally, those orders go to the vendor's system, running on an application server, that processes them. We have created an environment to host such application by installing application servers and DBs on the Business Grid nodes (see Figure 2). In this way all

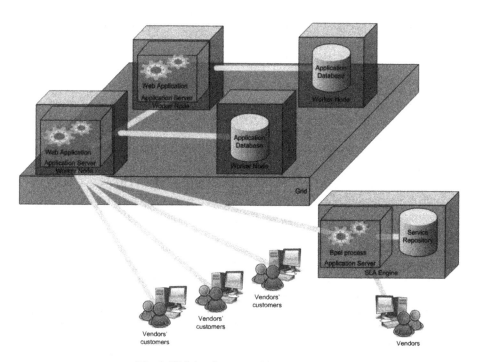

**Fig. 2.** Web hosting scenario representation

---

[1] A gLite Worker Node (WN) is a single unit of computation, containing a set of clients needed to run jobs.

customers' orders are processed by the vendor's system running on the application servers hosted on our Business Grid solution.

This scenario allows experimenting with such type of businesses to show the ability of the proposed system to cope with them.

The ORACLE SOA suite comes with a demo application, which is a commercial application for a hardware vendor webssite implemented through a BPEL process. This demo was chosen for our scenario.

A potential online vendor accesses the infrastructure through a web interface by filling a form with his/her requirements. The system verifies that the service can be performed and sends an offer. After accepting the offer, the vendor sends his/her application in a WAR/EAR format along with the database scripts that are needed to create the necessary DB tables and procedures. Those files are then stored on the gLite SE. The *monitoring service* detects the new SLA and informs the *QoS service*. The *QoS service* chooses the resources (i.e. gLite WNs) to run the service based on the indications of the *performance prediction service*. The deployment phase then starts by performing an installation of the vendor's application, a DB creation and relative configurations in a fully automated way. After the deployment phase, *sensors* are attached to the application and its services. Those *sensors* then send data read to the *service repository*, which are used by the *monitoring service* to assess the SLA compliance during its lifecycle. If current WNs are not enough to guarantee the SLA requirements a dynamic workload balancing is performed by the *monitoring* and *QoS services* adding more worker nodes as needed to fulfill the SLA constraints. Vice-versa, if an SLA, considering its actual load, has assigned too many WNs an action to release the WNs that are not necessary is performed.

### 3.3 Scenario Assessment

The first test we carried out aimed to assess basic functionalities of the system. The vendor's requirement was to support a maximum of 300 transactions per second. Initially, the vendor's application runs on a single worker node (WN1). We setup the network threshold on WN1 of 150 KB/s, after which the system detects that the SLA does not have enough resources and an action has to be performed. We have simulated accesses to the vendor's website using a tool called JMeter [10].

In the first phase we simulate traffic for 10 concurrent users performing an average of 7 operations each. WN1 is able to take on the all load, according to the threshold we setup.

In the second phase JMeter increases the number of concurrent users to 40, in order to overload WN1. As a consequence, the *monitoring service* spots this situation, understand that the involved SLA has rights for more resources and informs the *QoS service*. The latter chooses another WN to install the vendor's application and re-start the deployment phase. Following the steps previously described, when this phase completes there are 2 WNs to serve all users' requests. The traffic towards the vendor's website is then divided between WN1 and WN2.

Finally in the third phase JMeter reduces the traffic by simulating again 10 concurrent users. In this situation there is an overallocation of resources. The *monitoring service* captures this new state and again informs the *QoS service*. The *QoS service* then starts an undeployment phase where the vendor's application is uninstalled from

WN2 along the associated *sensors*. WN1 is able to address all users' requests to the vendor's website. Table 1 shows the data of the total network traffic sent and that relative to WN1 and WN2. Those data are also graphically reported on Figure 3.

**Table 1.** Network traffic data of Web application hosting scenario

| Time (mins) | Total Network Traffic sent (KB/s) | WN1 Network Traffic sent (KB/s) | WN2 Network Traffic sent (KB/s) |
|---|---|---|---|
| 1 | 0 | 0 | 0 |
| 2 | 0 | 0 | 0 |
| 3 | 0 | 0 | 0 |
| 4 | 51.04 | 51.04 | 0 |
| 5 | 52.46 | 52.46 | 0 |
| 6 | 223.46 | 223.46 | 0 |
| 7 | 273.1 | 219.65 | 53.46 |
| 8 | 251.06 | 145.63 | 105.43 |
| 9 | 239.99 | 113.54 | 126.45 |
| 10 | 246.3 | 118.76 | 127.54 |
| 11 | 245.34 | 109.87 | 135.46 |
| 12 | 180.94 | 86.57 | 94.37 |
| 13 | 115.28 | 76.53 | 38.75 |
| 14 | 56.37 | 56.37 | 0 |
| 15 | 59.88 | 59.88 | 0 |
| 16 | 51.24 | 51.24 | 0 |

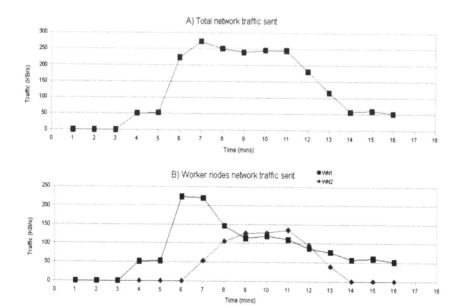

**Fig. 3.** A) Total network traffic sent in reply to vendor's website customers' requests. B) Traffic sent by WN1 and WN2.

As we can see, initially until minute 5 (phase 1) WN1 serves all requests to the vendor's website. After minute 5 starts phase 2 until minute 11. Here the traffic grows more than the threshold (150 KB/s) and more resources are added to serve users' requests, according to the vendor's SLA. From minute 6 to minute 12 WN2 is active and serves users' requests along WN1. In fact, the total traffic is split between the two nodes. At minute 12 starts phase 3 where the users' request decreases drastically and the vendor's application is removed from WN2. The situation then returns to its initial state.

Although only a simple scenario was used we can say that the system behaves correctly and delivers QoS services. Obviously, more tests will be needed for which more complex scenarios will be setup. For example, if traffic is very bursty, deployment and undeployment phases will be quite frequent. Tests to understand those situations will be needed.

## 4  Future Scenarios

Further scenarios will be implemented in the future. One of the goals of the S-Sicilia project is to show the flexibility of the system to support very different applications. A part from the Web hosting scenario which will be further developed to add more complexity, other applications will be integrated within the system.

We have already implemented a virtualization solution that runs on our gLite based infrastructure. Virtualization has a lot of advantages, because allows setting up customized environments tailored to the users' needs. For example, a user might have specific requirements for its application in terms of operating system, or his/her application might be a legacy system with specific requirements. Virtualization is the perfect choice in those situations. Also new range of applicability of the virtualization approach are being studied. Different companies showed interest in this approach and have provided some application to experiment.

INTERGRAPH [11] is providing SmartPlant Foundation SPF (Engineering Database), SmartPlant P&ID (CAD 2D), SmartPlant Instrumentation  and Marian (Material management and procurement). ST Microelectronics [14] will provide its software suite for microchip design and simulation. Other agreements for experimentation have been reached with INSIRIO [12] and INQUADRO [13] to supply further applications. In the future, the virtualization solution will be integrated within the S-Sicilia infrastructure.

## 5  Conclusions and Future Work

This paper presented the S-Sicilia project. Issues related to Business Grids were discussed. New business models, service composition, SLA management, security, trust, privacy are some of those issues. The relative projects conducting research on those aspects were also mentioned. Our system aims to deliver solutions targeting SME companies with specific needs and can be a point of reference for the development of the business mechanisms that will lead to the global adoption of the Grid paradigm.

We have presented the system infrastructure. The system sits on top of a Grid infrastructure based on the gLite middleware. The Grid infrastructure is mainly used for scientific applications, but we have extended it to provide business solutions. The business layer is based on a SOA approach. Basic services composing our system were introduced. Addition of *sensors* at gLite level were also introduced. Users access the system through web interface, establishing a contract containing the service requirements, parties commitments, service performances, terms of service violation and service price. A web hosting scenario was also shown. In this scenario we offer a service that allows a web vendor to have his/her web application hosted on our infrastructure. An initial assessment of the basic functionalities to deliver the user's contracted quality was discussed.

The future steps of our work will be to implement some of the logic behind the scenes. For example, we are working on a mapping mechanism that will allow to get the raw resources based on high level requirements. Tests are being carried out for the purpose. Moreover, we want to increase the complexity of our web hosting scenario. We want to start experimenting with an increasing number of concurrent SLAs and see when and where the system breaks. Improvements will be definitely needed.

Another important aspect that we are working on is the use of a different approach for the definition of SLAs. Currently we are using WSLA of IBM, but the adoption of WS-Agreement is under study. WS-Agreement [32] is getting more consensus from the research community. Recent works [33][34] have shown how it can be extended to allow service runtime re-negotiation.

Finally, we have discussed further scenarios through which we will be able to demonstrate the flexibility of our solution. Companies interested in those services have already agreed to provide their applications for experimentation. The implementation and assessment of those scenarios is also a priority for us.

**Acknowledgments.** This work makes use of results produced by the PI2S2 Project managed by the Consorzio COMETA, a project co-funded by the Italian Ministry of University and Research (MIUR) within the Piano Operativo Nazionale "Ricerca Scientifica, Sviluppo Tecnologico, Alta Formazione" (PON 2000-2006). More information is available at http://www.pi2s2.it and http://www.consorzio-cometa.it.

# References

1. The COMETA Consortium, Consorzio Multi Ente per la promozione e l'adozione di Tecnologie di calcolo Avanzato, http://www.consorzio-cometa.it
2. The S-Sicilia project, http://www.consorzio-cometa.it/s-sicilia, s-sicilia.unime.it
3. Oracle and COMETA Consortium Combine Approach to Grid Computing for Sicilian Pilot Project,
   http://www.oracle.com/corporate/press/2006_dec/cometa.html
4. Ludwig, H. et al.: Web Service Level Agreement (WSLA) Language Specification,
   http://www.research.ibm.com/wsla/WSLASpecV1-20030128.pdf
5. Oracle SOA suite, An SOA Suite of Oracle's Most Popular Best-of-Breed Technologies,
   http://www.oracle.com/technologies/soa/soa-suite.html
6. ORACLE DB 10G, http://www.oracle.com/database/index.html
7. Oracle BPM, Business Process Management,
   http://www.oracle.com/technology/products/ias/bpel/index.html

8. Oracle ESB, Enterprise Service Bus, http://www.oracle.com/appserver/esb.html
9. gLite, User Guide, https://edms.cern.ch/file/722398/gLite-3-User Guide.html
10. Apache JMeter, http://jakarta.apache.org/jmeter
11. INTERGRAPH, Leading global provider of spatial information management (SIM) software, http://www.intergraph.com
12. Insirio, Business Solution Integrator, http://www.insirio.it
13. InQuadro, Insirio Innovazioni, http://www.inquadro.it
14. ST Microelectronics, http://www.st.com
15. Globus, Globus Toolkit, http://www.globus.org
16. Gria, Service Oriented Collaborations for Industry and Commerce, http://www.gria.org
17. Unicore, Uniform Interface to Computing Resources , http://www.unicore.eu
18. EGEE, Enabling Grids for E-sciencE, http://public.eu-egee.org
19. Gridpedia, The European Grid Marketplace, http://www.gridipedia.eu
20. Digipede, Distributed computing solutions for real-word business problems at any scale, http://www.digipede.net
21. DataSynapse, The leader in Real-Time Infrastructure Software, http://www.datasynapse.com
22. Sun Grid, Sun Utility Computing, http://www.sun.com/service/sungrid/index.jsp
23. Platform, HPC Management Software, http://www.platform.com
24. Altmann, J., Ion, M., Mohammed, A.A.B.: Taxonomy of Grid Business Models. In: 4th International Workshop, GECON 2007, Rennes, France, August 28 (2007)
25. Altmann, J., Routzounis, S.: Economic Modeling of Grid Services. e-Challenges 2006, Barcelona, Spain (October 2006)
26. Altmann, J., Courcoubetis, C., Darlington, J., Cohen, J.: GridEcon – The Economic-Enhanced Next-Generation Internet. In: Veit, D.J., Altmann, J. (eds.) GECON 2007. LNCS, vol. 4685, pp. 188–193. Springer, Heidelberg (2007)
27. TrustCom, An environment for trust, security and contract management in B2B collaborations, http://www.eu-trustcom.com
28. NextGrid, Architecture for Next Generation Grids, http://www.nextgrid.org
29. GRASP, Grid Based Application Service Provision, http://www.eu-grasp.net
30. Akogrimo, Access to Knowledge through the Grid in a mobile World, http://www.akogrimo.org
31. Amazon EC2, Amazon Elastic Compute Cloude, http://www.amazon.com/gp/browse.html?node=201590011
32. Web Services Agreement Specification (WS-Agreement), http://www.ogf.org/documents/GFD.107.pdf
33. Di Modica, G., Tomarchio, O., Vita, L.: A framework for the management of dynamic SLAs in composite service scenarios. In: Workshop on (NFPSLA-SOC2007) in conjunction with ICSOC2007, Vienna (Austria) (September 2007)
34. Di Modica, G., Regalbuto, V., Tomarchio, O., Vita, L.: Enabling re-negotiations of SLA by extending the WS-Agreement specification. In: IEEE Int. Conf. on Service Computing (SCC 2007), Salt Lake City, Utah (USA) (July 2007)
35. Djemame, K., Gourlay, I., Padgett, J., Voss, K., Kao, O.: In: Buyya, R., Bubendorfer, K. (eds.) Market-Oriented Grid Computing. Wiley, Chichester (to appear, 2008)
36. GridEcon, Grid Economics Business Models, http://www.gridecon.eu

# Monitoring and Reputation Mechanisms for Service Level Agreements*

Omer Rana[1], Martijn Warnier[2], Thomas B. Quillinan[2],
and Frances Brazier[2]

[1]School of Computer Science/Welsh eScience Centre, Cardiff University, UK
o.f.rana@cs.cardiff.ac.uk
[2]Department of Computer Science, VU University, Amsterdam, The Netherlands
warnier@cs.vu.nl, tb.quillinan@few.vu.nl,
frances@cs.vu.nl

**Abstract.** A Service Level Agreement (SLA) is an electronic contract between a service user and a provider, and specifies the service to be provided, Quality of Service (QoS) properties that must be maintained by a provider during service provision (generally defined as a set of Service Level Objectives (SLOs)), and a set of penalty clauses specifying what happens when service providers fail to deliver the QoS agreed. Although significant work exists on how SLOs may be specified and monitored, not much work has focused on actually identifying how SLOs may be impacted by the choice of specific penalty clauses. A trusted mediator may be used to resolve conflicts between the parties involved. The objectives of this work are to: (i) identify classes of penalty clauses that can be associated with an SLA; (ii) define how to specify penalties in an extension of WS-Agreement; and (iii) specify to what extent penalty clauses can be enforced based on monitoring of an SLA.

**Keywords:** Quality of Service, WS-Agreement, Service Level Agreement Monitoring.

## 1  Introduction

A Service Level Agreement (SLA) is an agreement between a client and a provider in the context of a particular service provision. SLAs may be between two parties, for instance, a single client and a single provider, or between multiple parties, for example, a single client and multiple providers. SLAs specify Quality of Service (QoS) properties that must be maintained by a provider during service provision – generally defined as a set of Service Level Objectives (SLOs). Often an SLA is only relevant when a client *directly* invokes a service (rather than through an intermediary – such as a broker). Such direct interaction also implies that the SLOs need to be measurable, and must be monitored during the provision of the service.

---

* This paper extends preliminary work reported at the USAGE OF SERVICE LEVEL AGREEMENTS IN GRIDS WORKSHOP [17].

J. Altmann, D. Neumann, and T. Fahringer (Eds.): GECON 2008, LNCS 5206, pp. 125–139, 2008.
© Springer-Verlag Berlin Heidelberg 2008

From an economics perspective, one may associate a cost with an SLA – which is the amount of money a client needs to pay the provider if the agreement has been adhered to (i.e. the requested quality has been met). The cost needs to be agreed between a client and a provider – and may be based on a posted price (provider publishes), or negotiated through single/multi-round auctions (English, Dutch, Double, etc). How this price is set has been considered elsewhere [3], although the mechanism for doing this can also be determined through equilibrium pricing (based on supply-demand) or through auctions (based on client need). An SLA must also contain a set of penalty clauses specifying the implications of failing to deliver the pre-agreed quality. This penalty may also be defined as a cost – implying that the total revenue made by a provider would be the difference between the cost paid by the client and the discount (penalty) imposed on the provider. This type of analysis assumes that failure to meet an SLA is a non-binary decision – i.e. an SLA may be "partially" violated, and that some mechanism is in place to determine how this can be measured.

Although significant work exists on how SLOs may be specified and monitored [14], not much work has focused on actually identifying how SLOs may be impacted by the choice of specific penalty clauses. A trusted mediator may be necessary to resolve conflicts between involved parties. The outcome of conflict resolution depends on the situation: penalties, impact on potential future agreements between the parties and the mandatory re-running of the agreed service, are examples. While it may seem reasonable to penalize SLA non-compliance, there are a number of concerns when issuing such penalties. For example, determining whether the service provider is the only party that should be penalized, or determining the type of penalty that is applied to each party. Enforcement in the various legal systems of different countries can be tackled through stipulating a 'choice of law clause', that is a clause indicating expressly which countries' laws will be applied in case a conflict between the provider and the client would occur. Automating conflict resolution process could provide substantial benefits. Broadly speaking there are two main approaches for contractual penalties in SLAs: reputation based mechanisms [13,18] and monetary fines. It is useful to note that often obligations within an SLA are primarily centered on the provider towards the client. An SLA is therefore an agreement between the provider to offer particular QoS to a client for some monetary return. We do not consider scenarios where there is also an obligation on the client towards the provider. An example of such a scenario could be where a provider requires the client to make input data available by a certain time frame to ensure that a particular execution time target is met. If the client is unable to meet the deadline for making such data available, the penalty incurred by the provider would no longer apply.

The use of reputation-based mechanisms to promote data integrity in distributed architectures has been explored by [9]. Knowing the reputation of a client can provide insight into what access may be granted to that client by a provider. Maintaining a measure of each client's reputation allows clients to make decisions regarding the best service provider for a specific task. In this case, reputation is a numerical value quantifying compliance to one or more SLAs. This value represents the previous behaviour of the provider in the system, and can be used by other clients to determine whether or not to interact with that provider. The higher this value, the more likelihood that the provider will act correctly in the future. Applying a numerical weight to users allows a more informed decision to be made when negotiating SLAs in the future. As users (clients and providers) interact with one another in the system, their reputation changes to reflect how they perform. For example, if a service provider consistently provides poor service (that is, violating its SLAs), its reputation will decline.

While reputation based mechanisms work relatively well in community based environments – where each participant monitors and judges other participants – in commercial environments reputation based mechanisms are rarely used. This can partly be attributed to the unbalanced nature of the relationship between clients and service providers. Monetary fines give a higher degree of expected QoS for service providers and (especially) clients. Monetary fines are also used in this paper. Such approaches are not new, other works in this area, such as [7,8], provide only a partial solution to this problem. For example, they do not have a mechanism for conflict resolution.

The remainder of the paper is organized as follows: Section 2 starts with some background on Service Level Agreements, violations for SLAs and WS-Agreement. Section 4 discusses issues associated with penalties and Section 3 explains how monitoring of SLAs can be performed. The paper ends with a discussion.

## 2  Background

This section provides background on SLAs, violations for SLAs and WS-Agreement.

### 2.1  SLAs

An SLA can go through various stages once it has been specified. Assuming that the SLA is initiated by a client application, these stages include: discovering providers; defining the SLA; agreeing on the terms of the SLA; monitoring SLA violations; terminating an SLA; enforcing penalties for SLA violation.

The discovery of suitable providers phase involves choosing possible partners to interact with. This involves searching a known registry (or a distributed number of registries) for providers that match some profile – generally using predefined meta-data. The outcome of this stage is a single (or list of) providers that offer the capability a client needs.

Once a service provider(s) has been identified, the next stage involves defining the SLA between the client and the provider. The SLA may be between a single client and provider, or it may be between one client and multiple providers. In the subsequent analysis, we assume a two party SLA (i.e., one involving a single client and a single provider).

The definition of the SLA impacts the other stages in the SLA lifecycle – as the mechanisms used to identify particular Service Level Objectives (SLOs) will determine how violations will be identified in the future. Hence, an SLA may be defined using (name, value) pairs – where name refers to a particular SLO and value represents the requested quality/service level. An alternative is to use constraints that are more loosely defined – such as the use of (name, relationship, value) triples. In this context, provided the relationship between the name and value holds, the provider would have fulfilled the SLA requirements. Examples of relationships include less_than, greater_than or a user defined relationship function that needs to be executed by both the client and the provider.

Other schemes have included the use of server-side functions—an SLA being defined as a function $f(x_1, x_2, ..., x_n)$, where each $(x_i)$ corresponds to a metric that is managed by the service provider. Using this approach, a client requests some capability from the service provider that is a function of what is available at the service provider. For instance, if the service provider has 512MB of available memory at a particular point in time, the client requests 50% of this. In this context, $f(x)$ is evaluated based on currently available capacity at the service provider [20]. An SLA must also be valid within some time period – a parameter that also needs to be agreed upon by the client and the provider.

Agreeing on SLA terms takes place once a description scheme has been identified. The next step is to identify the particular SLOs and their associated constraints. There needs to be some shared agreement on term semantics between the client and the provider. There is, however, no way to guarantee this, unless both the client and provider use a common namespace (or term ontology), and therefore rely on the semantic definitions provided within this namespace.

Agreeing on SLO terms may be a multi-shot process between the two parties. This process can therefore be expressed through a 'negotiation' protocol (a process requiring a provider to make an 'offer' to the client, and the client then making a 'counter offer'). The intention is to either reach convergence/agreement on SLOs – generally within some time bounds (or number of messages) – or indicate that the SLOs cannot be met. Also associated with an SLA must be the 'penalty' terms that specifies the compensation for the client if the SLA was not observed by the service provider. These penalty terms may also be negotiated between a client and a provider – or a fixed set of penalty terms may be used.

Monitoring SLA violation begins once an SLA has been defined. A copy of the SLA must be maintained by both the client and the provider. It is necessary to distinguish between an 'agreement date' (agreeing of an SLA) and an 'effective date' (subsequently providing a service based on the SLOs that have been agreed). A request to invoke a service based on the SLOs, for instance, may be undertaken at a time much later than when the SLOs were agreed.

As outlined in Section 3, during provision it is necessary to determine whether the terms agreed in the SLA have been complied with during provision. In this context, the monitoring infrastructure is used to identify the difference between the agreed upon SLO and the value that was actually delivered during service provisioning – which is 'trusted' by both the client and the provider. It is also necessary to define what constitutes a 'violation'. Depending on the importance of the violated SLO and/or the consequences of the violation, the provider in breach may avoid dispatch or obtain a diminished monetary sanction from the client. In some instances, a client may be willing to avoid penalizing the provider if some of the SLOs are not fully adhered to compared to others.

An SLA may be terminated in three situations: (i) when the service provision identified in the SLA has completed; (ii) when the time period over which the SLA has been agreed upon has expired (could be due to a successful or unsuccessful service provision); (iii) when the provider is no-longer available after an SLA has been agreed (for instance, the provider has crashed or is off-line). In all three cases, it is necessary for the SLA to be removed from both the client and the provider. Where an SLA was actually used to provision a service, it is necessary to determine whether any violations had occurred during provisioning. As indicated above, penalty clauses are also part of the SLA, and need to be agreed between the client and the provider.

These stages demonstrate one cycle through the creation, use and deletion of an SLA.

## 2.2   Violations

One of the main issues that the provider and the consumer will have to agree during the SLA negotiation is the penalty scheme or the sanctionary policy in use. Both the service provider and the client are free to decide what kinds of sanctions they will associate with the various types of SLA breaches, in accordance with the weight of the quality attribute that was not fulfilled. According to the Principles of European Contract Law [4], the term 'unfulfillment' is to be interpreted as comprising: (1) defective performance (parameter monitored at lower level) (2) late performance (service provided at the appropriate level but with unjustified delays) (3) no performance (service not provided at all). Although a mapping from these concepts to technical SLOs is not possible, we derive the following broad categories motivated by the above concepts:

- 'All-or-nothing' provisioning: provisioning of a service meets all the SLOs – i.e., all of the SLO constraints must be satisfied for a successful delivery of a service;
- 'Partial' provisioning: provisioning of a service meets some of the SLOs – i.e., some of the SLO constraints must be satisfied for a successful delivery of a service;
- 'Weighted Partial' provisioning: provision of a service meets SLOs that have a weighting greater than a threshold (identified by the client). This type of analysis is based on the assumptions that SLOs that have a weighting/priority greater than a threshold are considered to be more significant for a client than others.

Monitoring can be used to detect whether an SLA has been violated. Typically such violations result in a complete failure – making SLA violations an 'all-or-nothing' process. In such an event a completely new SLA needs to be negotiated, possibly with another service provider, which requires additional effort on both the client and the service provider. Based on this all-or-nothing approach, it is necessary for the provider to satisfy all of the SLOs. This equates to a conjunction of SLO terms. An SLA may contain several SLOs, where some SLOs (e.g. at least two CPUs) may be more important than others (e.g. more than 100 MB hard disk space). During the SLA negotiation phase, the importance of the different SLOs may be established. Clients (and service providers) can then react differently according to the importance of the violated SLO. In the WS-Agreement specification [1], the importance of particular terms is captured through the use of a 'Business Value'.

Weighted metrics can also be used to ensure a flexible and fair sanctionary policy in case an SLA violation occurs. Thus, instead of terminating the SLA altogether it might be possible to re-negotiate, i.e., with the same service provider, the part of the SLA that is violated. Again, the more important the violated SLO, the more difficult (if not impossible) it will be to re-negotiate (part of) the SLA. The WS-Agreement specification supports the definition of a "Business Value" for particular SLOs (see section 4.2). These values reflect the relative importance placed on a particular term by a user, and may be used to support such a sanctioning policy.

## 2.3  WS-Agreement

WS-Agreement [1] provides a specification for defining SLAs, and comes from the Open Grid Forum (OGF). WS-Agreement is an XML document standard, that is, interactions between clients and providers are performed using an XML standardized format. There are two types of XML documents in WS-Agreement: *templates* and *agreements*. One basic element is that agreements need to be confirmed by both parties. Including penalties in a WS-Agreement, for example, cannot be one-sided. The WS-Agreements needs to be confirmed by the client. The existing WS-agreement specification, however, will need to be extended to include this step. Mobach *et. al.* [15] proposed this extension in the context of the WS-Agreement specification.

Figure 1 shows the extended interactions between a service provider (SP) and a consumer (C) described by [15]. The advertisement phase uses WS-Agreement template documents; the request and offer phase use WS-Agreement agreement documents. Templates describe the different services that the provider supports. When a negotiation takes place, the service provider sends these templates to the consumer. The consumer then makes an offer to the provider and, if acceptable, the agreement is created by the provider based on the offer. In figure 1 the initial template is generate by the provider, in accordance with the WS-Agreement specification.

Templates and agreements both use the concept of negotiation *terms*. Terms define the service description and guarantees about the service. Guarantees are made relating to the service, such as the quality of service and/or the resource availability during service provision.

1. SP → C  : Advertisement
2. C  → SP : Request
3. SP → C  : Offer
4. C  → SP : Acceptance/Rejection

**Fig. 1.** Negotiation using WS-Agreement

Agreements have a name defined by the provider and a context that contains meta-information about the agreement. This meta-information can include identifiers for the service provider and the agreement initiator; the name of the template that the agreement is based on; references to other agreements, and the duration of the agreement [15], as agreements have a fixed period when they are valid. Functional and non-functional requirements are specified in the *Terms* section. This is divided into the *Service Description Terms* (SDT) and *Guarantee Terms* (GT). A SDT holds the functional requirements for the delivery of services, and may refer to one or more components of functionality within one or more services. There may be any number of SDTs in a single agreement. GTs hold a list of services that the guarantee applies to, with the conditions that this guarantee applies, and any potential pre-conditions that must exist. Templates have a similar structure to agreements, with an additional *Creation Constraints* section. These constraints could include, for example, the maximum or minimum value for a service request. Creation constraints are an indication of the valid values for agreement requests. Creating an agreement that complies with these values does not guarantee the acceptance of the agreement by the service provider.

## 3  Monitoring

Monitoring plays an important role in determining whether an SLA has been violated, and thereby determine which penalty clause should be invoked as a consequence. From a legal point of view, monitoring appears as a pre-requisite for contract enforcement. In the present context, what needs to be put into effect are the consequences of breaching the agreed SLOs. In addition, service clients base their trust in service providers largely on the provided monitoring infrastructure. Traditionally, in the context of SLAs three monitoring modules can be distinguished [19,14]: A trusted third party (TTP); a trusted module at the service provider; a model on the client site.

The trusted third party provides an independent module that can monitor (and log) all communication between clients and service providers. Both the service provider and client commit for each SLA. It is important for the TTP to be trusted by *both* the client and the provider. It is therefore necessary to establish the choice of a TTP before monitoring commences. It is also possible for the TTP to be defined in the SLA, requiring both the client and the provider to confirm this. After successfully completing the SLA both parties receive a signed ticket from the TTP that can be used for non-repudiation and reputation building of the service provider. Notice that a TTP cannot monitor the internal state of either client or service provider.

Using a trusted module at the service provider's site as an outside observer is functionally the same as using a TTP with the extension that trusted modules *may* also have the ability to observe the internal state of a service provider. A module can monitor communication between client and service provider and can similarly provide (signed) tickets after successful completion of an SLA. Thus, the main difference between these approaches is that the trusted module is integrated into the service provider. This has as advantage that the internal state of the service provider can also be observed. The use of such a module provides weaker verification of SLOs than the use of an external TTP. There are two restrictions to using this approach:

– The service provider may not reveal it's internal state to the monitor module, and only allow a set of pre-defined variables to be monitored.
– The service provider may willingly or by error report incorrect information to the monitor module.

However, the service provider has the incentive to correctly report data to the monitoring module, to avoid incurring penalties for any SLO violations that it has not caused. Consider the following example: if the SLO is "execution time", a network latency may result in an extra delay in the client's experience of this SLO. However, as the provider is not responsible for managing the network, the additional latency should not lead to a penalty for the provider. A co-located monitor at the provider would enable the provider to confirm that it was not at fault.

The third option – using a model on the client side – requires a client to determine if SLOs diverge from the predicted behaviour, i.e., predicted by the model, of the service provider. Notice that in this case it is often impossible to prove to third parties that the service provider is misbehaving. The applicability of this method is limited, it can be used as a means for individual clients to establish their trust level in specific service providers, provided that a model that predicts the service provider's behaviour can be successfully constructed.

Monitoring facilitates a direct and automatic SLA enforcement at run-time and without undue delay (that is, once a SLA violation is recorded, the agreed sanction can be automatically triggered), it also facilitates a more traditional enforcement. In either case, if the provider or the client contests the automatic sanction imposed, it can use monitoring data to argue its case. It is therefore vital to monitor all those metrics that have legal relevance and to give the parties the possibility to retrieve such data in a format that is admissible as evidence.

In situations that require a high level of assurance, the monitoring modules discussed above (especially the first two) can be combined. In the next section a monitoring architecture is provided that combines a trusted third party together with the use of a trusted module at the client side.

### 3.1   A Monitoring Architecture

In most cases, monitoring is only useful at the service provider. It is here that the resources specified in the SLAs (number of CPUs, disk space etc.) are actually hosted/provided. The alternative, to use a TTP, requires a trusted module [16] to be installed on the service provider's side, which can be accessed by the TTP for monitoring purposes.

The module should be able to monitor all resources that the service provider offers, for example, number of CPU's, type of CPU or upload limit of the network connection etc. For obvious reasons it is important that only a TTP that is explicitly trusted by the service provider can actually view this kind of information. This can be ensured by supplying a TTP with a secret key that can be used for communicating with the module.

During SLA negotiation, it is required that: (1) the client can chose which TTP to use; and (2) to ensure that there is enough choice for a client, each service provider must provide reference to multiple external TTPs. Of course, this does not guarantee that the client will always find a TTP that it wants to use. Clients remain free to chose another service provider altogether, or ask a service provider to use an additional TTP the client does trust. Once a client and a service provider have created an SLA, the service itself is monitored by a TTP, using the trusted module at the service provider. Messages are exchanged between the Client (C), Service Provider (SP) and Trusted Third Party (TTP). Figure 2 gives a representation of the message exchange in the system.

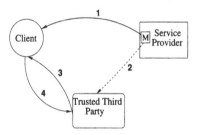

**Fig. 2.** Message Exchange

The messages are detailed in Figure 3. $SLA_1 \ldots SLA_n$ are SLAs, $T_P$ is the timestamp of principal $P$. $K_{TTP-M}$ is a shared key between the TTP and the trusted module M. The other messages are encrypted by the public key of the principal sending the message $(K_P)$.

Whenever a service provider provisions a service: (1) it is monitored by the module and sent to the TTP $(2_1 \ldots 2_n)$. The TTP stores a log of the information monitored for each SLA. Messages 3 and 4 are optional. They are only used if the client suspects a violation and requests the log ($log_k$ in Figure 3) from the TTP – containing monitored data up to that point in time. The protocol ensures that only trusted parties gain access to the monitoring information.

The monitoring "interval" is also an important consideration when verifying violations of an agreement. Associated with this is the requirement for understanding whether *spot* or *aggregate* data should be considered for an SLO – or whether both need to be considered. For instance, short peaks in load (a common occurrence in many systems) may not always signify *real* exceptional situations –

$$
\begin{array}{llll}
1. & \text{SP} & \rightarrow \text{C} & : \text{Service} \\
2_1. & \text{SP} & \rightarrow \text{TTP} & : \{\text{SLA}_1, \log_1, T_{M_1}\} K_{\text{TTP-M}} \\
& \multicolumn{3}{c}{\cdots\cdots} \\
2_n. & \text{SP} & \rightarrow \text{TTP} & : \{\text{SLA}_n, \log_n, T_{M_n}\} K_{\text{TTP-M}} \\
[\; 3. & \text{C} & \rightarrow \text{TTP} & : \{\text{SLA}_k, \log_k, T_{C_k}\} K_{\text{TTP}} \quad ] \\
[\; 4. & \text{TTP} & \rightarrow \text{C} & : \{\text{SLA}_k, \log_k, T_{\text{TTP}_k}\} K_C \quad ]
\end{array}
$$

**Fig. 3.** Where $k, n \in \mathbb{N}$ and $k < n$. Message exchange between the Service Provide (SP) with trusted module (M), Client (C) and Trusted Third Party (TTP).

and any adaptive behaviour at the service provider to these short peaks could lead to unstable behaviour [10]. For long running services (i.e. where the execution time of a service exceeds significantly the monitoring interval), it is therefore necessary to also determine what constitutes as a violation of an SLO.

## 4    Types of Penalties

Using penalty clauses in SLAs leads to two questions that need to be answered: what types of penalty clauses can be used; and how (if at all) can these be included in SLAs. The focus is on penalty clauses for service providers, since the 'burden of proof' and the interest in demonstrating that the agreed SLOs have been violated lies on the main beneficiary of the service, that is in the service client. One point should be kept in mind when designing 'penalty schemes'. Behind the imposition of any contractual sanctions lies the idea that faulty behavior of a provider should be deterred. As such, it is always possible for the service provider to contest its liability in the unwanted result (SLA breach) and claim that a 'force majeure' situation occurred. Although the situation is impossible to be dealt with through automatic enforcement, monitoring the message exchanges among the provider and the client can give an indication whether the SLA violation was the consequence of a 'misconduct' from the provider (either intentional or negligent). The parties are advised to stipulate either in the SLA or a written document (such as a Collaboration Agreement) how they choose to deal with the situation where the provider's faulty behavior cannot be documented, and a 'force majeure' situation did occur. Assuming only monetary fines are used, a penalty clause in an SLA may consist of the following:

- a decrease in the agreed payment for using the service, i.e., a direct financial sanction;
- a reduction in price along with additional compensation for subsequent interaction;

During the negotiation phase, client and provider can agree on a direct financial sanction. Usually, the amount to be paid depends on the value of the loss suffered by the client through the violation (which should cover entirely) and if agreed, a fixed sum of money that has to be paid as 'fine' for the unwanted behavior. Due to the difficulties in proving and documenting the financial value of the loss, during the SLA formation phase the parties may choose an 'agreed payment for non performance' that is a fixed sum of money that will have to be paid upon nonperformance, regardless of the fact that no financial loss was suffered by the client. During the formation phase client and provider can agree on a direct financial sanction (referred to as a 'fine' below) if an SLA is not (completely) fulfilled. The service provider can deposit the fine at a TTP, that acts as a mediator, before the service provision commences. On successful completion of the service provision (based on the SLA) the TTP returns the deposit to the service provider, otherwise the client receives the deposit as compensation for the SLA violation. Similarly, a fine can be combined with a discount for future services with the same provider. Note that this requires a trusted monitor, as a client can never prove by itself that an SLA was (partially) violated. However, for this to work properly –and especially automatically– a micro payment [11] system may be required – such as Paypal.

## 4.1  Negotiating Penalties

In section 2.3, the messages that are exchanged within the system are described. Supporting penalties within this framework can be easily achieved using the *terms* section of WS-Agreement templates and agreements. This allows the use of the extended negotiation protocol defined by [15].

While negotiations can be managed in the existing framework, this does not adequately reflect the complexity of penalty negotiation. For example, if a mutually trusted third party cannot be agreed upon by both consumer and provider, there is little point in proceeding with the SLA negotiation. Similarly, if an SLA cannot be agreed upon, there is no need to negotiate the penalty clause. Therefore it is instead proposed to separate these three stages into distinct negotiation steps. Each of these steps follows the same steps as shown in Figure 1: Advertisement; Request; Offer, and Acceptance/Rejection. These steps can be considered negotiations for three separate services.

For example, negotiations to select a TTP proceeds as follows: In the *Creation Constraint* section of the WS-Agreement template, the TTPs trusted by the service provider are listed. When the consumer receives this template, it creates an agreement offer specifying the TTP that they have selected. The offer is then processed by the provider. If it is acceptable, the provider produces the agreement document. This is passed to the consumer for acceptance/rejection. Negotiations for the SLAs and penalties are handled using the same process.

One concern with this approach is the verification that a SLA template refers to the TTP agreement previously negotiated and, similarly, the penalty template to the SLA and TTP agreements. This is achieved by the use of the references to the prior agreements within the *context* section of proceeding templates and agreements. Each penalty agreement then contains references to the TTP and SLA agreements. This ensures that a verifiable link is maintained throughout the service negotiation and provision.

Another approach to the multi-step process could be to specify the template and agreement documents as a single document, with separate services for each of the three stages. This would eliminate the need for three separate negotiations. However, this approach would make the templates more complicated.

## 4.2 Mapping to WS-Agreement

The WS-Agreement specification provides an XML schema [1] to represent the top-level structure of an agreement. This includes concepts such as an agreement identifier, guarantee terms in an agreement etc. Key to the discussion here is the use of a 'Business Value' (BV) and 'Preference' specification made available in WS-Agreement. A BV allows a provider to assess the importance of a given SLO to a client. Similarly, a provider may indicate to a client the confidence that a provider has in meeting a particular SLO. Based on the specification, a BV may be expressed using a **penalty** or **reward** type. The penalty is used to indicate the likely compensation that will be required of a provider if the SLO with which the penalty is associated is not met. A BV list is specified as:

```
<wsag:BusinessValueList>
<wsag:Importance>xs:integer</wsag:Importance>
<wsag:Penalty> </wsag:Penalty>
<wsag:Reward> </wsag:Reward>
<wsag:Preference> </wsag:Preference>
<wsag:CustomBusinessValue>
  </wsag:CustomBusinessValue>
</wsag:BusinessValueList>
```

Notice that a BV list consists of both a penalty and a reward – to enable a provider to assess the risk/benefit of violating a particular SLO. **Preference** is used in the BV list to provide a more detailed sub-division of how a business value is impacted by different alternative actions of a provider. Essentially, **Preference** allows a service provider to consider different possible alternatives for reaching the same overall SLO requirement. For instance, if a client requests access to a particular number of CPUs, it is possible to fulfill this requirement based on CPUs from one or more providers. **Preference** allows the provider to chose between the available options to improve its own revenue or meet other constraints that it has (provided this is not prohibited by the service provision agreement or other agreements between the parties involved).

A **Penalty** in WS-Agreement may be associated with one or more SLOs, and occurs when these SLO(s) are violated. According to the WS-Agreement specification, assessment of a violation needs to be monitored over an **AssessmentInterval** – which is defined either as a time interval or some integer count. Essentially, this means that a penalty can only be imposed if an SLO is violated within a particular time window, or if a certain number of service requests/accesses fail. **ValueUnit** identify the type of penalty – in this case a monetary value – that must be incurred by the service provider if the penalty occurs. In the current WS-Agreement specification, the concept of a **ValueExpr** is vague – as being either an integer, float or a 'user defined expression'. This implies that a user and provider may determine a dynamic formula that dictates the penalty amount depending on the particular context in which the WS-Agreement is being used. In WS-Agreement the ability to also specify a Reward, in addition to a penalty provides an incentive mechanism for a provider to meet the SLO.

```
<wsag:Penalty>
   <wsag:AssesmentInterval>
       <wsag:TimeInterval>xs:duration
        </wsag:TimeInterval> |
       <wsag:Count>xs:positiveInteger</wsag:Count>
   </wsag:AssesmentInterval>
   <wsag:ValueUnit>xs:string</wsag:ValueUnit>
   <wsag:ValueExpr>xs:any</wsag:ValueExpr>
</wsag:Penalty>

<wsag:AssesmentInterval>
    <wsag:Count>4</wsag:Count>
</wsag:AssesmentInterval>
<wsag:ValueUnit>US Dollar</wsag:ValueUnit>
<wsag:ValueExpr>500</wsag:ValueExpr>
```

Although useful, the description of penalty and rewards in WS-Agreement is still very simple and cannot account for the varying types of penalties that can be defined in other types of agreements [17]. For instance, it is not currently possible to define variations in penalties at different quality levels. In addition, the extent to which terms and conditions specified in WS-Agreements are legally binding is currently subject of research [5].

## 5   Discussion and Conclusion

The use of penalties in SLAs has obvious benefits for both clients and service providers. Monetary sanctions (and optionally reputation based mechanisms) can be used as, pre-agreed, penalties. It has been shown how the WS-Agreement specification can be used to specify penalties and rewards, in the context of a particular resource sharing scenario. Both of these approaches require the participation of a Trusted Third Party. The types of monitoring infrastructure that can be used to validate SLOs during service provisioning are identified. As monetary sanctions are the *de facto* standard in industry for penalty clauses, these are preferred over reputation based solutions, though the latter can be used if so required.

A particular focus has been discussion of the types of violations that can occur in SLOs during provisioning. Three types of violations that may lead to penalties – an 'all or nothing', 'a partial' or a 'weighted partial' violation of a contract, have been identified. It is useful to note that flagging a violation incurs a cost for the client (as well as the provider). It is therefore in the interest of the client to continue with service provision, even if some of the SLOs are not being observed fully – a trade off discussed in this paper. A key contribution of this work is a model that demonstrates how a client may provide weighting to certain SLOs over others, the legal basis on which this model is based and subsequently how this approach can be used alongside WS-Agreement.

**Acknowledgments.** This research has arisen as a result of collaboration between the EU "SORMA" project (IST 034286), support provided by the NLnet Foundation (http://www.nlnet.nl) and in part by the NWO TOKEN programme. Part of this work was also supported by the EU FP7-IST-215890 "ALIVE" project. We are grateful to Dana Cojocarasu (Research Center for Computers and Law, University of Oslo, Norway) for contribution and discussion regarding European law for electronic contracts.

# References

1. Andrieux, A., Czajkowski, K., Dan, A., Keahey, K., Ludwig, H., Nakata, T., Pruyne, J., Rofrano, J., Tuecke, S., Xu, M.: Web Services Agreement Specification (WS-Agreement). In: GRAAP Working Group at the Open Grid Forum (September 2006)
2. ARAD Automatic Real-time Decision-making (2002), http://www.haifa.il.ibm.com/projects/software/arad/papers/ARAD-May-2002.pdf
3. Becker, M., Borrisov, N., Deora, V., Rana, O.F., Neumann, D.: "Using k-Pricing for Penalty Calculation in Grid Market". In: Proceedings of IEEE HICSS 2008 Conference, Hawaii (January 2008)
4. Bonell, M.J.: The UNIDROIT Principles of International Commercial Contracts and the Principles of European Contract Law: Similar Rules for the Same Purposes (1996)
5. Boonk, M., Brazier, F., de Groot, D., van Stekelenburg, M., Oskamp, A., Warnier, M.: Conditions for Access and Use of Legal Document Retrieval Web Services. In: Prooceedings of the Eleventh International Conference on Artificial Intelligence and Law (ICAIL 2007). ACM Press, New York (2007)
6. Chen, Y., Iyer, S., Liu, X., Milojicic, D., Sahai, A.: SLA Decomposition: Translating Service Level Objectives to System Level Thresholds. In: HPL-2007-17 (2007)
7. Clayton, B.C., Quillinan, T.B., Foley, S.N.: Automating security configuration for the grid. Journal of Scientific Programming 13(2), 113–125 (2005)
8. Foley, S.N.: Using trust management to support transferable hash-based micropayments. In: Proceedings of the 7th International Financial Cryptography Conference, Gosier, Guadeloupe, FWI (January 2003)
9. Gilbert, A., Abraham, A., Paprzycki, M.: A System for Ensuring Data Integrity in Grid Environments. In: Proceedings of the International Conference on Information Technology: Coding and Computing (ITCC 2004), Las Vegas, Nevada, USA, April 5–7 2004, pp. 435–439 (2004)
10. Gmach, D., Krompass, S., Scholz, A., Wimmer, M., Kemper, A.: "Adaptive Quality of Service Management for Enterprise Services". ACM Transactions on the Web 2(1) (February 2008)
11. Hauser, R., Steiner, M., Waidner, M.: Micro-payments Based on IKP. IBM TJ Watson Research Center (1996)
12. Joita, L., Rana, O.F., Chacin, P., Chao, I., Freitag, F., Navarro, L., Ardaiz, O.: Application Deployment on Catallactic Grid Middleware. IEEE DS-Online 7(12) (2006)

13. Kamvar, S.D., Schlosser, M.T., Garcia-Molina, H.: The Eigentrust Algorithm for Reputation Management in P2P Networks. In: Proc. of the 12th Int. World Wide Web Conference, Budapest, Hungary, May 20-24 2003. ACM Press, New York (2003)

14. Keller, A., Ludwig, H.: The WSLA Framework: Specifying and Monitoring Service Level Agreements for Web Services. Journal of Network and Systems Management 11(1), 57–81 (2003)

15. Mobach, D.G.A., Overeinder, B.J., Brazier, F.M.T.: A WS-Agreement Based Resource Negotiation Framework for Mobile Agents. Scalable Computing: Practice and Experience 7(1), 23–36 (2006)

16. Pearson, S., Balacheff, B.: Trusted computing platforms: TCPA Technology in Context. Prentice Hall PTR, Englewood Cliffs (2002)

17. Rana, O., Warnier, M., Quillinan, T.B., Brazier, F.M.T., Cojocarasu, D.: Managing Violations in Service Level Agreements. In: the Proceedings of the Usage of Service Level Agreements in Grids Workshop. IEEE/ACM Grid Conference, Austin, Texas, September 2007. ACM Press, New York (2007)

18. Sabater, J., Sierra, C.: Social regret, a reputation model based on social relations. SIGecom Exch. 3(1), 44–56 (2002)

19. Sahai, A., Machiraju, V., Sayal, M., van Moorsel, A., Casati, F.: Automated SLA Monitoring for Web Services. In: Feridun, M., Kropf, P.G., Babin, G. (eds.) DSOM 2002. LNCS, vol. 2506. Springer, Heidelberg (2002)

20. Yarmolenko, R.S.V.: An Evaluation of Heuristics for SLA Based Parallel Job Scheduling. In: 3rd High Performance Grid Computing Workshop (in conjunction with IPDPS 2006), Rhodes, Greece (2006)

21. Wustenhoff, E.: Service Level Agreement in the Data Center. In: Sun Microsystems Professional Series (April 2002)

# BEinGRID: Development of Business Models for the Grid Industry

Katarina Stanoevska-Slabeva[1], Davide Maria Parrilli[2], and George Thanos[3]

[1] Mcm Institute of the University of St. Gallen, Blumenbergplatz 9, CH-9000 St. Gallen
[2] Interdisciplinary Centre for Law and ICT, K.U.Leuven – ICRI -IBBT,
Sint-Michielsstraat 6, B-3000 Leuven
[3] Network Economics and Services Group, Athens University of Business and Economics,
76 Patission Str. Athens, Greece
Katarina.Stanoevska@unisg.ch,
davide.parrilli@law.kuleuven.be, gthanos@aueb.gr

**Abstract.** Driven by the increasing demand, grid technology is entering the business market in form of utility computing, grid middleware and grid-enabled application. However, the business market is interested in complete grid solutions. This means that for a successful take up of grid technology on the business market the establishment of grid value networks is required. This again can only be achieved by implementation of sound business models for each player providing part of a grid solution. This paper discusses the business models of providers of grid-enabled application.

**Keywords:** Grid Business Models, Business Grids, Grid enabled Application.

## 1 Introduction

Newest market research studies report a growing awareness for the potential of grid technology by industry and increased interest for utility computing and grid solutions for business application. This trend has been in particular enforced by well established Internet companies as for example WebEx, Amazon, AOL, who offer their services in form of utility computing [1]. Another player driving utility computing are telecommunication companies. For example T-Systems in Germany is rolling out in cooperation with SAP an SAP on-demand service. A growing interest for grid computing can also be observed with Independent Software Vendors (ISV) [1]. This is mostly evident in vertical markets with strong grid interest or for applications that are suitable for grid (for example data mining). First steps towards grid friendly licensing models can be observed at some vendors even though there is the fear of cannibalizing existing business models for packaged application.

Driven by the growing interest and demand on the market, grid technology is entering a new level of maturity and is offered on the business market in three forms [3]: 1) as open source or packaged grid middleware; 2) as utility computing, that is as hardware and software infrastructure provided according to the Software as a Service (SaaS) paradigm, and 3) in the form of grid enabled application. However, business

J. Altmann, D. Neumann, and T. Fahringer (Eds.): GECON 2008, LNCS 5206, pp. 140–151, 2008.
© Springer-Verlag Berlin Heidelberg 2008

customers are interested in complete grid solutions. This means that for a successful take up of grid technology on the business market the establishment of grid value networks [15] is required that will be able to provide complete solutions and a critical mass of offerings on all levels of the value network. This again can only be achieved by implementation of sound business models for each player providing part of a grid solution. In particular, new business models are required from two perspectives: the grid utility computing providers and providers of grid enabled applications. The business models of these two players of the grid market are closely related to each other. On the one hand grid enabled application are an important driver for the demand of grid resources offered as a service. On the other hand grid infrastructure offered as a service is a necessary prerequisite for grid enabled application. Thus, a critical mass of grid enabled application is needed for the next step of the grid market evolution. However, while there is a growing body of literature on business models or specific components of them for the utility computing market [3], [15], there is less consideration of business models from the perspective of providers of grid enabled applications. This paper provides a contribution in this context and discusses the main aspects of business models of ISV evolving their products from pre-packaged applications towards grid-enabled application.

The content of the paper is structured as follows: Section 2 provides an overview of definitions and the research approach. Section 3 provides an overview of business models of pilot applications developed as part of the BEinGRID project. Section 4 provides a generic concept for components of business models for grid enabled application. Section 5 concludes the paper with a summary and outlook.

## 2 Research Approach

The research presented in this paper followed the following approach:

1. First the most important terms (grid-enabled applications and business models) involved in the research were defined and an analysis approach was chosen.
2. Then business models of technology and application providers were analyzed based on case studies of grid pilots from the project BEinGRID. BEinGRID (www.beingrid. com) is an Integrated Project (IP) that is funded by the European commission under FP6. One of the main objectives of the project is to evaluate the applicability of grid technology in business through grid business experiments. In the heart of the project there are 18 business experiments that are piloting grid technology in various key industrial sectors. In this paper the business models of pilots focusing on grid-enabling application were analyzed.
3. Finally the findings of the analysis were aggregated to a generic business model for providers of grid-enabled application.

The resulting business model can be applied by providers of grid-enabled applications as a checklist for developing successful business models.

## 2.1 Grid-Enabled Application Definition and State-of-the-Art

The term grid-enabled application is used in this research paper to denote software application that have been offered on the market as pre-packaged software and that are being extended in a way that they can run in a distributed manner in a grid environment. To grid-enable a pre-packaged software product therefore means that a previously pre-packaged centralized application is enabled to run either on a distributed grid infrastructure or to be offered as an online service based on the Software as a Service paradigm (SaaS) (see also [4]).

In principle, the idea of providing applications in a SaaS manner is not a new concept. A similar concept for software delivery was introduced by [5] in 1998 under the term "Application Service Provisioning (ASP)". ASP evolved from IT outsourcing and is based on the idea that a web-enabled application can be provided online through IP-based telecom infrastructure [6] by a central application service provider [9]. At the beginning the ASP model was a typical one-to-many delivery model, which means that the application is operated in a centralized manner by the application service provider and is offered in the same manner to many customers. The main advantages of the ASP business model for customers are: cost savings and no need for developing and maintaining an own infrastructure and skills.

Even though at the first glance the business models of ISVs offering grid-enabled application and of ASPs seem similar, there is a significant difference. The core competence of the ISP is the development of the application itself and not its distribution. On the contrary, the core competence of the ASP is the online provision of applications that are mostly developed by other ISV. Despite of the difference regarding their business models, key learning's from the experiences with the ASP business model can be applied during development of business model for grid-enabled application. Even though ASP was foreseen to be successful, it did not take up on the market and its adoption has been very slow [7]. The main reasons for the failure have been: the inability of early ASPs to produce customized services, the centralized approach for computing, which requires the sending of input and output data and the general lack of trust in the ASP paradigm [6], [7], [9].

At present, the business models of grid-enabled application and ASPs are converging. The convergence of web services and grid computing technologies is expected to solve current ASP delivery problems [6], [9]. The ASP business model is evolving from one-to many to a many-to-many model, where several service offerings are bundled and can flexibly be applied by the user [7].

## 2.2 Definition of Business Models and the Business Model Analysis Framework

There is a considerable body of literature related to business models. The definitions of business models range from very broad ones as for example the definitions proposed by [10] or [11] to very specific ones (see for example [12] or [13]). [10] for instance defines in a most basic sense business models *"as the method of doing business by which a company can sustain itself - that is, generate revenue"*. While such definitions try to delimit the scope of the meaning of the concept business models, they do not provide insights into components of business models in such a way that it can be used for assessing the activities of a company in more detail. A more concrete definition is the definition of Timmers [14]. According to Timmers, a business model is "*... an architecture for the products, services and information flows, including a description of various business actors and their roles, a description of the potential benefits for the various business actor, and a description of the sources of revenues.*" [14]. The definition provided by Timmers was used as starting point for the development of the so called MCM business model analysis framework. The MCM-Business Model Framework provides a generic overview of components of business models based on Timmers that need to be considered during a business model analysis or design. It has been used successfully for structuring the analysis of business models of different type of digital products [15]. The components of business models denoted by Timmer's definition were extracted and enhanced with further aspects affecting business models (for example "Social Environment"). Further components of business models have been synthesized based on an in-depth analysis of the body of literature about business models [10], [11], [12], [14]. The resulting MCM-Business model analysis framework is presented in figure 1:

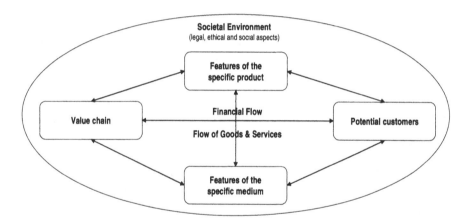

**Fig. 1.** MCM-Business Model Analysis Framework

The elements of the framework that need to be considered during analysis or design of a business model are explained in more detail below:

The **social environment** component of a business model reflects all outside influences on the business models, such as the legal and ethical aspects as well as the competitive situation in the market. It refers to the social and regulatory context in which a business model is developed and implemented.

The component **features of the medium** expresses the possibilities for transaction and interaction over a specific medium. For example different applications are possible based on grid or a centralized infrastructure.

The component **potential customer** covers all aspects of target groups and customers as well as the expected added value provided by the product or service subject of business model development. The different business models certainly address different target groups, and do address different needs of the customer. Choosing the right target customers and designing the product according to their needs are key success factors.

The component **value chain** reflects the involved players necessary for the production and delivery of the offered product or service and their interrelationships. A typical grid value network consists for example of a content owner, content aggregator, content provider, portal owner and of course the user (for a complete generic grid value chain see [15]).

The component specific **features of the product** express the exact design and the way the service is experienced by its customers. It also explains what the specific benefits are, and how the customer might be contributing.

The component **financial flow** explains the earning logic of the business model and makes it clear which elements of the value chain contribute from a financial perspective.

The component **flow of goods and services** identifies all the processes within the company and the value chain necessary for the creation of the product or service.

The components of a business model are interrelated among each other. For example the target group of customers and their needs is influencing the product design. The product design requires a certain value network and also needs to consider legal and ethical requirements. The agreed upon relationships among the involved players of the value network are the foundation for the financial flow and the flow of goods and services. The different components need to be smoothly integrated into a business model that offers the opportunity for sustainable business and profit for all involved players.

## 3   Case Studies of Grid-Enabled Applications Business Models in the BEinGRID Project

The business model analysis framework was applied for an in-depth analysis of the intended business models of ISVs participating in experiments of the BEinGRID project and developing a grid-enabled version of their product. Out of the 18 pilots six are aiming towards business models for grid-enabled application:

- Business experiment (BE) BE16 has developed a grid-enabled extension of an existing application for ship design and simulation so that it can be offered in cooperation with an infrastructure provider in a SaaS manner.
- BE18 grid-enabled an existing application for processing of seismic data and plans to offer the service over the Internet in particular to small and medium size enterprises.
- BE07 grid enabled an existing application for generation of global aerosol maps using information coming from different satellite sensors.
- BE03 has grid-enabled an application for 3D rendering and animation.
- BE12 and BE17 are grid-enabling existing application for supply chain management.

The in-depth analysis of the business models of the above BEs has revealed several advantages and obstacles that need to be considered during the design of the business model. The main advantages are: From the perspective of the ISV the enhancement of existing application clearly provides a valuable extension of the existing application portfolio. In addition to that most of the above BE can achieve a broad competitive advantage, as most of them can leverage a first-mover advantage. In particular for the small ISV (BE12 and BE17) to grid-enable their application provides a clear competitive advantage and also a needed precondition to stay on the market. To offer the grid-enabled version of the application also results in an image gain for the companies. For most of the companies the grid-enabled version of the application is applied to approach a new category of target customers - small and medium size companies.

The main obstacles that need to be overcome are the following: At present all providers of grid-enabled application need to establish sound business relationships with utility computing providers, in order to be able to offer a complete solution. This means that the establishment of the whole value chain is necessary. Another major obstacle is the fear of cannibalization effects for the existing centralized application. As the described application show, the applications that are being grid-enabled are applications that are needed by the customer companies occasionally. This means that by talking advantage of a SaaS offering customers might try to optimize the usage and pay less than for the licenses for the centralized application.

The above findings have been considered for the development of generic business models.

## 4 Development of Generic Business Models for Grid-Enabled Application

Based on the findings from the case studies general guidelines for the development of the business models were developed. Considering the above obstacles the main emphasize in this paper was on the following components of the business model: design of the product, design of the value chain and legal aspects. The findings are explained in more detail in the sections below.

### 4.1 Design of the Product

The design of the grid-enabled application needs to address in particular the cannibalization problem. A careful strategy is necessary, in order to keep existing customers that do not want or cannot use the grid-enabled application and to meet the requirements of new customers (see also [16]). An important question is: Are different versions for different customer segments and licensing strategies possible and in which form? The problem can be illustrated on the following example:

**Example:** One ISV offers an application with a given set of functions to the market. A grid-enabled version of the application is developed. However not all of the existing customers have a grid infrastructure and cannot apply the new functionality. They would like to stay with the centralized version of the application. A small number of the customers has already an own grid infrastructure and would like to take advantage of the new functionality. This are also the customers that have a high volume of transaction and would also be willing to pay more for the enhanced application. The ISV gets furthermore requests by smaller companies for an occasional use of the application based on the SaaS paradigm. After a certain time a cooperation with a grid infrastructure provider is agreed upon and the application is also available on a SaaS basis.

The question now is how the different categories of the products should be defined and which licensing and pricing strategy should be defined? A low price for the SaaS application might result in the effect that existing customers of the centralized application - in particular those that use the application occasionally - switch to the SaaS application and save the licensing costs for the central version of the application. In order to avoid such effects, a carefully designed packaging of the functionality of the different versions of the application together with the licensing and pricing strategy is necessary. The different options regarding versioning of the products are discussed below.

*Versioning option 1:* Offering the application in form of commercial software with and without grid enhancement and without SaaS option (c.f. 2):

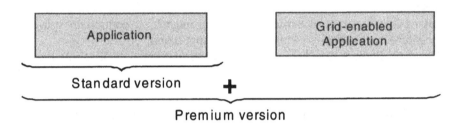

**Fig. 2.** Standard and premium version of a grid-enabled application sold as commercial product

The versioning example given in figure 2, enables to keep the existing customer base and the established licensing models for the existing application and provide a premium version for customers that have an own grid infrastructure. This versioning option provides the basis for diversified licensing strategies, to target customers with different needs as well as for additional revenues as the grid-enabled application can be offered with adding additional licenses for it.

*Versioning option 2:* In case the application is available as centralized application, grid-enabled application and SaaS, several different options for versioning and packaging are possible. One possible example is given in figure 3 below.

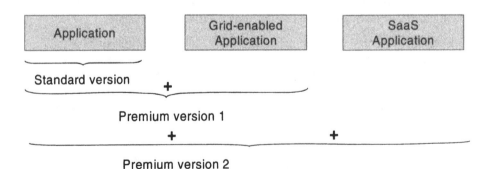

**Fig. 3.** Example of versioning strategies based on three product categories

As in versioning option 1 there might be a standard and a premium version if it is bought by the customer together with the grid enhancement. The question here is how the SaaS version can be included in a way that it might be suitable to also attract new customers, for example SMEs that cannot afford the premium 1 version, but at the same time not provoke a massive switch from the lucrative licenses for the central application by existing customers. One option is that customers opting for the premium version 1 can add also access to the SaaS version and pay additionally per use, if in addition to their own grid they use also the SaaS. A similar option might be available for the customers with the standard version of the application. The question is how to differentiate the SaaS version. One possibility would be to limit the functionality of the SaaS version or to differentiate a "light" version with respect to the output options or other functionality that are available. For example, an SME that wants the functionality as SaaS might get the output data only in a basic format, while premium customers get it in a pre-defined format. Similar differentiation of the quality of the service can be made also based on other features of the product and service (see also [16]). How exactly the existing functionality can be packaged in the three product categories and which versions are possible depends on the modularity of the software, the existing customer base and the potential for segmentation of the customers depending on their willingness to pay and their specific needs. A good knowledge of the usage patterns of customers as well as their willingness to pay is therefore a clear advantage in determining the right versioning and pricing strategy.

## 4.2 Price Strategies of the BEinGRID Business Experiments

The pricing strategy involves two components: the pricing model and the definition of the prices. The major general pricing models for grid enabled applications are Pay-per-use pricing models. Thereby the price might include infrastructure and access to the application or be provided separately for grid computing infrastructure and for the application. In this pricing model the price per usage includes also the license. A benchmark for pricing in this area might be the published price of SUN of 1$/hour computing resources or the pricing strategy of Amazon: 0.20$ per GB stored or to hire a complete virtual PC for $0.10 per hour.

The definition of concrete pricing depends on the specific product. In case where different versions of the product are involved, pricing should not affect the product strategies. For example: BE01 found during the competitive analysis that a license for computational fluid dynamics software can vary from £10'000 to £15'000 per single CPU license and go up to £100'000 for 64 CPUs. In case such an application is grid enabled, the question is what the right price might be. Several aspects need to be considered: The typical usage patterns of an average customer, the market prices for similar services and the costs of the provider. For example let's assume that in case of SaaS the same number of CPUs is used. How can the license per CPU be expressed per hour of usage? If a price that is too low is chosen than the ISV does not have interest to provide the application as SaaS as he will lose revenue. In case data about the usage patterns of customers are available the actual average usage per year could be transformed in a price. For example, the provider knows that an average customer is using the application 50% of a person's yearly working time per user. This would mean that the application is used by a typical user for 840 working hours (assuming a yearly total of working hours of 1680). Thus, in order to get the same revenue from the user based on a SaaS version of the application a price of £12 per hour for the application would be required (assuming a basic license of £10'000 for a single CPU). In a similar way based on average usage patterns and total number of users a potential price might be calculated.

### 4.3 Design of the Value Chain

As mentioned above, in order to bring a grid-enabled application on the market, it is necessary to assure the availability of a grid infrastructure by bundling it with offerings of utility computing. The ISV can achieve this in two ways - either by developing know-how and deploying an infrastructure by himself or by partnering with a provider of utility computing. Option two has obviously more advantages. However, it cannot be implemented in all cases. For example BE12 and BE17 are very small companies and have small customers and are located in Italy so that a low volume of total transaction can be expected. Such a low volume of expected transaction is not relevant for the utility computing provider, so that a partnership could not be established. The ISVs need to provide a grid infrastructure themselves.

In case a partnership can be established, an important design option is the question who of the two players will orchestrate the offering and have the customer ownership [see also 17]. The application provider should strive towards partnerships where he can keep the customer ownership.

### 4.4 Legal Aspects

The analysis of the project's cases shows that in addition to business aspects, major legal issues have to be addressed as well [18].

It is pivotal to address, as starting point, what is, in legal terms, the agreement that encompasses the provision of SaaS. This, of course, depends on the applicable national legal framework but, in general it means to set up an ASP contract. The provision of SaaS implies that there is no physical item delivered to the end user and that, unlike in the contract between a customer and a software house for the writing of a specific computer programme, the software provider keeps the ownership of the application. In case of due diligence, for instance, this element has to be taken into account, as the software can be considered as an asset (and not a liability) of the targeted company only if this undertaking has the ownership of the software.

The service provider will limit as much as possible the rights of the client, which could use the SaaS only during its ordinary course of business, thus he will be liable for breach of contract if, in practice, he sublicenses the supplier's applications. It is pivotal to say that the parties, by virtue of their contractual freedom, would have the possibility to adapt the above clause to their exigencies, and they could opt, for instance, for a transferable or exclusive license. As regards the code provided to the client, in a typical SaaS scenario the object of the contract will concern the object code and not the source code.

The contractual freedom of the parties plays a fundamental role also as regards confidentiality obligations. This issue is particularly complex and the experience gained shows that the relative clause should address at least the following issues:

- Extension of the confidentiality obligations of the supplier and the client as regards, basically and respectively, the data of the customer and the executable code of the software;
- Duties of the parties;
- Contractual and Court remedies, taking into account that the latter are heavily influenced by the applicable national legal framework;
- Exceptions to the rule, i.e. situations in which there are no confidentiality obligations.

We have developed the following template that encompasses the abovementioned elements and that is suitable to be adopted in case of SaaS in a Grid environment: "Customer shall not sell, transfer, publish, disclose, display or otherwise make available any portion of the executable code of the Application to others. Client agrees to secure and protect the Application and the Service in a manner consistent with the maintenance of Supplier's rights therein and to take appropriate action by instruction or agreement with its users to satisfy its obligations hereunder. Client shall use its best efforts to assist Supplier in identifying and preventing any unauthorised access, use, copying or disclosure of the Application or the Service, or any component thereof, or any of the algorithms or logic contained therein. Without limitation of the foregoing, Client shall advise Supplier immediately in the event Client learns or has reason to believe that any person to whom Client has given access to the Service has violated or intends to violate the confidentiality of the executable code of the Application or the proprietary rights of Supplier, and Client will, at Client's expense, cooperate with Supplier in seeking injunctive or other equitable relief in the name of Client and Supplier against any such person.

Client agrees to maintain the confidentiality of the executable code of the Application using at least as great a degree of care as Client uses to maintain the confidentiality of Client's own confidential information (and in no event less than a reasonable degree of care). Client acknowledges that the disclosure of any aspect of the executable code of the Application, including the documentation or any other confidential information referred to herein, or any information which ought to remain confidential, will immediately give rise to continuing irreparable injury to Supplier inadequately compensable in damages at law, and Supplier is entitled to seek and obtain immediate injunctive relief against the breach or threatened breach of any of the foregoing confidentiality undertakings, in addition to any other legal remedies which may be available. In addition, Supplier may immediately terminate this Agreement, including all license rights granted herein, in the event Client breaches any of its confidentiality obligations regarding the Application or the Service.

Furthermore, Supplier agrees that it shall not disclose to any third party or use any information proprietary to Client including information concerning the Client and the users, trade secrets, methods, processes or procedures or any other confidential information of the other party which it learns during the course of its performance of the Service, except for purposes related to Supplier's rendering of the Service to Client under this Agreement or as required by law, regulation, or order of a court or regulatory agency or other authority having jurisdiction thereover. In addition, Client may immediately terminate this Agreement in the event Supplier breaches any of its confidentiality obligations set forth herein. Notwithstanding the foregoing, the confidentiality obligations set forth in this Article will not apply to any information which the recipient party can establish to have: (i) become publicly available without breach of this Agreement; (ii) been independently developed by the recipient party outside the scope of this Agreement and without reference to the confidential information received under this Agreement; or (iii) been rightfully obtained by the recipient party from third parties which are not obligated to protect its confidentiality."

It is furthermore interesting to consider and define the liability of the software supplier. In this field, in fact, the ASP agreement (and the other related contracts entered into by the concerned parties) has the duty to shift and balance the risk and the corresponding liabilities between the software provider, the Grid provider and the end user. In principle, in fact, the former should avoid to be liable (if it does not own and manage the Grid infrastructure) for technical failures of the Grid itself. In other words, he should be liable only for deficiencies that are under his control. At the same time, provided that the majority of disputes concern the gap between the concrete performance of the service and the level expected by the client, the use of Grid technology should reduce this risk and, at the same time, as explained above, could extend the burden of liability of the software provider. For this reasons, the software provider should limit his responsibility to the functionality of the application and the service to the exclusion of the client's requirements. As regards the remedies at disposal of the customer, then, they usually include Service Credits (and, with this regard, it is possible to wonder whether the customer, in a Grid environment, will require higher credits in case of failure to meet the promised level of services), damages (regulated by the applicable national laws) up to, in the most serious cases, termination of the contract.

## 5 Summary and Conclusion

The goal of the paper was the discussion and development of a generic business model framework for providers of grid enabled application. Based on five in-depth case studies first major advantages and obstacles for developing business models for grid-enabled application were identified. Then following the business model analysis framework, general guidelines for the design of the product, the value chain and the legal issues related to provisioning applications in a SaaS manner have been developed. The core consideration has been the avoidance of cannibalization efforts with centralized applications.

**Acknowledgement.** The research presented in this paper was part of the project BE-inGRID (034702), which is supported by the European Commission in the sixth Framework Program.

## References

1. The 451 Group, Grid computing preview, Section 7.2 in Review/Preview 2006-2007, The 451 Group, pp. 83–89 (2007)
2. MomentumSI, Implementing a Successful Service-Oriented Architecture (SOA) Pilot Program, Actional Corporation (2005)

 3. Forge, S., Blackmann, C.: Commercial Exploitation of Grid Technologies and Services - Drivers and barriers, Business Models and Impacts of Using Free and Open Source Licensing Schemas. Final Report of the European Study No. 30-CE-065970 /00-56
 4. Snjeepan, V., Matsunaga, A., Zhu, L., Lam, H., Fortes, J.A.B.: A Service-Oriented, Scalable Approach to Grid-Enabling of Legacy Scientific Application. In: Proceedings of the IEEE International Conference on Web Services (ICWS 2005) (2005)
 5. Heart, T., Pliskin, N.: Is e-commerce of IT application services alive and well? Journal of Information Technology Theory and Application 3(4), 33–41
 6. Xu, H., Seltsikas, P.: Evolving the ASP Business Model: Web Service Provision in the Grid Era. In: Proceedings of the Second Intzernational Conference on Peer-to-Peer Computing (2002)
 7. Desai, B., Currie, W.: Application Service Providers: A Model in Evolution. In: Proceedings of the ICES 2003, Pittsburgg (2003)
 8. Stanoevska-Slabeva, K., Talamanca, C.F., Thanos, G., Zsigri, C.: Development of a Generic Value Chain for the Grid Industry. In: Veit, D.J., Altmann, J. (eds.) GECON 2007. LNCS, vol. 4685, pp. 44–57. Springer, Heidelberg (2007)
 9. Mittilä, T., Lehtinen, K.: Customizing the Application Service Provider Offering. (2005), http://www.ebrc.fi/kuvat/1066.pdf
10. Rappa, M.: Managing the Digital Enterprise.(2005), http://digitalenterprise.org/index.html
11. Afuah, A., Tucci, C.L.: Internet Business Models and Strategies. McGraw-Hill, New York (2001)
12. Osterwalder, A.: The Business Model Ontology. Ph.D. Thesis at the HEC Lausanne (2004)
13. Staehli, P.: Geschätsmodelle in der digitalen Ökonomie. Josef Eul Verlag, Lohmar, Köln (2002)
14. Timmers, P.: Business Models for Electronic Markets. International Journal on Electronic Markets and Business Media 8(2), 3–8 (1998)
15. Hoegg, R., Stanoevska-Slabeva, K.: Towards Guidelines for the Design of Mobile Services. In: Proceedings of the ECIS 2005 conference (June 2005)
16. Shapiro, C., Varian, H.R.: Information Rules - A Strategic Guide to the Networked Economy. Harvard Business School Press, Boston Massechusets (1999)
17. Tapscott, D., Ticoll, D., Lowy, A.: Digital Capital - Harnessing the Power of Business Webs. Harvard Business School Press (2000)
18. Raysman, R., Brown, P.: Computer Law: Drafting and Negotiating Forms and Agreements. Law Journal Press, New York (2003)

# Edutain@Grid: A Business Grid Infrastructure for Real-Time On-Line Interactive Applications

Justin Ferris[1], Mike Surridge[1], E. Rowland Watkins[1], Thomas Fahringer[2], Radu Prodan[2], Frank Glinka[3], Sergei Gorlatch[3], Christoph Anthes[4], Alexis Arragon[5], Chris Rawlings[6], and Arton Lipaj[7]

[1] IT Innovation Centre, University of Southampton, UK
{jf,ms,erw}@it-innovation.soton.ac.uk
[2] Institute for Computer Science, University of Innsbruck, Austria
{tf,radu}@dps.uibk.ac.at
[3] Institute of Computer Science, University of Münster, Germany
{glinkaf,gorlatch}@math-uni.muenster.de
[4] Institute of Graphics and Parallel Processing, University of Linz, Austria
canthes@gup.jku.at
[5] Darkworks S.A., France
a.arragon@darkworks.com
[6] BMT Cordah Ltd., UK
chris.rawlings@bmtcordah.com
[7] Amis d.o.o., Slovenia
arton.lipaj@amis.net

**Abstract.** Grid infrastructures are maturing to a point where they are attracting the interest of businesses in many application domains. While many large-scale on-line gaming platforms exist, they fail to take into consideration the potential business to business relationships when it comes to dynamic on-line game hosting. This work presents an initial implementation of the edutain@grid architecture to support business value chains identified for on-line gaming and e-learning application hosting. An analysis of business actors and value chains is presented briefly before a detailed description of the edutain@grid implementation. We also consider first results concerning how best to construct appropriate value chains using bipartite and bi-directional Service Level Agreements.

**Keywords:** Business models, Service Level Agreements, Grid, Trust, Security, Value chains.

## 1 Introduction

Emerging Grid technologies [1] have the capability to substantially enhance on-line games and similar applications. Just as the World Wide Web enables people to share content over standard, open protocols, the Grid enables people and organizations to share applications, data and computing power over the Internet in order to collaborate, tackle large problems and lower the cost of computing.

The edutain@grid project [2, 3] aims to develop a novel, sophisticated and service-oriented Grid infrastructure which provides a generic, scalable, reliable and secure

J. Altmann, D. Neumann, and T. Fahringer (Eds.): GECON 2008, LNCS 5206, pp. 152–162, 2008.

service infrastructure for a new class of 'killer' applications of the Grid: Real-Time, On-Line, Interactive Applications (ROIA). ROIA include a broad sub-class of commercially important applications based on virtual environments, including massively multiplayer on-line gaming applications (MMOG), and interactive training and other e-learning applications. The edutain@grid project is aiming to provide an infrastructure to make such applications easier to develop, more economic to deploy and operate, and more capable of meeting the Quality of Experience expected and demanded by end-users.

Grid middleware systems such as Globus [4], gLite [5] and UNICORE [6] enable high-throughput applications by sharing computational resources for processing and data storage to meet the needs of individual and institutional users. ROIA such as multiplayer on-line computer games are soft real-time systems with very high user interactivity between users. Large numbers of users may participate in a single ROIA instance, and are typically able to join or leave at any time. Thus ROIA typically have extremely dynamic distributed workloads, making it difficult to host them efficiently. Initiatives such as Butterfly Grid [7] and Bigworld [8] have applied Grid computing to on-line gaming with some success, enabling 'scalable' or 'elastic' terms for hosting such games. However, these 'scalable' hosting services are only as scalable as the hoster supporting them, and typically don't guarantee how far this will be. The edutain@grid project addresses these challenges using 'business Grid' developments such as GRIA [9, 10], but extending them to support scalable, multi-hosted ROIA applications, allowing scaling beyond the limits of any one hoster.

The rest of this paper is organised as follows. In section 2 we present an overview of the business models and actors supported by edutain@grid, and highlight some of the business issues addressed by the project. Section 3 describes the implementation of the edutain@grid framework in more detail, and discusses the initial results and their implications. Section 4 provides a summary of the overall work on edutain@grid value chains to date, and discusses the direction of future work.

## 2   Business Actors and Value Chains in Edutain@Grid

To ensure business models for Grid-based ROIA will be economically viable, it is necessary to analyse the value chains (i.e. business actors and value flows) in which ROIA (specifically on-line games and e-learning applications) will be operated and used. The goal of edutain@grid is to support value chains corresponding to commercially viable scenarios, preferably in such a way that the same ROIA application software need not become locked into one particular business scenario.

The business actors (roles) supported by the edutain@grid infrastructure must be generic enough to meet the needs of both application sectors, and flexible enough to allow business models to be tuned to best fit the market conditions which may vary even within each sector. The analysis revealed an extensive hierarchy of business roles, as shown in Figure 1. These include 'providers' who host services through which the ROIA is delivered to users, 'consumers' who access the ROIA by connecting to these services, and 'facilitators' who play other business roles in the creation of ROIA application software, its distribution to providers and consumers, and the operation of ROIA instances.

Three important sub-classes of ROIA providers were also identified that have to be supported by the project:

- Hoster: is an organisation that hosts core, usually computationally intensive processes that support a ROIA virtual environment including interactions of users with this environment and with each other.
- Co-hosters: are other hosters participating in the same ROIA instance – where more than one hoster is involved in a single ROIA instance, each hoster will regard the others as 'co-hosters' of the ROIA instance.
- Coordinator: is an organisation that makes a ROIA instance accessible to its consumers, and coordinates one or more hosters to deliver the required ROIA virtual interactive environment.

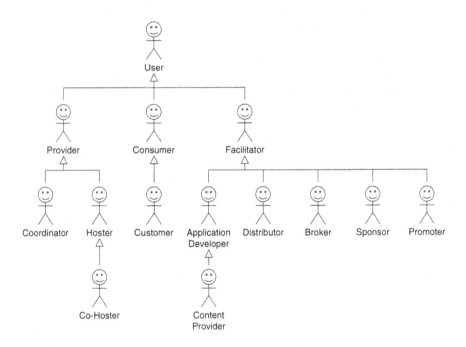

**Fig. 1.** Business Actors in edutain@grid

Today, on-line game hosters exist, but there are no 'co-hosters' or 'coordinators' because there is only one hoster per game instance. The edutain@grid infrastructure breaks away from this limitation, enabling new business models to manage risks of ROIA hosting and delivery, and provide genuine scalability for ROIA provision.

To achieve these benefits, edutain@grid allows actors to combine in a wide range of 'value chains' through which ROIA software and services are produced, deployed and delivered to the end users. The links in these value chains are defined through business agreements: either Service Level Agreements (SLA) or in some cases software licence agreements. These agreements are always bipartite, following the pattern used in the NextGRID project [11, 12] and used with GRIA in the SIMDAT project

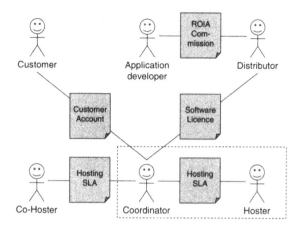

**Fig. 2.** A typical edutain@grid value chain

[13]. Each agreement is between two parties only, and defines the service provided by one party and the obligations on both sides as to how this service will be delivered and used. The details of each agreement depends partly on the topology of the value chain through which funds flow from the customers (who ultimately pay for everything) to the other actors. The edutain@grid project allows for a wide range of topologies, of which a typical example is shown in Figure 2.

In this example, the ROIA application is commissioned by a distributor from an application developer. The distributor licenses coordinators to use and sub-licence the software. The coordinators pay hosters for the capacity to run ROIA services, and sell access to these services to customers, sub-licensing the required software to each as part of the deal with each. In the example shown, the coordinator also hosts some of the resources needed to run the ROIA, shown by the dotted line indicating that the coordinator and one of the hosters are actually the same organisation. Other co-hosters can be brought in to handle peaks in demand, or if the ROIA becomes so popular that one organisation cannot host it all any more.

## 3  Implementation and First Results

### 3.1  Scope and Architecture

The edutain@grid project has produced a first implementation of the framework to support these business actors and value chains. The prototype focuses on the core edutain@grid actors: the coordinator, the hoster (or co-hoster), and the customer. The framework is based on a Service Oriented Architecture, organised in four layers, as shown in Figure 3. The real-time layer provides a framework [14] for ROIA developers to create scalable applications capable of running across multiple sites. The management layer deals with the allocation and management of resources (and ROIA processes) by hosters. The business layer handles setting up and enforcing the terms

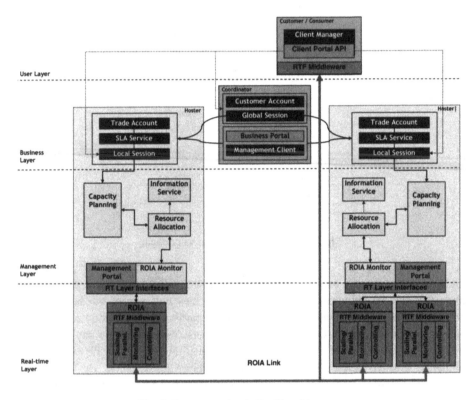

**Fig. 3.** Prototype edutain@grid architecture

of SLA (including hosting SLA and customer agreements). The business layer is also responsible for enforcing security policies, including the need to sign up to an appropriate SLA before accessing ROIA functionality. There is also a client layer which provides programming interfaces to use services from the other three layers.

### 3.2 Business Layer

The business layer is responsible for establishing and managing value chains through which ROIA services can be provided and consumed. This is based on management services from the GRIA 5.2 middleware [10] with some custom ROIA services developed by the edutain@grid project.

In this first edutain@grid prototype implementation, facilitator roles have not been considered, and it has been assumed that customers will only pay for themselves to access ROIA. This makes it possible to use a lightweight user authentication mechanism based on their ability to pay, because no consumers should have access unless they are paying. This authentication procedure is handled by the Customer Account service which is run by the coordinator. It acts as a WS-Trust token validator service allowing other business layer services to validate credentials supplied to them (which may include self-signed tokens), by comparing them with the credentials used by that Customer when setting up their account. The Trade Account service has a similar role at the hoster site, authenticating coordinators based on their ability to pay for services, and allowing them to establish SLA with the SLA service if this is the case. The Global and Local Session services are then used to mediate access to ROIA instances. The Global Session service provides the entry point for customers and coordinates the involvement of hosters, including setting up security policies at each hoster to restrict access to genuine Customers. The Local Session is used to manage and provide access to ROIA processes contributed by its hoster. The Global Session service is also responsible for propagating information between the co-hosters where more than one hoster (and Local Session) is involved in a single ROIA instance.

Finally, note that even with a fixed set of possible actors, a large variety of value chains and business models is possible, and different arrangements may be needed to suit different applications or even the same application in different market conditions. The edutain@grid infrastructure therefore has to be flexible and able to support a range of topologies and business models, even if each application uses only a single agreement topology and business model.

### 3.3 Management Layer

The management layer is responsible for predicting the QoS that can be delivered by available resources, monitoring and managing these resources to enforce QoS terms, and translating monitoring events back into business layer terminology so it can be provided to business layer services that handle SLA negotiation and cross-hoster coordination. This allows the negotiation and enforcement of QoS parameters such as minimum latency, maximum user load, or minimum update rate in highly scalable ROIA that may involve thousands or someday millions of online user connections to hosts running in multiple hoster sites.

Even when using the Grid to provision resources, delivering the required real-time QoS needs remains a challenging task since MMOGs (especially FPS games) are highly dynamic and users may become concentrated in each other's proximity within a short period of time causing excessive server load and loss of QoS. To address this, it is possible to change parallelisation strategies using rezoning or zone replication and instancing, but this is an expensive operation that may take many seconds. The management layer must therefore anticipate potential QoS breaches so corrective action can be initiated before the breach has occurred.

To solve these challenges, the management layer will use a resource provisioning strategy based on four distinct services:

- A monitoring service that interacts with the real-time layer and logs ROIA execution information such as the number, position and interactions of entities within the virtualised environment.
- A load prediction service that estimates the future distribution of entities based on historical monitoring information, allowing server congestion hot-spots to be predicted ahead of time.
- A capacity management service that estimates ROIA session load based on entity distribution and interaction data, and plans the use of resources to fulfil QoS requirements while maintaining hoster-specified metrics (e.g. utilisation).
- A resource allocation service that provisions the required CPU, memory and network resources required by each ROIA session.

In future the management layer will also provide support for competitive as well as collaborative interactions within virtual organisations of users, including prevention of cheating within the ROIA.

## 3.4  Real-Time Layer

The real-time layer provides special services to facilitate the development of ROIA that are executable in a grid environment under soft real-time constraints. These services are combined in the C++ based *Real-Time-Framework* (RTF) [15] and include, among others, a grid-aware communication infrastructure, integrated business- and management-related monitoring and controlling facilities, as well as a sophisticated API for the systematic, high-level development of scalable, distributed ROIA. The RTF integrated services will enable a ROIA developer to create ROIA using high level abstractions to deal with the distributed and dynamic nature of the application, as well as the resource management and deployment aspects of the underlying infrastructure (Grid).

The real-time layer provides the communication infrastructure to connect the resources used by ROIA processes, based on a communication protocol which is highly optimized with respect to the low-latency and low-overhead requirements of typical ROIA. This infrastructure is Grid-aware, so communication endpoints can be transparently redirected to a new resource, if, e.g., parts of the ROIA are relocated to a new Grid resource for load-balancing reasons. Security aspects are taken care of by supporting authentication and encryption of real-time communications. This is mandatory as customers that connect through the Internet will be charged for using a ROIA, and must be traceable via their real- or pseudo-identities as established in the business layer.

The RTF offers an API which provides the development of ROIA using different parallelization approaches: zoning, instancing and replication for the scalable application distribution across multiple resources. The API provides an abstraction from the underlying resources: RTF (re)distributes the zones, instances and replication instances [16, 17] transparently for the customers during runtime, as advised by the business- or management layer. This redistribution functionality is realized in a non-disruptive way which ensures that a ROIA, which often requires the adherence of client-server response times of 100ms and less, is not interrupted during the redistribution process.

The high level of abstraction allows RTF to monitor certain real-time application metrics transparently for the developer. These metrics include, e.g., the number of transferred in-application events, the number of in-application objects, minimal response time for client requests, the number of connections, communication latency and bandwidth usage, and the virtual environment update frequency. These and other metrics are provided to the business and management layer through a dedicated interface at the border of the real-time layer, which decouples the real-time sensitive ROIA within the real-time layer from the slower, upper management and business services.

The integrated monitoring functionality of RTF provides the management and business layer with the information that is required for appropriate management and business decisions. The monitoring also is required to observe the QoS-related terms of an SLA and to check if a certain term was breached. The available distribution steering functionality of RTF provides decision opportunities to the hoster and coordinator: they can reallocate their resources as required and most commercially viable for them [18]. Dynamic resource allocation is very important as the customer demand for the access to a ROIA typically varies depending on daytime or holidays. This advantage also applies if the user base is not changing and allows a hoster to tremendously improve his resource utilization.

## 3.5 Initial Results

At this stage, the edutain@grid framework is being used to perform experiments to determine what types of hosting SLA terms will be most useful in on-line gaming applications, what kinds of resource management strategies can deliver QoS promised in these SLA, and what kinds of dynamic adaptation facilities from the real-time layer will allow applications to exploit the provisioned resources efficiently. The challenge is to define terms that coordinators find useful in managing the risks of over/under-estimating user demand, yet allow hosters to retain control over their own resources and implement efficient (ideally autonomic) management processes to control QoS by exploiting application-level adaptive behaviour. Since edutain@grid allows co-hosting scenarios, this involves going well beyond existing (even Grid-based) on-line game hosting environments, as it is necessary to take account of possible interactions and dependencies on co-hosters.

The GRIA middleware supports SLA terms based on arbitrary (capacity-oriented) quality of service metrics, but up to now these have been used only with traditional data storage and processing applications using traditional metrics such as disk storage and CPU time. Only a few users have defined metrics on less traditional items such as the number of floating software licences that can be used for commercial codes [19]. In edutain@grid, it is already clear that these types of metrics are not very useful (or valuable) in a multi-hosted ROIA scenario, as they make it too difficult for the coordinator to work out whether their customer expectations can be met, and force the hoster to cede too many internal resource management decisions to the coordinator. Experiments are now focusing on quite higher level QoS terms for hosting SLA which allow the coordinator to manage ROIA Quality of Experience, but without needing to control (or even understand) the resources and management strategy at each hoster.

This also means the project has to investigate how a hoster could manage resources to deliver the required ROIA performance, when the limits on usage are defined in terms of customer and application behaviour. It is clear that if very few customers are connected to the ROIA, the hoster can use the freedom inherent in such an SLA to reduce the resources allocated – e.g. by running multiple ROIA processes on a single host. However, a ROIA may be come computationally expensive for purely internal reasons – e.g. through an increased level of interaction. If the SLA doesn't specify a limit on resources, the hoster would be obliged to allocate more resources to maintain the specified ROIA performance. It is also possible for the ROIA itself to induce SLA breaches. For example, if two co-hosters agree to support up to (say) 600 user connections each, they will be able to support (say) 1000 customers between them. But if the ROIA causes all the customers' virtual avatars to gather in one zone of the ROIA virtual environment, then they may all end up having to connect to just one hoster, breaching the limits agreed by the coordinator with that hoster. The hoster would be within their rights to start refusing connections, destroying the Quality of Experience for many of the customers.

The edutain@grid project is now starting to investigate how advanced (including predictive) resource management mechanisms and application adaptation can be used to address both types of problems. For example, is it possible to predict a gathering of on-line gamers in one location, and inform the coordinator in time for hosting SLAs to be re-negotiated, possibly involving additional hosters? If the management layer can predict problems well enough to do this, how would the QoS terms need to change to reflect a predictive exception handling facility for an otherwise constrained level of service?

## 4  Summary and Future Work

The edutain@grid project aims to create a new class of 'killer application' for the Grid: Real-time On-line Interactive Applications (ROIA). This class spans several commercially important applications, including on-line gaming and simulator-based training, both of which are being used in validation case studies in the project.

The project has investigated the need for value chains between business actors to deliver ROIA in a Grid-based environment. The analysis has led to a separation between the roles of the hoster (who hosts ROIA services) and the coordinator (who sells ROIA access to customers and guarantees their Quality of Experience), which makes it possible to support co-hosted (and hence more scalable) ROIA, as well as conventional single-hosted ROIA (in which a business acts as both hoster and coordinator). The edutain@grid architecture has been designed to be flexible enough to support a wide range of value chain topologies among the roles identified, and to accommodate facilitators such as brokers where such roles are economically viable.

The initial implementation of the edutain@grid framework is now complete, and experiments are being conducted to investigate how business values can be expressed in SLA terms that allow service providers to retain flexibility and control costs, while being attractive to service consumers. Initial findings suggest that the hosting SLA between ROIA coordinators and hosters should be expressed in terms of the outcomes for the coordinator, as more conventional SLA terms based on resource committed by the hoster are of lower value to the coordinator and force the hoster to lose control over aspects of their resource management.

Future work will focus on the analysis of business models constructed using these value chains and SLA terms, operational management of ROIA and resources to address outstanding challenges such as dynamic ROIA-induced load, customer load imbalances, and their relationship to application adaptation and scalability features provided by a generic, abstract real-time application framework. These challenges are already faced in on-line gaming applications, but today the only solution is to restrict customer interactions in the game environment. The edutain@grid approach offers the prospect of Grid-based ROIA with few restrictions, which should also stimulate much greater commercial investment in the Grid itself.

**Acknowledgments.** The work described in this paper is supported by the European Union through EC IST Project 034601 'edutain@grid'.

# References

1. Foster, I., Kesselman, C. (eds.): The Grid2: Blueprint for a New Computing Infrastructure, 2nd edn. Morgan Kaufmann Publishers Inc., Elsevier, Boston (2004)
2. Fahringer, T., Anthes, C., Arragon, A., Lipaj, A., Müller-Iden, J., Rawlings., C., Prodan, R.: The Edutain@Grid Project. In: Veit, D.J., Altmann, J. (eds.) GECON 2007. LNCS, vol. 4685, pp. 182–187. Springer, Heidelberg (2007)
3. The edutain@grid website, http://www.edutaingrid.eu/index.php
4. Foster, I., Kesselman, C.: Globus: A Metacomputing Infrastructure Toolkit. International Journal Supercomputer Applications 11(2), 115–128 (1997)
5. Czajkowski, K., Ferguson, D.F., Foster, I., Frey, J., Graham, S., Sedukhin, I., Snelling, D., Tuecke, S., Vambenepe, W.: The WS-Resource Framework (March 2004)
6. Breuer, D., Erwin, D., Mallmann, D., Menday, R., Romberg, M., Sander, V., Schuller, B., Wieder, P.: Scientific Computing with UNICORE. In: Wolf, D., Münster, G., Kremer, M. (eds.) Proceedings of NIC Symposium 2004. NIC Series, vol. 20, pp. 429–440. John von Neumann Institute for Computing, Jülich (2003)
7. IDC Case Study, Butterfly.net: Powering Next-Generation Gaming with On-Demand Computing, http://www.ibm.com/grid/pdf/butterfly.pdf
8. Big World Technology, http://www.bigworldtech.com/index/index_en.php
9. Surridge, M., Taylor, S., De Roure, D., Zaluska, E.: Experiences with GRIA — Industrial Applications on a Web Services Grid. In: Proceedings of the First International Conference on e-Science and Grid Computing, pp. 98–105. IEEE Press, Los Alamitos (2005)
10. http://www.gria.org
11. Snelling, D., Fisher, M., Basermann, A.: NextGRID Vision and Architecture White Paper. This is updated periodically: at the time of writing the published version dates from 30 July 2006 (2006)
12. Mitchell, B., Mckee, P.: SLAs A Key Commercial Tool. In: Cunningham, P., Cunningham, M. (eds.) Innovation and the Knowledge Economy: Issues, Applications, Case Studies. IOS Press, Amsterdam (2005)
13. Phillips, S.C.: GRIA SLA Service. In; Cracow Grid Workshop, Cracow, Poland, pp. 15–18 (October 2006)
14. Müller, J., Gorlatch, S.: Scaling Online Games on the Grid. In: Proceedings of the Fourth Annual International Conference in Computer Game Design and Technology, 15-16 November (2006)
15. Glinka, F., Ploss, A., Gorlatch, S., Müller-Iden, J.: High-Level Development of Multi-Server Online Games. International Journal of Computer Game Technology – Networking for Computer Games (August 2008)
16. Müller-Iden, J., Gorlatch, S., Schröter, T.: Parallelization and Scalability of Multiplayer Online Games via State Replication. In: Grandinetti, L. (ed.) High Performance Computing and Grids in Action, March 2008, pp. 384–402. IOS Press, Amsterdam (2008)

17. Müller, J., Gorlatch, S.: Enhancing Online Computer Games for Grids. Parallel Computing Technologies. In: Malyshkin, V.E. (ed.) PaCT 2007. LNCS, vol. 4671, pp. 80–95. Springer, Heidelberg (2007)
18. Müller, J., Gorlatch, S.: Scaling Online Games on the Grid. In: Proceedings of GDTW 2006 - Fourth International Game Design and Technology Workshop and Conference, Liverpool, UK, pp. 6–10 (2006)
19. The Simdat project, http://www.scai.fraunhofer.de/about_simdat.html

# BREIN, Towards an Intelligent Grid for Business

Eduardo Oliveros[1], Henar Muñoz[1], David Cantelar[1], and Steve Taylor[2]

[1] Telefónica I+D, Emilio Vargas 6, 28043 Madrid, Spain
[2] IT Innovation Centre, 2 Venture Road, Southampton, SO16 7NP, UK
{eod,henar,dcm}@tid.es, sjt@it-innovation.soton.ac.uk

**Abstract.** Nowadays companies' communication is mainly static and does not allow for the flexibility and adaptability required to meet changing requirements or to support unexpected situations. The BREIN project's main objective is to create an infrastructure that allows companies to collaborate in a dynamic business environment. Moreover, BREIN is strongly focused on SMEs which do not have enough knowledge or resources to participate in this kind of environments. To address this knowledge gap, the BREIN framework reduces relations' complexity and aims to provide a solution where essential requirements to build this collaborative environment such as self-management capabilities, security, trust and reliability are all integrated into one business network.

**Keywords:** Service Grid, Business Grid, Semantic Web, Multi-agents, Business relationship, Service Level Agreement, Security, Abstract workflow.

## 1 Introduction

The adoption of the Grid by companies in a business environment has not had the success anticipated based on the experience in science and academic institutions [4], where the Grid has been a complete success. However, it is well-known that some large companies are clear examples of Grid utilization (e.g. eBay [1] or MICRON [2]), which are making use of Grid technologies and semantic web to improve their internal business processes.

Most of the previous companies, which have successfully deployed Grid solutions, own important infrastructure and enormous technical and economical resources. Regarding business, some industrial sectors as aerospace or financial [7] are introducing Grid technology inside their businesses. However, they are still few examples and implementations of Grid crossing different administrative domains.

The main reasons of this low usage of Grid across different enterprise administrative domains can involve [4]: i) the high knowledge and resources required, ii) the lack of interest in Grid capacities and iii) the necessity of having high-level services that provide complex functionality and solve part of the business needs of a company.

However, recent new business models are arising as Software as a Service [9], which allows most enterprises to be part of value systems without the necessity of investing in infrastructure, allowing all of these enterprises to interact creating a broad and heterogeneous collaborative environment. In this matter, some new important requirements arise. The most important of these is security, but also interoperability, reliability, trust among participants and simplicity are essential.

J. Altmann, D. Neumann, and T. Fahringer (Eds.): GECON 2008, LNCS 5206, pp. 163–172, 2008.
© Springer-Verlag Berlin Heidelberg 2008

BREIN focuses on addressing these requirements, providing a solution with SMEs in mind that reduces the complexity of using the Grid and enables the participation of companies of any size in this collaborative environment.

The remainder of this paper is as follows: In Section 2, we introduce the new business models arisen together with the main barriers. Section 3 deals with a description of the BREIN project, and its general benefits are provided in Section 4. Section 5 defines the two end-user scenarios involved in the project and their impact affecting the project. Finally, Section 6 presents the conclusions gathered.

## 2  New Business Models

The introduction of Information and Communication Technology (ICT) and Internet inside the business is changing the way that enterprises are doing their work, creating new opportunities for the society of information provides. Using the Web infrastructure, intranets support intra-organizational business processes, extranets connect enterprises to their channel partners and the Internet links the enterprises to their customers, other institutions and agencies [10]. In addition, customers are demanding more complex and integrated services, tailored to their specific needs.

Moreover, outsourcing is becoming increasingly popular since companies can outsource some work to third-party more expert enterprises [5]. Outsourcing provides an efficient and cost effective infrastructure that is far cheaper and offers far better economies of scale than the customer's own processes, as it lets each party in the relationship concentrate on their core business. In this matter, each enterprise specializes in concrete tasks and its business model should take into account the different enterprises making up the value chain. The most general pattern is that an organization buys in components, goods or services as "raw materials", adds value to them to produce their goods or services and sells these to their customers.

Thus, the supply chain of business model is more and more complicated, which implies the complexity of business relationships. All these changes are supposing a constant readjustment of business models, which is viewed by companies like an opportunity that they try to take advantage, integrating their business, selling products of third companies that supplement their offer, and incorporating technologies that facilitate agility and flexibility to changes.

However, this complexity can exclude SMEs from these models, since they can not afford the infrastructure investment in software and hardware and do not have technical resources to deal with the installation and maintenance of this infrastructure. In order to solve these problems, new payment models have arisen like pay-per-use, which can be used in models such as "Software as a Service" (SaaS) and customer's access and use these services over the Internet [9]. It implies that software providers require new computing capacity to be offered on demand. On one hand, the provider could buy those machines required, but due to the variable nature of computing demands, the capacity requirements are difficult to plan for, creating the risks of under-provisioning or the wasting of resources. On the other hand, it could use computing capacity offered by providers of computing services [14]. In this matter, Service Providers can outsource computing to other Service Providers, acting as customer for this bipartite relationship [12]. In addition, SMEs can move away from their limited area of business (interests) and offer adapted services to interested customers, which gives them a more diverse, stable and stronger business opportunities and with that to compete on the market.

The following figure [8] shows the value system illustrating the new business models discussed above. Mainly, it involves providers of resources (machines, hardware), service providers (computing and software), and finally the customer, who is able to use these services.

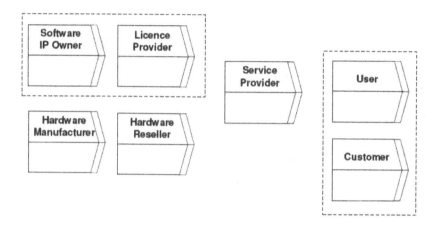

**Fig. 1.** Value system example [8]

Attracted by the potential for B2B relationships among companies to bundle more elaborate and profitable services, entrants to the service market are increasing. As new enterprises are continually joining the service market place, business value systems are being more and more complex. This creates new requirements such as: i) enterprises interoperability to solve the heterogeneity problems due to different information exchanged among enterprises, ii) relationships management considering SLA management, accounting, billing…, iii) task automation to reduce time and effort, iv) dynamic enterprise relationships and business processes, to achieve flexibility, dynamic and agility in execution and v) security mechanism to assure enterprise data privacy, authentication, authorization and trust.

Addressing these requirements will assist an SME enormously to get involved with these new business models by permitting them to use service-based infrastructures with low entry costs.

Technically, a Service Oriented Architecture permits dealing with the outsourcing of work as services. It promotes the idea of assembling application components into a network of services that can be loosely coupled to create flexible, dynamic business processes and agile applications that span organizations and computing platforms [5].

The use of SOA is an evolution from the traditional architectures of applications or maps of systems that we find in the departments of information systems, toward an architecture of processes and services that increase companies' flexibility, so they can better address changes of business (fusions of companies, temporary alliances among companies to attack determined markets, regulatory aspects of each country, internal reorganizations in one company,...).

Moreover, Grid technologies provide mechanisms for sharing and coordinating the use of diverse resources and thus enable the creation, from geographically and organizationally distributed components, of virtual computing systems that are sufficiently integrated to deliver desired qualities of service [6]. In this model, a service provider hosts and manages the Grid solution dedicated for serving customers.

To sum up, with the growing demand for fast, reliable and electronic business provisioning, the according middleware needs to hide complexity from the users that don't need to see it whilst retaining full control from both the provider and consumer sides of a business relationship. This is one of the main objectives of BREIN, and BREIN intends to address this by providing tools that permit different business actors to do what they are good at. For example we want to let engineers use fluid dynamics codes (their field of expertise), and let their managers control the business side. This means that each actor is operating within a field they know and understand, and can collaborate to increase efficiency and thereby wealth.

# 3 General Description of BREIN

The research Project BREIN, partially funded by the EC under the FP6, has as its main objective the creation of an infrastructure that will support collaboration among companies in a dynamic and changing environment. The project has a strong focus on business requirements established by the definition of two scenarios (Virtual Engineering and Airport Resource Management) driven by two main end-user stakeholders in the project: ANSYS Europe Ltd and Stuttgart Airport.

BREIN aims to develop a framework that will extend the possibilities of using the Grid for use inside new target areas from the business domain. Thus, BREIN is dealing with all necessary functionality in a business Grid to enable enterprises to simplify their relationships complexity by using its infrastructure. To this end, BREIN will give the best support possible to enhance business and to optimize business execution whilst minimising interaction and knowledge about the underlying technical nature of the system from the individual participants.

To build this framework, BREIN will combine concepts provided by different research areas and apply them to a Grid situation. These areas include: semantic web, multi-agent and workflow technologies in order to enable interoperability, flexibility and adaptability.

A key concept in our approach is that of the "bipartite (that is two-party) agreement", which is the contract established between two parties, deriving from a negotiation and describing the service, its quality and the terms under which it is delivered. This model closely follows real B2B practice and does not impose any restriction on the aspect of the value chain or the pricing model of each participant. It does not require the previous establishment of a virtual organization beforehand and defining the participants in the process. Therefore, there is no central component that manages the Virtual Organization lifecycle, and each participant establishes bipartite relationships with other participants, to govern their business interactions and the services traded between them.

To create this eco-system of collaborative business the use of standards is essential for interoperability, but even using standard communication protocols is not enough for two organizations to collaborate – they also need to understand each other. Also required is a common understanding of the concepts and terms that are going to describe the services provided, outcomes, and also the terms of the agreement and the compensation in case of breach of contract.

Another fundamental concept in Grid is virtualization. This provides companies with means of provisioning for a service in any way they see fit, as long as it is compliant with the terms of the agreements they have with their customers. A provider could change their internal infrastructure and their clients will not perceive any change. This provides the freedom of managing the internal resources without any restriction and facilitates the adaptation to changing business circumstances.

## 3.1 General Benefits Provided by BREIN

BREIN is currently working on achieving the enough dynamicity and flexibility to address the complex relationships among stakeholders in the new value chain provided [16] by these new business models described above. Dynamicity is addressed by separating customer goals with processes execution, which means that business processes are not defined statically, but are determined at runtime. Flexibility is obtained since BREIN allows the system to be able to react to failures in execution or SLA violations. Concretely, BREIN plans to deliver the following technological innovations.

### 3.1.1 Dynamic Workflow
Workflow allows customers to connect services from providers together to deliver more complex, flexible services directly addressing their business requirements. BREIN addresses dynamic workflow by making a distinction between *abstract* and *concrete* workflow. The abstract workflow is defined by a high level language close to the human language, where the user is able to define their requirements in terms of processes goals. On the other hand, concrete workflow is executable involving actual services, SLAs, security etc, and is translated from abstract workflow by the process of evaluation. This means that the same abstract workflow may be executed at different providers every time it is executed, as the binding to the providers can be done at runtime. This gives a great deal of flexibility, and robustness is achieved through the replacement of a non-performing provider with another at runtime.

### 3.1.2 Enhanced SLA Management
The delivery of business services is typically bound by Service Level Agreements (SLAs), describing the expected functionality and potential reactions to missing the obligations. The management of such a service level agreement is a complex task as the overall service quality depends on several aspects such as system behaviour, network reliability, external dependencies and even unexpected events. The BREIN approach is to enhance existing work in SLA [17] by exploiting semantic descriptions of the services offered and their dependencies, as well as to use concepts from the multi-agents domain enabling a faster enactment of necessary actions and decisions without necessary human intervention.

The service provider's management of SLAs is also considered in the project. A single SLA cannot be managed in isolation from all other SLAs offered at the same time by the same provider – all SLAs offered by a provider must to be in line with their management policies, priorities, and business and provisioning strategies. These policies can be priority driven (based on the overall business goals/objectives of the service provider) and with that, they will influence the decisions taken by the provider. This could mean, for example, that SLAs with a certain customer are treated with higher priority than others.

### 3.1.3 Planning Support

The concept in BREIN is to allow the definition of goals to be achieved and allow intelligent components to map the goals to a composition of available services. With that, BREIN automatically enables reaction to service failures, driven by policies or in general changes in the execution in the environments. This capacity of automatic reaction and self-management is essential to increase reliability for consumers, and this will in turn benefit providers. When outsourcing a task, a customer is relying on external companies. This situation can be very risky, and guarantees are required to ensure that the service providers will perform as expected. SLA terms assist the customer in that they encapsulate the vested interest for the provider in correctly providing the service: if they provide the service correctly, they will get paid, and if they do not, they will have to pay a penalty for example. In addition, the customer can insulate themselves from risk though having alternative strategies. This may range from different providers to perform the same abstract task, to complete alternative workflows that achieve the same goal.

It is not expected to solve this problem in a fully generic way but to find mechanisms that allow understanding simple compositions of service to be equal and to build the case for further research in this area. These solutions as well as reference implementations will be a highly valuable result.

### 3.1.4 Security

The BREIN vision is to support dynamic collaboration creation by allowing a user to collaborate with other on a B2B level, and with the BREIN framework triggering the necessary actions based on this. Security is considered from the first design stages, and is predicated on the SLA and the business relationships. This is because the SLA and business relationships provide a binding contractual foundation. In effect, these elements provide a root of trust for collaboration. Trust is defined from the point of view of the trusting party: it is the confidence that another party (the trustee) will behave as the trustee expects. To increase this confidence, it is helpful to give the trustee a vested interest in behaving as the trustee expects, and SLAs and business relationships provide the mechanism for this. There are payments for correct behaviour and penalties (and possibly court proceedings) for violations.

Access control is considered from a fine-grained, least privilege perspective. A user will only have access to exactly what they need to do their work, and no more. This means that there is no Unix login, but access is constrained to an individual data set or running job and the actions permitted on these items are tightly constrained as well.

# 4   BREIN Lifecycle and Validation Scenarios

For the demonstration of the capabilities and functionalities that may be available using the BREIN framework, two complimentary scenarios have been defined with different (but nevertheless compatible) scopes, contexts and approaches. Both scenarios cover the formation, cooperation, interoperation and integration between different service providers that create a Virtual Organization (VO) [6] for the purpose of addressing the goal defined by the customer. The goal of this VO is to enable customers to request the remote execution of a workflow containing several services that may be provided by different providers. However, the customer goal and its business policies may be at least different or even contradictory to the business policies of each service provider. This view of BREIN is shown in the next figure, which also includes some of the main building blocks of the framework [12].

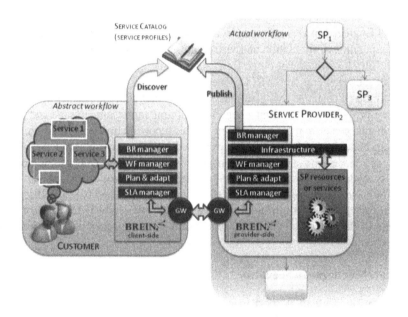

**Fig. 2.** BREIN diagram

In the VO normal operation, the BREIN platform and its components will be firstly involved in the discovery of the services that will be included in the overall process to achieve the VO goal, by means of the already mentioned generic workflow. The negotiation and subsequent selection make use of semantics in the terms already described of establishing a common language for the description of both the service and its SLAs. With this input, BREIN permits negotiation with several service providers and establishment of the VO by an agreement between all the stakeholders, assigning every node of the workflow to a specific service provided by a single service provider, once its capabilities and SLAs are compatible with the ones stated in the abstract workflow.

If there is not any violation in the process, the workflow will be executed without any interruption. In the case of any violation, the client-side planning process will adapt the process by renegotiating and reassigning another service provider for the service that has failed or violated the agreement, trying to reach the VO goal with the minimum side-effects. This will be underpinned in BREIN by means of intelligent agents technology, which eases these processes by means of its main features [13]: (1) autonomy as agents does not require human interaction, (2) reactivity to environment events (i.e. SLA violation), (3) pro-activeness exhibiting goal-directed behaviours (replace service who might violate some SLA with another one, trying to accomplish the overall goal) and (4) social ability to interact with other intelligent agents (negotiations within BREIN customers and providers).

### 4.1 Virtual Engineering Design Scenario

The Virtual Engineering Design scenario covers a typical Grid use case that involves several computational, simulation and visualization services for performing engineering design. These services can range from a simple computing provision to complex geometry or mesh generation for CFD codes. As described above, the customer wants to reduce time and cost, and this goal must be reconciled with the business policies of each service provider – to maximize benefit by optimizing resource usage and avoiding performance peaks, and the mechanism for this reconciliation is negotiation.

The main benefits of BREIN that are exploited by this scenario are (1) reliability, by means of the security and the proven grid reliability when some computational resource is needed, (2) auto-management in terms of automatic response to unexpected or new events by means of the intelligent agents implemented in BREIN (this also increases reliability from the customer's perspective) and (3) business orientation, thanks to the workflow and SLA negotiation support underpinned by semantic technologies.

### 4.2 Airport Management Scenario

The inclusion of Stuttgart Airport in a research project about Grid initially seems confusing because this scenario goes away from the classical view of Grid. However, the Airport scenario addresses resource management and provisioning aspects, which are critical to Grid service provision. The only difference is that in the Airport, resources are, luggage handling, buses, gangways, cleaning services, catering etc, rather than the traditional Grid resources of CPUs, memory and storage. The Airport is a good example of a big collaborative environment where market-based resource management techniques can equally apply to an airport or a computational cluster, and lessons can be learned from one scenario that can apply to the other. It is in this sense that the scenarios, while apparently very different, are described as complimentary.

This scenario covers the use of the airport as a virtual hub in which every service provider, by means of the different companies that operate in the airport (i.e., commercial companies or public authorities), collaborate with each other to accomplish the overall goal: to efficiently and optimally manage all the organizational and logistics processes. As in the virtual engineering scenario, the overall goal may or may not be compatible with every stakeholder individual goals (i.e., pilots and control agencies attach great importance to security issues, which is not usually compatible with the airline individual goal of reducing transfer and waiting times), and negotiation is required to manage these conflicts.

Optimal management of all the airport processes could lead to a new business opportunity: once the airport can efficiently manage, for instance, flights and planes, a new offering combining two flights almost in real time could be offered, and this is the overall goal of the Airport scenario. In the normal operation of the airport when no incidents may occur, the behaviour of the BREIN platform and its components will be to monitor the overall planning and schedule for every service resource. When events happen that could cause, for instance, a flight delay caused by an issue in a passenger bus, the BREIN platform will directly and automatically perform the correct adjustments and adaptations underpinned by intelligent agents, for rescheduling and reassignment the resources of the affected services to hopefully maintain and reach the overall goal despite the unexpected events, or to minimize the impact of the unexpected events.

## 5  Conclusions

Overall, BREIN's remit is to facilitate the participation of SMEs by simplifying the access of them to a collaborative business Grid. BREIN's research goal is to investigate the integration of a set of different disciplines with the aim of addressing some of the major barriers preventing companies' participation in a collaborative business Grid. To address this, BREIN has a set of characteristics that can help to shorten the time for the adoption and utilization of this environment, being some key aspects carried out by BREIN:

- The incorporation of security policies in a virtualized environment;
- The freedom of evolving and adapting internal infrastructure without affecting the external offering to customers; and
- The possibility of defining the business processes in an abstract way, without defining concrete service providers or services.

The system will plan the execution of the process depending on the availability of services and the experience on previous business relationships. This abstract description gives also the freedom to the platform to replan part or all of workflow when reacting to unexpected situations.

The Semantic Web and the Multi-agents technologies are key elements of the architecture and enablers of the advanced functionality described in this paper. These technologies provide the means for a common understanding among customers and service providers about the description of the SLA and intelligent negotiations of SLAs, together with the possibility of defining process and policies in an abstract way, so that different offers from different providers can be compared in a like-for-like way. The combination of these factors increases the simplicity and reliability for users of a business Grid, and thus will promote the uptake of it for non-expert users.

# References

1. eBay Looks to the Semantic Web, `http://www.semanticweb.com/article.php/3738251`
2. A Peek into Micron's Grid Infrastructure, `http://www.gridtoday.com/grid/633762.html`
3. Crash: Amazon's S3 utility goes down, `http://www.techmeme.com/080215/p47#a080215p47`
4. Challengers, Interaction of European and International Grid Communities, Conclusions of the first consultation workshop, Italy (October 2006)
5. Papazoglou, M.P., Traverso, P., Dustdar, S., Leymann, F.: Service-Oriented Computing: State of the Art and Research Challenges. Computer 40(11), 38–45 (2007)
6. Foster, I., Kesselman, C. (eds.): The Grid: Blueprint for a New Computing Infrastructure. Morgan Kaufmann Publishers, San Francisco (1999)
7. Fernández, M., et al.: Report on business and market context V1.1, D2.2.1 BREIN deliverable (2007)
8. Leukel, J., et al.: The BREIN value chain and scenario-specific supply chain definition, BREIN deliverable, D3.3.1 (2007)
9. Jacobs, D.: Enterprise software as service. Queue 3(6), 36–42 (2005)
10. Strader, T.J., Lin, F., Shaw, M.J.: Information Infrastructure for Electronic Virtual Organization Management. Decision Support Systems 23, 75–94 (1998)
11. Papazoglou, M.P., Heuvel, W.J.: Service oriented architectures: approaches, technologies and research issues. The VLDB Journal 16(3), 389–415 (2007)
12. Laria, G.: Overall architecture v1, BREIN deliverable D4.1.2 (2007)
13. Wooldridge, M., Jennings, N.R.: Intelligent Agents: Theory and Practice. Knowledge Engineering Review 10(2) (1995)

# SORMA – Business Cases for an Open Grid Market: Concept and Implementation

Jens Nimis[1], Arun Anandasivam[2], Nikolay Borissov[2], Garry Smith[3], Dirk Neumann[4], Niklas Wirström[5], Erel Rosenberg[6], and Matteo Villa[7]

[1] FZI Forschungszentrum Informatik Karlsruhe, Germany
nimis@fzi.de
[2] Institute of Information Systems and Management (IISM)
University of Karlsruhe, Germany
{anandasivam,borissov}@iism.uni-karlsruhe.de
[3] School of Systems Engineering, University of Reading, UK
garry.smith@computer.org
[4] Department of Information Systems, University of Freiburg, Germany
dirk.neumann@vwl.uni-freiburg.de
[5] Swedish Institute of Computer Science, Sweden
niwi@sics.se
[6] Correlation Systems Ltd., Isreal
erel@cs.co.il
[7] TXT e-Solutions, Italy
matteo.villa@txt.it

**Abstract.** Economic mechanisms enhance technological solutions by setting the right incentives to reveal information about demand and supply accurately. Market or pricing mechanisms are ones that foster information exchange and can therefore attain efficient allocation. By assigning a value (also called utility) to their service requests, users can reveal their relative urgency or costs to the service. The implementation of theoretical sound models induce further complex challenges. The EU-funded project SORMA analyzes these challenges and provides a prototype as a proof-of-concept. In this paper the approach within the SORMA-project is described on both conceptual and technical level.

**Keywords:** Grid Computing, Market, Business case.

## 1 Introduction

Until now, the exchange of computing resources has been mainly driven by voluntary sharing in non-profit settings via small-scale Grid networks. The free sharing concept is, however, not applicable in large-scale scientific and commercial networks. Participants tend to free-ride aiming to reduce costs [1]. In particular, they will consume without offering own resources. Technical scheduling algorithms for fair sharing are often centralized, and have problems, when organizational boundaries are crossed, and information about demand and supply

J. Altmann, D. Neumann, and T. Fahringer (Eds.): GECON 2008, LNCS 5206, pp. 173–184, 2008.

can be manipulated. More precisely, if demand exceeds supply, the scheduling algorithms fail to allocate the resources efficiently.

Economic mechanisms enhance technological solutions by setting the right incentives to reveal information about demand and supply accurately. Market or pricing mechanisms are ones that foster information exchange and can therefore attain efficient allocation [14]. By assigning a value (also called utility) to their service requests, users can reveal their relative urgency or costs to the service [9,13]. The mediated resource allocation and delivery over the market will allow better utilization of available resources, which automatically directs those resources provided to the clients, who value them most.

The EU-funded project SORMA[1] is designing and implementing an Open Grid Market and will test it in real world use cases. To establish an Open Grid Market in practice, there are several obstacles that have to be overcome. The bidding process cannot be managed manually as it is too complex and time-consuming, so there is a need for intelligent tools, which simplify access to Grid-based systems in a way that businesses are empowered to make use of them. In essence, these intelligent tools must support the automation of the bidding process, which is dependent on the resource supply situation and business policies. Additionally, the Open Grid Market has to be equipped with intelligent monitoring tools that gather resource information frequently in order to correct unexpected events such as demand fluctuations or failure to share resources. Other aspects like the structured design of market mechanisms, contract management and a market information service are part of the Open Grid Market as well.

In this paper, we focus on the implementation and the first running prototype in SORMA. Our scenario is based on the business cases from our partners TXT e-Solution and Correlation Systems. In their applications the Grid is applied to process amounts of forecast data and to analyze video streams in real-time as described in Section 2. Section 3 gives an overview of the architecture and describes the prototypical implementation of the selected entities. Section 4 concludes with a summary and an outlook.

## 2   Pilot Applications

SORMA comprises an application infrastructure integrating theoretic economic models to construct a general Open Grid Market platform. The assessment of the SORMA platform as well as the developed theoretic models is realized via two pilot Grid applications that will be run on the final SORMA system. The pilots are a Supply Chain Management software and a geospatial data analysis software provided by SORMA partners TXT e-Solutions[2] and Correlation System Ltd.[3], respectively.

---

[1] http://www.sorma-project.eu

[2] http://www.txtgroup.com/

[3] http://www.correlation-systems.com/

## 2.1   Supply Chain Management with TXTDemand

TXTDemand is a demand forecasting tool and part of TXT's Supply Chain Management suite. It combines complex forecasting algorithms as well as algorithms for the analysis of historic data and current sales data with interactive revision tools. Business analysts from the customers of TXT have access to TXTDemand to get support in their daily tasks of defining demand and replenishment strategies. Time-critical jobs process previous days' sales data over night and create initial forecast plans, which are analyzed by the business experts during the following day. This application has recently adopted a grid-based architecture in order to solve performance problems when used in business scenarios involving very large amounts of data. The Grid support is required in the following two situations:

- The night BATCH phase, where data is processed off-line, implies "slowly" changing request of grid resources, since the number of records to process is more or less stable over time. Daily or weekly, there can be small variations that require negotiation of new resources on the Grid market. Execution duration is a critical factor here, since it should start and also finish at a quite precise time.
- In the INTERACTIVE phase end-users need to access the application on-line. In this case, the request for Grid resources depends on everyday human activities, so there can be unpredictable peaks of requests within a short period of time. In contrast to the BATCH phase, start and finish times cannot be planned, while again execution duration needs to be kept as low as possible.

In the scenario TXT assumes to have customers, who do not have the technical infrastructure (or are not economically interested into having it) for running the application, thus they rely on third party's resources (resource providers). The role of TXT is to act as an application broker by offering ASP service to its customers. The application portions jobs to be run on the Grid. Therefore, a market is required to achieve the best price for each job-part and to prioritize time-critical jobs by adjusting the price. The market has to support third party framework agreements (i.e. concerning Service Level Agreement (SLA) issues, security, etc.) in order to provide a substantial level of quality of service (QoS). The prices for the jobs can be defined dynamically in an agreement depending on submission time, execution time and duration. A bid generator facilitates the strategic price adaptation. As outlined in Figure 1, the customer is not aware of the Grid market. Instead TXT buys the required Grid resources on the market on demand. The goal is to ensure a better QoS to customers to reduce cost and to enhance the resource utilization.

In some business situations, customers may want to host the application. Yet, they may need to outsource the computational power required for the most CPU- and data-intensive computations. Then, TXT can no longer act as a broker, but TXTDemand application at customer's site will need to negotiate directly on the SORMA market to find a suitable resource provider. This scenario poses

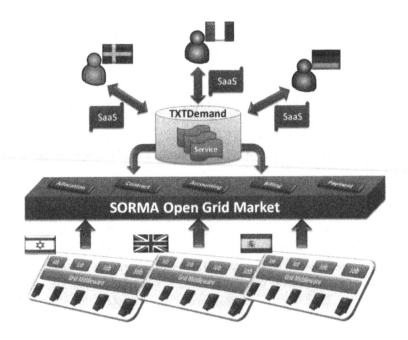

**Fig. 1.** Integration of TXTDemand with the Open Grid Market

more technically challenging requirements, as the market access and negotiation process need to be fully automated. Moreover, the business benefits for both TXT and its customers is harder to demonstrate. The access to the SORMA market via the TXTDemand application enables the customer to lower their investments in hardware infrastructure.

## 2.2   Real-Time Geographical Data Analysis

Correlation Systems Ltd. is a provider of geospatial data analysis tools and applications. The core software platform of Correlation Systems provides an execution environment for geospatial data analysis, geographic data mining and a self-learning behavioral analysis system. The software is able to receive geospatial information from multiple types of data sources including GPS receivers, cellular networks, analytical video surveillance systems etc. The data from the different sensors are aggregated to a video stream with additional information. The transformation from incoming sensor data to a video stream consumes vast amounts of computing power. Since data can be split into smaller chunks and thus the jobs can be parallelized, a Grid network can significantly improve the response time of the application. Customers can view the results using a graphical interface (Figure 2). Furthermore, customers can define alert rules to receive pictures, if a predefined event occurs in the stream. In this case, the picture is further analyzed and results in a picture with more detailed information, which requires more computing power.

Both processes are characterized by a large number of atomic operations where the processing results may influence on the next processing steps. For example, while processing a video stream the system receives N frames per second, where the pre-processing is responsible for the following tasks:

- Detection of motion
- Detection of object (i.e. body, face)
- Localization of the objects.

Pre-processing is performed in sequence, where a following processing step is only performed, if the previous one has completed successfully and has delivered a result that gives reason for further processing steps. Data reduction may be performed in case of a lack of resources, by reducing the data rate of the video stream. Due to the characteristics of the process, it is important to minimize the overhead related to each specific transaction and if necessary to conflate smaller processing steps into larger ones in order to minimize transaction costs. The system is required to be fully automatic, i.e. users may define their strategy or rules regarding the resource allocation, however all decisions on the actual resource allocation are required to be performed in real-time.

## 3    Architectural Design of the Open Grid Market

The holistic approach of SORMA comprises several aspects like resource monitoring, market mechanisms, automated bidding, SLA or payment. Special business cases as defined in Section 2 require a generic market platform, where the exchange of resources and service are executed in a standard manner among different computer systems. Standard communication protocols and the virtualization from the underlying resource managers outline the openness of the market to offer access to the platform for other Grid systems like Amazon's Elastic Compute Cloud or Sun Microsystems' network.com [18]. A distinct definition of each component with specified tasks in the Market platform is inevitable for building a modular and flexible Open Grid Market. The logical architecture of the Open Grid Market represents entities and their dependency on other entities (Figure 3). The flow of information or control are depicted by arrows. An arrow from an entity A to an entity B means that A sends information to B or passes control to B.

### 3.1    Layered Architecture

Layer 4 represents the human interaction with the Grid application. At the provider side a provider IT specialist makes use of the intelligent tools in layer 3 to model the provider's business strategies and the offered Grid resources as well as to elicit the preferences of the user by the software agent. *Grid resource* in this context means a physical resource, a raw service or a complex service [6]. SORMA will initially focus on the trading of "physical resources", but from a logical architecture standpoint, it is correct to consider that any type of resource

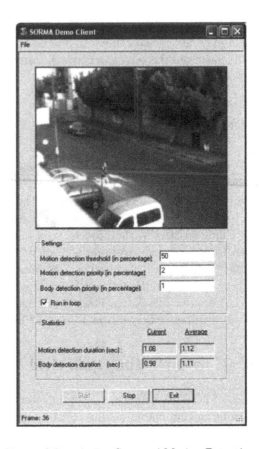

**Fig. 2.** Demo Client of Correlation Systems' Motion Detection Application

or service could be offered at this layer. On the consumer side it has to be distinguished between the Grid application's end user(s) and the consumer's IT support staff who will use the intelligent tools to model an application's resource requirements and the consumer's preferences.

On Layer 3 SORMA provides Intelligent Tools for consumers and providers in order to easily access the SORMA market. Four modeling entities allow consumers and providers to define their bidding strategies. Providers can choose between pricing policies to increase revenue, whereas consumers specify important technical requirements for their jobs. The bid and offer generator are applying machine learning strategies to adjust the bidding price. The aim is to achieve a better price on the market.

Layer 2 is the place, where the offered resources or services are assigned to the Grid applications of the consumers, following certain market organizations. A major role on Layer 2 is assigned to the *trading management*. It is the access point for the consumers to the Open Grid Market, where they can find the offered services and place their according bids. Therefore as a first step, the trading management matches the technical descriptions of the request (received from the consumers' bid generation) to the suitable technical descriptions of the

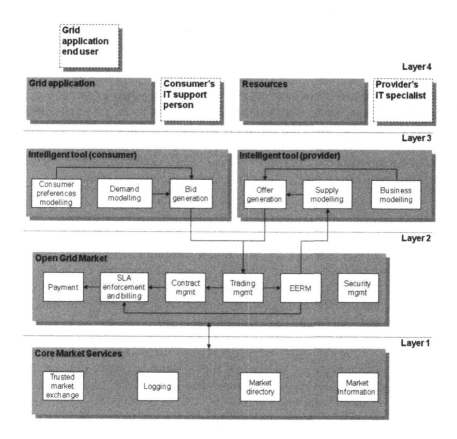

**Fig. 3.** Architecture of the Open Grid Market

offered resources (collected from the associated Grid market directories). In the second phase the trading management orchestrates the bidding process from the (possibly competing) consumers according to a given market mechanisms (e.g. English auction). If the bidding process finishes successfully the corresponding bid and offer are submitted to the contract management and the participants are informed.

The trading management is supported by the *contract management, SLA enforcement & billing* and the *payment component*. The interface between the resources and the market platform is provided by the *Economically Enhanced Resource Management (EERM)*. This component provides a standardized interface to typical Grid middleware (e.g. Unicore, Globus Toolkit or Sun Grid Engine) and shields clients from resource platform specific issues by virtualization. Another essential task of EERM is to monitor the resource usage and check the compliance with the SLA. Information about resource usage deviating from the agreement have to be cleared or even punished according to the SLA. Since standard Grid middleware does not provide all the infrastructure services necessary for an open marketplace, on Layer 1 the available information of standard Grid middleware is augmented by additional infrastructure services including real-time logging, market information (historical information about former transactions) and market directory (current information about resources, prices etc.) For more details on the implemented SLAs we refer the reader to [5,8,17].

The security management component on Layer 3 is intended as the entry point for a single sign-on mechanism and is responsible for a tamper-proof identity management for the consumers, the suppliers and the constituent components of the SORMA system. Thus, all components that are developed as part of the SORMA system will have to provide security connectors to build the technological bridges from the respective layers to the security management.

## 3.2   Prototypical Implementation

One goal within the SORMA project besides theoretical models is to develop a running prototype as a proof-of-concept. Thus, we emphasis in this section the current implementation. The Demand and Supply Modelling Components support the users of the Intelligent Tools (Layer 3) to specify the technical aspects of their resource requests and offers respectively. This support comprises three main parts:

1. a user interface based on Gridsphere [19] to allow the input of the technical resource specifications on consumer and supplier side with a standard webbrowser (see Figure 4),
2. a matchmaking library that technically matches resource requests to offers to fulfil the request
3. and at its heart a specification language that is able to express the resource specifications for the resources traded on the SORMA marketplace on different layers (from raw resources to complex services) [6].

As discussed in the last section, the Open Grid Market implemented by SORMA supports a wide variety of goods, namely physical resources, raw services and complex application specific services. Thus, one approach towards SORMA resource modeling could be to develop a single comprehensive new

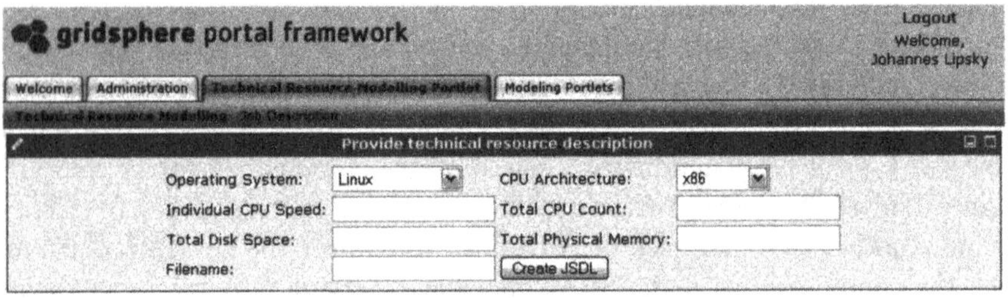

**Fig. 4.** Gridsphere User Interface for Technical Resource Specification

language from the scratch that is especially tailored towards the SORMA requirements. In general, such languages tend to be complex and are often not easy to reuse in other environments [6]. The approach followed in SORMA is to use established standards and technologies and to adapt them according to the SORMA requirements in order to have a modular compact and yet expressive set of languages. Prominent representatives for the distinct goods are the Job Submission and Description Language (JSDL) [2] for raw resources, parts of the Common Information Model (CIM) standards [11] or the Web Service Resource Frameworks (WSRF) [3] for generic service description, and the Web Ontology Language for Services (OWL-S) [27] as well as the Web Service Modeling Language (WSML) [10] for application specific complex services. As all these languages are mutually independent it is necessary to define a connector language between them that allows relating the description on the different layers with another. Therefore, a connector language called Resource Dependency Language (RDL) has been developed to define the consecutive and parallel processing steps within one layer and indicate the dependencies between different layers.

The matchmaking library matches technical request descriptions with technical offer descriptions on the marketplace in order to find possible offer candidates that technically could satisfy the request. It has to be considered that the matchmaking only covers the technical aspects of the resource and not the economic parameters. The Trading Management performs economic matchmaking and is described later in this document. There are two possibilities for matchmaking: Boolean matchmaking that only returns if a certain offer fulfils a request or not (return values $\in \{0, 1\}$) or fuzzy matchmaking that states how good an offer fulfils a request (return values $\in [0, 1]$). While the evaluation logic of Boolean matchmaking is easy to derive from the evaluation results of the three layer languages and from the structure of the connector trees, fuzzy matchmaking needs the definition of fuzzy evaluation rules for all four languages. Some of the language layers already have basic support for fuzzy matchmaking. For example JSDL allows exact matching for CPUs with a specified clock speed, as well as matching for all CPUs that have a clock speed greater than a specified threshold.

Bidding for heterogeneous and dispersed services can be a complex and time-consuming process based on the applied bidding strategies and market mechanisms. Agents should be able to make autonomous decisions, choose the appropriate market for their bids and send out bids automatically according to a predefined strategy. Market-based allocation of computational resources is widely explored in the literature. Thus, the allocation process is controlled by market mechanisms e.g. Vickrey, English, Dutch, and double auctions [12] as well as combinatorial mechanisms [4,24,25]. Prominent examples of market mechanisms for scheduling of computational resources like CPU and Memory are based on proportional share mechanisms [15], where the users receive a share of the computer resource proportional to their valuations fraction of the overall valuation across all users. A related and implemented mechanism is the so-called pay-as-bid mechanism proposed in [23,26], where the user pays the price he has bid.

We assume that agents are self-interested. Hence, they aim to implement a strategic behavior in order to maximize their utilities. In this context the mechanism design and auction literature investigated various bidding strategies for market-based scheduling [16,20,22]. Such strategic behavior is ranging from the selection of the right auction to the published/requested resource configuration or the definition of the willingness-to-pay/reserve price. Consumers and providers are faced with multi-attribute decisions. Personalized bidding agents will be configured with a set of strategies and learning algorithms in order to automatically execute the providers' or consumers' preferences. In his thesis [20], Phelps classified bidding strategies into non-adaptive e.g. Truth Telling, Equilibrium-Price and Zero Intelligence strategy and adaptive strategies e.g. Zero-Intelligence Plus, Kaplans Sniping Strategy, Gjerstad-Dickhaut and Reinforcement-learning.

Three bidding strategies were implemented in SORMA: Truth-Telling as a non adaptive strategy, Zero-Intelligence Plus and Q-Strategy with adaptive bidding strategies. Each consumer and provider is using SORMA intelligent tools to specify her demand or supply regarding technical requirements for computational resources, their QoS and the price. The bid and offer generator component as a part of the intelligent tools is implemented within SORMA's Bidding Agent Framework [7]. Furthermore, the preferred bidding strategy can be configured by policies, which are defined by a rule description language and executed within a rule engine. Policies represent utility and pricing functions. Through the utility function, the participant specifies the overall objectives as a mathematical function that is to be maximized by its bidding agent. The pricing policy enables a static specification of a valuation or price calculation function for calculating the bid and reporting the bid to the Open Grid Market. The bid message contains the technical and economic preferences for both the provider and consumer.

The trading management is responsible for executing and providing evidence of economic matchmaking in SORMA. C-Space (Conversation Space) constitutes the Trading Management in SORMA. It is a framework for creating and executing conversations. A conversation follows a certain protocol that determines who can say what, and when. The protocols are defined by users in terms of Java classes that are submitted to C-Space and run in the C-Space trusted infrastructure. These protocols support different kinds of auctions or other trading mechanisms, for instance direct bargaining. We use the abstraction of conversations to emphasize the generality of the framework. All network communication between users and the trusted infrastructure consists of encrypted and signed SOAP messages according to the WS-Security specification. The user's trustworthy certificate issued by Certificate Authorities is monitored and validated by the Security Management component.

## 4   Conclusion

Exchanging computing power, storage space or memory over a large-scale network enables to run complex applications and services in an acceptable period of time. The process of exchanging resources can be facilitated by a platform offering a market for these resources. The design of this platform is, however, quite challenging. Providers and consumers need intelligent tools to participate in the market for automatic management. The user should initially configure his preferred strategy and the intelligent tool will autonomously update the price and other parameters. Depending on the applied market mechanism, participants have to dynamically adapt their strategies according to their outcome. The underlying platform infrastructure has to be flexible in the sense of extendability. New market mechanisms or SLA requirements should not trigger a complete redesign of the infrastructure. A flexible infrastructure with modular components and standardized message protocols allows a fast adaption and a new design of markets on demand. In this paper, we presented the first prototype implementing the concept of the Open Grid Market. The architecture gives an overview about the interplay of the components. We use a layered structure to identify resource-centric, user-centric components and market-centric components. Currently, we have implemented on the user side the components comprising bid and offer generator as well as demand and supply modeling. On the market-centric side the trading management component and the EERM are running successfully. For more information on the EERM component, we refer to [21].

As a next step the SLA enforcement and the contract management component need to be scrutinized to finalize the preliminary version. A visualization of the SLA component based on AJAX technology is already available. On Layer 1 the trusted market exchange and market information component, which are currently under development, are necessary to provide essential information to the intelligent tools.

# References

1. Anandasivam, A., Neumann, D.: Reputation-based pricing for grid computing in escience. In: Proceedings of the 16th European Conference on Information Systems (ECIS) (2008)
2. Anjomshoaa, A., Drescher, M., Fellows, D., Ly, A., McGough, S., Pulsipher, D., Savva, A.: Job submission description language (jsdl) specification (2005), www.gridforum.org/documents/GFD.56.pdf
3. Banks, T.: Web Services Resource Framework (WSRF) - Primer v1.2. Technical Report. Technical report, OASIS Open (2006)
4. Bapna, R., Das, S., Garfinkel, R., Stallaert, J.: A Market Design for Grid Computing. INFORMS Journal on Computing (2007)
5. Becker, M., Borissov, N., Deora, V., Rana, O.F., Neumann, D.: Using k-Pricing for Penalty Calculation in Grid Market. In: Hawaii International Conference on System Sciences, Proceedings of the 41st Annual (2008)
6. Blau, B., Schnizler, B.: Description languages and mechanisms for trading service objects in grid markets. In: Multikonferenz Wirtschaftsinformatik 2008, GITO-Verlag, Berlin (2008)
7. Borissov, N., Blau, B., Neumann, D.: Semi-automated provisioning and usage of configurable web services. In: Proceedings of the 16th European Conference on Information Systems (ECIS) (2008)
8. Brunner, R., Chao, I., Chacin, P., Freitag, F., Navarro, L., Ardaiz, O., Joita, L., Rana, O.F.: Assessing a Distributed Market Infrastructure for Economics-Based Service Selection?. LNCS. Springer, Heidelberg (2007)

9. Buyya, R., Abramson, D., Venugopal, S.: The Grid Economy. In: Proceedings of the IEEE, pp. 698–714 (2005)
10. de Bruijn, J.: The Web Service Modeling Language (WSML) (2005), http://www.wsmo.org/wsml/
11. Distributed Management Task Force. Common Information Model (CIM) Specification (2007), http://www.dmtf.org/standards/cim/
12. Grosu, D., Das, A.: Auctioning resources in grids: model and protocols: Research articles. Concurrency and Computation: Practice & Experience 18(15), 1909–1927 (2006)
13. Irwin, D.E., Grit, L.E., Chase, J.S.: Balancing Risk and Reward in a Market-Based Task Service. In: Proceedings of the 13th IEEE International Symposium on High Performance Distributed Computing, vol. 4(06), pp. 160–169 (2004)
14. Lai, K.: Markets are dead, long live markets. SIGecom Exch. 5(4), 1–10 (2005)
15. Lai, K., Rasmusson, L., Adar, E., Zhang, L., Huberman, B.A.: Tycoon: An implementation of a distributed, market-based resource allocation system. Multiagent Grid Syst. 1(3), 169–182 (2005)
16. Li, J., Yahyapour, R.: Learning-Based Negotiation Strategies for Grid Scheduling. In: Proceedings of the International Symposium on Cluster Computing and the Grid (CCGRID 2006), pp. 576–583 (2006)
17. Macias, M., Smith, G., Rana, O.F., Guitart, J., Torres, J.: Enforcing Service Level Agreements using an Economically Enhanced Resource Manager. In: Workshop on Economic Models and Algorithms for Grid Systems (EMAGS 2007), Texas, USA (2007)
18. Neumann, D., Stoesser, J., Weinhardt, C.: Bridging the Adoption Gap–Developing a Roadmap for Trading in Grids. Electronic Markets 18(1), 65–74 (2008)
19. Novotny, J., Russell, M., Wehrens, O.: Gridsphere: An advanced portal framework. Euromicro, 412–419 (2004)
20. Phelps, S.: Evolutionary mechanism design, ph.d. thesis. Technical report, University of Liverpool, Department of Computer Science (2007)
21. Puschel, T., Borissov, N., Macias, M., Neumann, D., Guitart, J., Torres, J.: Economically Enhanced Resource Management for Internet Service Utilities. In: Benatallah, B., Casati, F., Georgakopoulos, D., Bartolini, C., Sadiq, W., Godart, C. (eds.) WISE 2007. LNCS, vol. 4831, pp. 335–348. Springer, Heidelberg (2007)
22. Reeves, D.M., Wellman, M.P., MacKie-Mason, J.K., Osepayshvili, A.: Exploring bidding strategies for market-based scheduling. Decis. Support Syst. 39(1), 67–85 (2005)
23. Sanghavi, S., Hajek, B.: Optimal allocation of a divisible good to strategic buyers. In: 43rd IEEE Conference on Decision and Control-CDC (2004)
24. Schnizler, B., Neumann, D., Veit, D., Weinhardt, C.: Trading grid services–a multi-attribute combinatorial approach. European Journal of Operational Research 187(3), 943–961 (2008)
25. Stoesser, J., Neumann, D., Anandasivam, A.: A truthful heuristic for efficient scheduling in network-centric grid os. In: Proceedings of the 15th European Conference on Information Systems (ECIS) (2007)
26. Stosser, J., Bodenbenner, P., See, S., Neumann, D.: A Discriminatory Pay-as-Bid Mechanism for Efficient Scheduling in the Sun N1 Grid Engine. In: Hawaii International Conference on System Sciences, Proceedings of the 41st Annual, pages 382 (2008)
27. The OWL Services Coalition. OWL-S: Semantic Markup for Web Services (2003), http://www.daml.org/services/owl-s/1.0/owl-s.html

# GridEcon: A Market Place for Computing Resources

Jörn Altmann[1,5], Costas Courcoubetis[2], George D. Stamoulis[2], Manos Dramitinos[2],
Thierry Rayna[4], Marcel Risch[1], and Chris Bannink[3]

[1] International University in Germany, School of Information Technology
Campus 3, 76646 Bruchsal, Germany
jorn.altmann@acm.org, marcel.risch@i-u.de
[2] Network Economics and Services Group (N.E.S.), Department of Informatics,
Athens University of Economics and Business (AUEB),
76 Patision Street, Athens, GR 10434, Greece
{courcou,mdramit,gstamoul}@aueb.gr
[3] Logica Management Consulting
Prof. W.H. Keesomlaan 14, 1180 AD Amstelveen, The Netherlands
chris.bannink@logica.com
[4] Internet Centre, Imperial College London
South Kensington Campus, 180 Queen's Gate, London SW7 2AZ, UK
t.rayna@imperial.ac.uk
[5] TEMEP, School of Engineering, Seoul National University
San56-1, Sillim-Dong, Gwanak-Gu, Seoul, South-Korea
jorn.altmann@acm.org

**Abstract.** This paper discusses the rationales for a Grid market and, in particular, the introduction of a market place for trading commoditized computing resources. The market place proposed makes computing resources from different providers substitutable through virtualization. This includes the definition of a spot and future market as well as the parameters that a market mechanism for computing resources should consider. The above market place is complemented by a set of value-added services (e.g. insurance against resource failures, capacity planning, resource quality assurance, stable price offering) that ensure quality for Grid users over time. The market place technology for all of the above services has been designed by the GridEcon project, contributing to a broader adoption of Grid technology and enabling a service-oriented knowledge utility environment.

**Keywords:** Commercial Grids, Grid Computing, Business Models, Grid Economics, Utility Computing, Market Mechanisms, Grid Market Place.

## 1 Introduction

The Grid, as we use it in this paper, is a system of interconnected, virtualized computing resources. Those computing resources can be located in a few data centers around the world (owned by large enterprises) or can be highly distributed (owned by many end-users or small and medium-sized enterprises). These virtualized hardware resources provide interfaces to execute software (e.g. applications or middleware). There are many vendors that offer different kind of hardware virtualization software

J. Altmann, D. Neumann, and T. Fahringer (Eds.): GECON 2008, LNCS 5206, pp. 185–196, 2008.

1415. After the buyer purchased the right to execute the resources, it can upload an application or, first, a Grid middleware application and, then, an application on top of it. In our definition of the Grid, we explicitly exclude software resources or information resources.

During the past years, a few approaches have been undertaken to offer Grid technology for commercial purposes: The most successful approach is the one of Amazon, namely Amazon EC2 1. Besides this utility computing approach, there are three hardware vendors (HP 2, IBM 3, SUN 4) and one more Internet company entered the market (Google 5) that provides similar utility computing services. Since only these few players are in the market, the market structure for utility computing is an oligopoly.

In order to break the oligopoly market structure, GridEcon, an EC-funded project 1011, offers market place technology that allows many (small) providers to offer their resources for sale. The effect of a market place for computing resources can be illustrated with the following example. If computing resources are scarce due to low supply, the market price for computing resources will be high. Enterprises requiring resources during high price periods will invest in additional equipment. These additional resources can then be externalized when they are not needed, thereby increasing the overall capacity available on the market. The income generated by selling resources in the Grid market will act as an incentive to sell spare capacity if a market place is available.

The GridEcon project designs the technology that is needed to create an efficient market place for trading commoditized computing resources. The market place allows every owner of computing resources to offer spare computing resources as a standardized virtual machine. The challenge is to design this standardized virtual machine, which can be traded on the market place easily and allows establishing a competitive market. The market mechanism used has been designed to be simple for participants to use, and also economically sound. The later is concerned with inducing the right economic incentives to participants and avoiding unwanted strategic behavior leading to market dominance by large players. The GridEcon project also designed a series of value-added services on top of the market place (e.g. insurance against resource failures, capacity planning, resource quality assurance, stable price offering), ensuring quality of the traded goods for Grid users. The market place technology and the value-added services contribute to a broader adoption of Grid technology and enable a service-oriented knowledge utility environment.

This paper is structured as follows: Section 2 describes the rational for a market place for computing resources. In Section 3, the requirements for a spot and future market are discussed in detail. This includes the definition of a spot and future market as well as the prerequisites for a market mechanism for computing resources. Section 4 concludes the paper.

## 2 Markets and Market Places for Computing Resources

In general, a market describes the entirety of all transactions between a buyer and a seller in all forms. This includes direct transactions between a buyer and a resource provider as well as the transactions performed using the market mechanism provided within the market place. A market for computing resources comes into existence if there is discontinuous demand and redundancy of computing resources.

A buyer of a (virtual) computing resource in our Grid market is an entity that purchases the right to execute an application on a computing resource. Similarly, a seller of a computing resource sells the right of using a computing resource for a certain period of time.

A market place is an environment, which supports buyers and sellers in carrying out their trading transactions between each other 13. The rules of interaction between the players in the market place are set through the market mechanism. The market place helps finding trading partners more easily by storing information centrally and by offering procedures to facilitate the matching between supply and demand. It also makes sure that fraudulent transactions do not happen.

## 2.1 Rationale for a Market for Computing Resources

In general, a market for utility computing will only work if one of the following conditions are met: (1) the pattern of individual demand for resources show spikes; (2) the units of computing power that are needed are smaller than the purchase of a computer could provide. In addition to this, all of the following conditions exist: (3) adequate technology for implementing utility computing (e.g. definitions of standardized interfaces); and (4) none-constraining regulations.

The demand spikes, which have been mentioned in condition (1), could be a consequence of the type of business that the company performs. The business itself might bring uncertainty about the need for computing resources. An example for such a business could be a company that creates animated movies. When a movie has to be rendered, the demand for computing resources is very high, otherwise very low. To cover this uncertainty, until now, companies had to over-provision their IT resources, which is expensive.

If condition (2) applies, then, without utility computing, most users would not be able to afford computing resources because of the high cost of ownership and their sporadic usage patterns. Utility computing allows them to get access to a very large quantity of computing resources for a short time on a per-usage basis.

Condition (3) is a necessity in order to be able to substitute a computing resource of one provider with a similar computing resource of another provider. Without this condition, the effort to connect to another provider might be too high. In order to efficiently use utility computing, technology must be available that helps the provider to organize its tremendous amount of computing resources in an efficient way. It must be guaranteed that the management cost for using the Grid is not higher than administrating resources that are owned.

Government regulations mentioned in condition (4) can have a huge impact on the organization and efficiency of providing computing resources. These regulation issues must address areas such as data storage location, taxation, and access rights to computing resources. In order to make utility computing successful, a prerequisite is a set of supporting regulations.

If a market for computing resources is not available, an alternative solution is overprovisioning. That is, a user should have a permanent computing capacity that can meet the demand peaks, which in light of condition (1) are much higher than the average. However, besides the fact that this would defeat the purpose of utility computing, this is beyond the budget of many users and it causes economic waste of resource.

Another alternative is not to meet all demand for processing resources, which consequently leads to missing an opportunity for getting additional revenues.

## 2.2  Economic Implications of a Grid Market Place

The rationale for a market place for computing goods is the current utility computing market. It is an oligopoly. The advantage of the few providers of utility computing (e.g. Amazon, HP, IBM, Google, Sun) in this oligopoly is that they have brand recognition and are trusted entities. However, these few providers offer their resources at a price higher than in a competitive market structure.

A market place provides an alternative to the existing oligopoly of utility computing providers in the market. If buyers and sellers accept (i.e. trust) the market place for executing their trades, it will increase the supply of computing resources in the market. Consequently, It will lower the price for buying computing resources in the market. Computing resources become even affordable to enterprises with low budget. All quality of service issues would be resolved by the market place. Similar to the case of stock exchanges, there could be more than one market place for trading computing resources.

The market place that we envision in GridEcon is an environment that allows SMEs to trade their resources. However, there may be also larger companies that will benefit from such a market place and its services 12. For instance, it might be that large companies offer their spare capacity at the market place.

Eventually, we expect to see new business models arise. These business models will make entities act as brokers of computing resources to other companies, or offer other value-added services, complementing the market services.

## 2.3  Services for the Market Place for Computing Resources

In order to attract customers to the market place and get the market place concept accepted by users, the market place must offer a set of services that makes the use of the market place service convenient, secure, and less risky. This is the focus of the GridEcon project. The services, which we identified to be necessary for a market place environment, can be classified into core services and value-added services. The market place provider offers the market mechanism service and additional core services. These services are described in detail within the next subsection. The value-added services do not have to be offered by the market place provider but can be offered by independent service providers instead. The capacity planning service and the insurance service are briefly described in subsection 2.3.2. We are convinced, only if these services are present, a market place for commoditized computing resources will work.

### 2.3.1  Core Services of the Market Place for Computing Resources

*Resource Redundancy*
The market place might provide resource redundancy in order to achieve service reliability even if a resource provider dishonors his commitment. The market place might also provide extra resources in order to increase the probability of a liquid market in times when demand is not matched by supply. In these cases, the market place deals

with the risk of resource unavailability and will ease the bootstrap of a new market place.

*Monitoring of Computing Resource Offers*

In order to assure quality of the good offered (i.e. to assure that customers are truthful in declaring their computing resource postings), the market place provider may probe randomly the offered, not leased computing resources by running benchmark programs on them. In case that the computing resources have been sold on the market place, the market place requests ratings from the buyer of the resources, using a reputation system. The information within the reputation system is private to the market place. It will be used to decide whether to allow resource providers to sell goods in the market place in the future.

*Security*

The market place has to provide a secure environment. All communications among the market participants and the market place has to be encrypted. The market place also has to ensure that no viruses are spread between machines that are traded on the market place. It also builds in protection mechanisms that blocks buyers from getting access to resources of the provider beyond the border of purchased resources.

*Simplicity*

The market place has to enable access to computing resources in a transparent and simple way, using an intuitive user interface. Any transaction on the market place has to be simple, including the integration of the resource into the existing IT infrastructure of the buyer.

*Anonymity*

The market place has to ensure anonymity of sellers and buyers. This service is necessary in order to hide the identity of large providers/sellers. If the identity cannot be hidden, buyers and sellers might circumvent the market place and make the market transaction directly. If anonymity exists, buyers and sellers cannot trade directly with each other and more competition is guaranteed on the market place. However, buyers must be given the option of bidding for resources that will be provided by a single provider.

*Standardization of Computing Resources*

In order to offer commoditized computing resources, the market place must be able to cope with different hardware types available at the sellers' premises. Therefore, the market place requires sellers to virtualize their hardware and to run "standardized" virtual machines with certain performance characteristics (as defined by the market place provider). The market place accepts only offers of computing resources that comply with those performance standards. This makes all hardware resources comparable and substitutable.

The standardized resources are classified in terms of quality (e.g. CPU speed, bandwidth, main memory, disk space). However, in order to abstract from the detailed specification of the performance characteristics of virtual machines, those "standardized" Grid resources are given abstract names such as GEUnit1, GEUnit2, or GEUnit3.

### 2.3.2 Value-Added Services to the Market Place

*Capacity Planning*

The acceptance of Grid computing also depends on how simple is it to make optimized planning decisions about computing resource purchases. Therefore, to achieve acceptance, a capacity planning service needs to be in place that supports market place participants (i.e. sellers and buyers) in their decision making process for selling and buying resources on the market place. The capacity planning service has also to help customers on how to optimally shape their demand and to find the appropriate resources for their applications. The precision of the prediction of the capacity planner is based on input parameters, such as the current load, the past load, the current demand, the market price of computing resources, and the existing computing capacity.

*Insurance Contracts*

Uncertainty about resource failures can also have an impact on the acceptance of the market place. Those market participants, who are risk averse, will not participate in the market place if there is uncertainty about resource reliability. To overcome this, an insurance service must be in place. The insurance service provides an insurance contract to buyers for occurrences of resource failures. In case of a failure of a resource, the insurance provider replaces the failed resource with a fault-free resource (in case it owns resources) or simply compensates the buyer with the amount of money specified in the insurance contract.

## 3 Requirements for a Spot and Future Trading

Stocks are traded in markets called stock exchanges (e.g. New York Stock Exchange). Though all exchanges used to require physical presence of traders and trading was performed by means of open outcry, most modern stock markets rely on automated electronic trading systems. For instance, NASDAQ is an electronic stock trading platform, where all trading is done by means of computer systems 6.

### 3.1 Definition of a Spot Market

In order to set the requirements for a spot market for computing resources, a general definition of spot markets and an example are given. In general, the spot market is a securities market, in which goods, both perishable and non-perishable, are sold for cash and delivered immediately or within a short period of time. Contracts sold on a spot market are also effective immediately. The spot market is also known as the "cash market" or "physical market." Purchases are settled in cash at the price set by the market, as opposed to the price at the time of delivery. An example of a spot market commodity that is regularly sold is crude oil. Crude Oil is sold at the current prices, and physically delivered later 7.

The emergence of electricity wholesale markets is the consequence of privatization of the electrical power production companies. Like computation service, electricity is difficult to store (in large quantities), has to be available on demand, and (unpredictable) demand spikes may occur. Countries that have chosen to operate wholesale electricity markets where power companies offer their electricity output to meet the customers demand, have a number of mechanism to choose from. One model, which is used by the PJM 16 uses central scheduler to balance supply and demand and computes the market price, while the losses over the transmission network are also taken into account: At each network node a "shadow price" is computed, which reflects the cost of providing an additional MWatt-hour at this node.

Another model is that of conducting auctions in various time scales, i.e. auctions for yearly and daily provision of power, with additional spot market that resolves the need for accommodating short-term demand spikes. For example, this model is used by the European Energy Exchange (EEX) 17.

Finally, the Supply Function Equilibria has also been under investigation as the market mechanism of the power grids. It is also worth noting that there are several cases where regulators have intervened due to market failure, with the California market being the most prominent example 89.

## 3.2  Spot Market for Computing Resources

The spot market for computing resources also enables the trading of computing resources "as soon as possible". It employs a bid and ask mechanism (i.e. a stock market-like double auction mechanism) that enables the trading of computational power. The underlying principle for this mechanism is that of a standard spot market: All parties publicly announce the maximum price they are willing to buy for and the minimum price they are willing to sell for. The spot bids (respectively asks) are put in the spot queue for bids (respectively asks). Matters are more complicated for our system's spot market than in standard spot markets of storable commodities, since this good is non-storable and that the resource provisioning has to be transparent to the buyer.

## 3.3  Future Market for Computing Resources

The futures market for computing resources is actually a directory service containing the offers (respectively requests) for resources that are made available (respectively demanded) in a certain time interval. This index of offers and requests is searchable and visible to both bidders and providers. This market for futures complements the spot market. The futures and derivatives are contracts that denote the obligation of a buyer (respectively seller) to buy (respectively sell) at a certain agreed price.

## 3.4  Requirements for a Market Mechanism for Trading Computing Resources

After introducing briefly the spot and futures market for computing resources, we proceed to provide additional details regarding the unit that is to be traded in these markets (i.e. unit of trade), the format of spot market bids/asks and the futures market requests/offers, the matching algorithm to be adopted, and, finally, how bids and asks are routed in this system.

### 3.4.1  Unit of Trade

Prior to proceeding with the presentation of the GridEcon market mechanism, we define the unit that is to be traded in the Grid market place. Obviously, the unit must be suitable for the types of Grid applications currently existing or emerging. Computing resource providers offer different types of virtual machines (VMs) for leasing. It is expected that these resources be offered for a minimum desirable price and for a certain time duration within a specific time interval, depending on the providers' supply constraints. An assumption of our model for both the spot and the futures market throughout the paper is that time is discretized in time slots. Note that a virtual machine does not just correspond to a certain computational speed but rather to an entire configuration. The unit of trade, i.e. the VM, is defined through the CPU speed, the size of the main memory, and the size of the harddrive.

Depending on the nature of the tasks that consumers may wish to execute, their demand can be expressed in a multitude of ways. A general type of contract is specified by means of the number of VMs and the time duration. For instance, a company's Web server leases Grid resources when it is critically loaded. This type of consumer need can also be graphically depicted by means of a rectangle (see Fig. 1).

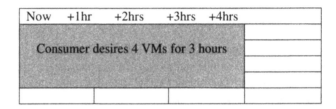

**Fig. 1.** A consumer's demand for 4 VMs over 3 hours is depicted as a rectangle

The height of the rectangle denotes the number of virtual machines required at any time of the interval, while the width of the rectangle denotes the amount of time for which these machines are needed.

Another type of contract could be specified by means of computational volume, i.e. a total number of VMs must be made available up to a maximum deadline constraint, so that a certain computationally intensive task can be executed in time. As opposed to the previous case, only the total quantity of computational power is of interest, while the rate of computation provided at the various time epochs is not. This could be the case for data parallel applications. In this case, the consumer needs do no longer correspond to rectangles but rather to areas of rectangles, possibly with a maximum width constraint (i.e. deadline). Since this type of contract can be also expressed (with some effort on the consumer side) in the market place through the earlier type of contract, we will focus on the earlier contract type.

### 3.4.2  Format of the Bid/Ask

A bid in our system describes the resources required by the buyer. The resources are specified according to:

(1)  The type of resource (VM) required,
(2)  The quantity of resources (the number of VMs) required,
(3)  The start time of the interval for using the resources (VM),
(4)  The time duration of using the resources,
(5)  The price expressed in €/min/unit, and
(6)  The time limit until which the bid is valid. If the time limit is reached without the bid being matched, the bid is removed from the system.

In order to keep the definition of the bid as general and flexible as possible, instead of allowing only fixed values for the number of VMs and the time duration, we allow that the bid can specify whether these constraint values should be met with equality or ≤ or ≥. Our system also considers two additional constraints regarding the total expenditure and the total volume of computation (see the "Rectangle" column in Table 1). Therefore, since each bid is associated with a set of relation constraints, this allows a richer ontology of bids. A meaningful subset of this ontology is depicted in Table 1.

**Table 1.** Meaningful combinations of constraints for bids

| Constraints: | Number of VMs | Time Duration | Total Expenditure | Rectangle |
|---|---|---|---|---|
| | = | = | Redundant | Redundant |
| **Relations:** | ≤ | ≤ | Optional | Required |
| | ≥ | ≥ | Required | Redundant |

There are two types of bids in our system, namely future and spot bids. Future bids (or equivalently requests) are the bids for which the start and end times are fixed. For instance, a request could be: "User X bids for 5 VMs of type A to be used for 5 hrs, starting at time 13:00, with price 0.5 €/min/unit". As opposed to requests, spot bids demand to utilize resources as soon as they are available. Spot bids are distinguished from requests by setting the start time to a specific value (e.g. 0) and by the fact that the start time and the end time are continuously moving as time passes. This is performed as long as the bid has not been matched (and up to the maximum time allowed by the expiry of the bid). For instance, a spot bid is: "User X bids for 5 VMs of type A to be used for 5 hrs, starting at time 0, with bid price 0.5 €/min/unit, and time limit 20:00". In this example, the bid could be executed with a start time of 20:00 the latest.

An ask in our system describes the resources offered, which are specified by the following five parameters:

(1) The type of resources (i.e. VM) offered,
(2) The quantity of resources (i.e. number of VMs) offered,
(3) The start time and the end time of the interval when the resources are available,
(4) The price, expressed in €/min/unit, and
(5) The time limit for which the ask is valid (the expiration time of the offer). That means, the ask will be removed from the system after this time limit.

Similar to bids, there are also two types of asks, namely future and spot asks. Future asks (or equivalently offers) are those for which the start time and the end time are fixed instants in the future. For offers, the end time equals the start time plus the duration, while the time limit also has the same value by default. For instance, an offer looks like: "Provider Y offers for leasing 2 VMs of type A to be used for 8 hrs, starting at time 15:00, with a price of 0.2 €/min/unit". On the contrary, spot asks offer resources that can be utilized as soon as there is demand for them. Such asks are distinguished from offers by setting the start time to a specific value (e.g. 0). Their main difference to offers is the fact that the start time and end time of asks are continuously moving as time passes.

This continues as long as the ask is not matched (up to the maximum time allowed by the expiry of the ask). Therefore, spot asks are more flexible than offers. They offer service of a certain duration over a larger time interval. For instance, a spot ask is: "Provider Y offers 2 VMs of type A to be used for 3 hrs, starting at time 0, with an ask price of 0.2 €/min/unit, and a time limit of 19:00".

### 3.4.3 Matching Algorithm

The matching algorithm defines how a bid (respectively request) in the spot market (respectively futures market) is matched by a set of asks (respectively offers). For simplicity reasons, it suffices to adopt a matching algorithm that passes the queues once. In our presentation below, we focus on the spot market. Indeed, the matching algorithm in the futures market is much simpler than that of the spot queue, since the time span of all requests and offers is fully specified, i.e. their start time and end time are decided upon their submission and cannot be changed subsequently, as opposed to spot bids/asks.

Trading in the spot market is performed by means of a continuous double auction mechanism. This is an extension of the standard spot market mechanism. Similarly to the standard mechanism, the spot bids and asks submitted by traders are placed in the *bid queue* and the *ask queue* respectively. Each queue is ordered according to the price and time of submission, with the *bid* queue being sorted in *decreasing* order of price, and the *ask* queue being sorted in *increasing* order of price. If two or more orders at the same price appear in a spot queue, then they are entered by time with older orders appearing ahead of newer orders. An order remains in the queue until it is removed by the system due to order expiration, removal by the user, or if a matching had occurred.

Moreover, the matching algorithm takes into account that spot asks may start providing resources at some later time than now, due to the flexibility associated with the provision of resources. Note that we refrain from adopting a combinatorial approach due to the high computational complexity.

The matching algorithm for the spot offers is as follows: It initially computes the candidate matches to an ask by means of creating a matrix. Each column of the matrix corresponds to a time slot (i.e. the time interval in which service can be provided). Each row corresponds to a provider that can offer service now, with the cheapest being on the top row. A cell of the matrix is marked if the provider can offer computing resources during this specific time slot.

Then, the algorithm attempts to perform a probabilistic matching. In particular, the algorithm starts with the cheapest ask and randomly fills some time slots of bids, so that the provider's resource availability becomes zero. This means the cheapest ask is fully utilized. It then proceeds with the next cheapest ask and does the same. Note, after the second step, there might be slots allocated to two candidate providers. For these slots, each provider is assigned a probability of moving from this slot. A provider is moved to an empty slot according to a transition probability, which is larger for providers of this slot if they could serve a target slot where the number of providers that could serve the target slot is small.

The algorithm terminates when all the slots are assigned to some provider and thus a match is found. In case there are slots where there is no provider serving it, while there are not any slots with more than one provider, the algorithm has failed to compute a match. Due to the fact that we use a probabilistic matching algorithm, the algorithm can be repeated for a maximum pre-specified number of times until it terminates. If it fails, then it attempts to compute a match for the next time slot, i.e. for the time interval [Now + 1 slot, Now + 1 slot + service duration]. This is repeated until a match is indeed found or the algorithm fails for all time slots (i.e. entire duration) for which the bid is valid.

### 3.4.4 Routing of Bids and Asks

It is the responsibility of the matching module to be invoked periodically, prior to the beginning of the next slot, in order to compute matches and remove expired bids and asks from the bid/ask queue of the spot market and requests and offers from the futures directory of the futures market. The results of the matching procedure are subsequently passed to the scheduler, the reservation system of the provider, and the accounting system of the market place.

## 4  Conclusion and Discussion

In this paper, we discussed the rationale for a Grid market for leasing computing resources as well as the relevant key requirements. The GridEcon market place has one major advantage over existing utility computing services (e.g. Amazon's EC2 service, Sun, HP, and IBM). It allows companies not only to access computing resources, but also to sell spare computing resources. However, in the GridEcon market place, not all providers need also to be consumers and vice versa. Furthermore, the low market power of the participant of the Grid market ensures that the price, though flexible, remains highly competitive. Therefore, not considering market lock-in (i.e. high switching cost), network externalities, or anti-competitive behavior of market leaders, a group of many small computing resource providers (i.e. any company with spare computing resources) could compete with IBM, Google, and Amazon.

The market place for computing resources has certain similarities to the electricity market place. Indeed, since the market price is directly related to demand and supply, it will provide incentives for companies to adapt their usage strategies (e.g. buy more and own less computing power; compute during the night only). Moreover, companies will adjust their in-house computing usage to the competitive market price. Since the market place allows reselling resources that have been purchased, a company can buy resources on the market for a longer time period and resell those resources that are not needed at a shorter time scale.

Finally, the Grid market opens opportunities for a wide range of services (such as insurances, and capacity planning). Those value-added services on top of the market place will provide functionality that addresses certain needs of users. Such additional services may also be developed in some of the aforementioned existing utility computing services. However, it is likely that these services will be developed in such a way that it ultimately increases the profit of the provider, which is of course detrimental to buyers of the computing resources.

**Acknowledgement.** This work has been funded by the European Commission within the context of the FP6 Project GridEcon, Grid Economics and Business Models, (FP6-2005-IST5-033634).

# References

1. Amazon, Amazon Elastic Compute Cloud (Amazon EC2) (June (2008), `http://www.amazon.com/gp/browse.html?node=201590011`
2. HP, Utility Computing Services (June 2008), `http://h20338.www2.hp.com/enterprise/cache/308072-0-0-0-121.html`
3. IBM, IBM E-Business On-Demand (June 2008), `http://www128.ibm.com/developerworks/ibm/library/i-ebodov/index.html`
4. Sun Grid (June 2008), `http://www.sun.com/service/sungrid/index.jsp`
5. Google, App. Engine (June 2008), `http://code.google.com/appengine/`
6. NASDAQ Stock Market (June 2008), `http://www.nasdaq.com`
7. International Monetary Fund (May 2008), `http://www.imf.org/external/np/pp/eng/2005/092105o.htm`
8. Joskow, P.L.: Restructuring, Competition and Regulatory Reform in the U.S. Electricity Sector. Journal of Economic Perspectives 11(3), 119–138 (1997)
9. Dekrajangpetch, S., Sheble, G.B.: Structures and Formulations for Electric Power Auctions. In: Electric Power Systems Research, vol. 54, pp. 159–167. Elsevier, Amsterdam (2000)
10. GridEcon (June 2008), `http://www.gridecon.eu`
11. Altmann, J., Courboubetis, C., Darlington, J., Cohen, J.: GridEcon – The Economic-Enhanced Next-Generation Internet. In: Veit, D.J., Altmann, J. (eds.) GECON 2007. LNCS, vol. 4685, pp. 188–193. Springer, Heidelberg (2007)
12. Techcrunch (May 2008), `http://www.techcrunch.com/2008/04/21/who-are-the-biggest-users-of-amazon-web-services-its-not-startups/`
13. Altmann, J., Ion, M., Mohammed, A.A.B.: Taxonomy of Grid Business Models. In: Veit, D.J., Altmann, J. (eds.) GECON 2007. LNCS, vol. 4685, pp. 29–43. Springer, Heidelberg (2007)
14. XenSource, Inc.(2008), `http://xen.org`
15. VMware, Inc (2008), `http://www.vmware.com/`
16. P.J.M. (June (2008), `http://www.pjm.com/contributions/pjm-manuals/pdf/m04.pdf`
17. European Energy Exchange (June (2008), `http://www.eex.com/en/document/32353`

# Grid4All: Open Market Places
# for Democratic Grids

Ruby Krishnaswamy[1], Leandro Navarro[2], René Brunner[2],
Xavier León[2], and Xavier Vilajosana[3]

[1] France Telecom R&D, France
ruby.krishnaswamy@orange-ftgroup.com
[2] Computer Architecture Department, Polytechnic University of Catalonia, Spain
{leandro,rbrunner,xleon}@ac.upc.edu
[3] Universitat Oberta de Catalunya, Spain
xvilajos@uoc.edu

**Abstract.** The Grid4All project is focused on the provision of the benefits and opportunities of Grids for everyone, including small organizations
such as schools, families, non-governmental organizations, or small businesses. This involves multiple relevant and related aspects despite the
scale of the global system: (i) self-management of applications as they
adapt to environmental changes, (ii) the complexity of developing and
using applications in that situation by multiple users, (iii) and the need
to organize, govern, and regulate the community. Grid4All[1] promotes the
concept of a democratic Grid, virtual organizations and self-management
systems, based on decentralized overlays. Thereby, the providers offer resources and services either for a shared-interest within a virtual organization (pooling) or for an open market across virtual organizations. These
two models of distributing resources that co-exist locally, contribute to
achieve global regulation. We propose an architecture according to these
ideas, which are inspired by real-world cases, which include a collection
of data sharing and execution services, used by collaborative applications.

**Keywords:** Economic-aware Grid Application, Markets and Market
Mechanisms for the Grid, Democratic Grid, Large-scale Grid Market,
Virtual Organizations.

## 1 Introduction

The idea of a public utility for digital data and computing is a natural evolution
beyond the widespread accessibility of Internet connections with higher capacity
and reliability to support the need for social interaction, sharing, and working
together. This model apply that to rent or share competitively computational
services is easier than having to acquire and maintain hardware and applications in advance. Therefore, The Grid or The Cloud opens an opportunity not

---

[1] More information at: http://www.grid4all.eu/

J. Altmann, D. Neumann, and T. Fahringer (Eds.): GECON 2008, LNCS 5206, pp. 197–207, 2008.

only to build a "virtual supercomputer", necessary to tackle scientific or industrial grand challenges, but also an opportunity for citizens, for the rest of us, to democratize this distributed computing global network in the sense of opening up participation by lowering the cost, facilitating the usage, supporting collaboration, and data sharing, increasing the flexibility of computing resources to adapt to demand, facilitating the transparency and control on how services and resources are shared and used.

There is an huge potential for empowering many people or small organizations equipped with low-performance PCs connected to the Internet as shown by many recent Internet-based services and applications such as Google Search, Yahoo Mail, SETI@Home, Flickr, and Google Docs. Moreover, commercially available platforms such as Amazon Web Services, SUN's Network.com, and Google Application Engine are expected to emerge.

The Grid4All project promotes the concept of a democratic Grid, accessible to modest groups of end-users such as schools, families, non-governmental organizations (NGO), or small businesses. It enables to put together people and computing resources to form Virtual Organizations (VO), a virtual collection of users or institutions that pool their resources into a single virtual administrative domain for a common purpose. Virtual Organizations can also trade resources among different VO on a decentralized market place.

Therefore, our use cases involve schools, learning institutions, families, and small businesses. Our scenarios do not only include distributed execution of bag-of-tasks computing-intensive applications, but they are also oriented towards facilitating collaborative work. In the area of data services, compared to previous Grids, the Grid4All architecture provides with a minimal administration enhanced support for content sharing and collaboration within groups. Semantic search and ontologies are used to locate and select among diverse resources and services.

The objective of this paper is to present the opportunity, the challenges, and the design for a Grid for domestic users or small organizations and how a scalable market place for resources is a key enabler. The rest of the paper starts describing an educational VO as one typical scenario. Based on the requirements it presents the Grid4All architecture. The corresponding Grid4All infrastructure is based on a component model supporting a number of properties required in a democratic Grid: usability, self-administration, dynamic behaviors, and security. We present several novel or improved collaborative applications that rely on and leverage self-managed software components and services. Furthermore, they apply network-wide shared data services for storage with support for flexible concurrent modification of application data and collaborative task execution.

## 2   Motivating Scenario

Among multiple scenarios for modest groups of people including schools, families, NGOs, or small businesses, we present in this section an educational scenario for remote collaborative learning tasks that shares many aspects with other cooperative work activities within the focus of this work. Our scenario takes its inspiration from iEARN, the International Educational, and Research Network [3]. iEARN is a world-wide educational network of people (young students, teachers, and families), who participate in diverse collaborative educational projects within regional or world-wide collaboration networks.

This scenario involves a network of schools engaged in collaborative activities. A collaboration consists typically of a course or a course project. It may involve students and instructors from multiple sites, spanning different departments, schools, countries, time zones or cultures. The member institutions may be schools at any educational level (primary, secondary or university). Participants work either from home or at their school.

A collaborative network pools resources from different providers for its activities. The providers include the schools, the students, the parents, and outside partners. The resources may be physical or virtual and include computational, storage, and other resources. Educational institutions already rely on specific digital tools, for instance to consult external experts, to perform digital experiments, and simulations, to communicate with other students, and to work remotely. These tools should be available in the collaboration and should be made aware of the collaboration context.

Collaborative work tools should allow a group of users (e.g., a class, or a set of instructors from different schools), to share computational or storage resources, to share and modify content together (e.g., to author a document collaboratively), and to make common decisions. However, the system must ensure that users access resources or information only if authorized.

Collaborative groups are fluid, short-lived or long-lived, and the membership of a group changes over the time. Groups are likely to overlap: some users will belong to several groups; the same content could be shared in different groups. However, content belonging to a group should be isolated from outside access. Content must be persistent and modifiable (subject to authorization).

Existing infrastructures of schools may vary significantly as it changes the demand imposed by users on it. For instance, one laptop per child (OLPC) based projects [6] rely on an ad-hoc network of personal computers without dedicated servers. In contrary, PlanetLab [7] consists of shared servers in a P2P manner but provides only best-effort quality service. Grid5000 [2] is similar but is a more stable environment with resource reservation.

Despite the differences, networks and computers usually remain unreliable given the usual lack of technical capacity to properly manage systems. Therefore, churn (computers connect and disconnect without notice), failures, and service degradation are arbitrarily frequent.

## 3   Main Requirements

The main challenges in this setting are:

- The work environment is dynamic and unpredictable because participants come and go. The load varies: just before an exam deadline, many students run simultaneously resource-intensive activities. Computing resources can fail. Nonetheless, the system should remain manageable, in order to ensure some level of dependability. For instance, a class project should not miss its deadline because of a glitch in the system. Otherwise, schools will be reluctant to use it.

- The responsiveness of the system should not degrade despite partial failures, network problems, and disconnected-mode work.
- The system must appear simple to its users and manual administration cost must be very low. The system should adapt automatically to problems, while collaboration should not tax the schools (usually very limited) support staff.
- Collaboration among distributed partners requires computer support. In that case, activities in a distributed school environment are not viable face-to-face (at the same place) and given the number and diversity of participants, there is need to use applications to support sharing, coordination and collaboration.
- A collaboration incorporates rules and policies. For instance the members may need to abide to predefined rules for that community, or to make contributions, either monetary or in kind (e.g., computational resources), and system may need to support or enforce this.
- Participants may move to multiple locations: in the school, at home, in a library, on the move or at work in other cities or countries elsewhere in the world.
- Participants must be able to work remotely in disconnected mode. It is not reasonable to expect that all participants are connected all the time.

# 4    A Democratic Grid Architecture

To overcome these challenges, the Grid4All architecture is based on the concept of virtual organization and it uses a component framework, which provides autonomic management mechanisms.

**Virtual Organizations.** A Virtual Organization (VO) consists of a set of resources and a set of users. Both resources and users may belong to different institutions; thus these sets may have cross institutional and administrative boundaries. The VO concept combines two related, but relatively orthogonal sets of mechanisms:

- Grouping and virtualisation of a set of resources (objects) that we call a virtual resource.
- Grouping and naming a set of users (subjects) that we call a user group.

The VO management system and the security infrastructure constitute one link between these two sets of concepts. The VO management system maintains the security associations between user groups and virtual resources, as prescribed by the VOs security policy. After a user executes an operation on a resource, the security infrastructure ensures that the operation is permitted according to the relevant policy.

The other link between the two concepts of virtual resources and users is that the VO management system also monitors users to ensure that they fulfil their obligations as stipulated by the appropriate policy. Indeed, the placement of both users and virtual resources within the VO is motivated by the two-way interaction with the VO management system indirectly monitoring both virtual resources and users.

**Component Framework.** Components are an effective approach for building and managing complex software systems. In this approach, all system elements are constructed or wrapped as components and management involves using primitives of the underlying component model (e.g., setting properties of components). We have adopted a component model that extends Fractal, a general and reflective component model intended for building dynamically reconfigurable systems, with remotely accessible components and over different machines distributed entities. The model adds composite bindings that support remote method invocation and group communication. This is particularly useful for building decentralized, fault-tolerant applications. Group bindings enable invocations to be delivered either to all group members (one-to-all style) or to any, randomly-chosen group member (one-to-any style).

**Autonomic Management.** The Grid4All scenario is very dynamic: members and resources can be constantly changing (we call this churn) as individual computers can join and leave continuously as members go off-line and on-line. Over the time, the total amount of available resources and members also changes; we call this evolution.

Within the democratic Grid, virtual organization will be created, grow, shrink, and die off as the members interest into the collaboration change. New applications and services will be added to an existing VO. Some VOs will prove popular, some will not. The democratic Grid evolves and changes at a high rate. Churn rates are expected to be high as different populations of user pools exist and share their resources.

Autonomic computing aims to automate system administration and management. By taking humans out of the loop, labour costs decrease, response to problems is faster and the availability improves. Grid4All takes the control loop approach to autonomic management. High-level management policies are expressed in a high-level language. These are translated into rules for the management runtime.

The runtime monitors the system and triggers events, which execute the associated rules. For instance, when a machine crashes, other interested machines receive the corresponding events and can recover.

The elements of the overall architecture of Grid4All VOs are presented in Figure 1. By an analogy with Foster et al.s decomposition of Grid systems [1], the Grid4All VO architecture can be decomposed as follows, from bottom to top:

The **Fabric** includes computers, storage capacities, files, application binaries and sources as well as other basic resources, which are provided to the VO by its

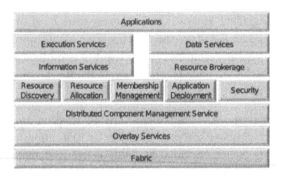

**Fig. 1.** Overall Grid4All architecture

members. In the following, the term resource without further qualification refers to a fabric resource.

The Core VO Support Architecture comprises the following basic services:

- Overlay Services deal with connectivity of VO resources and elements. Participation of nodes (i.e., computers) form a logical network is called an overlay. We use structured overlay networks because of their inherent self-management properties and scalability. These services provide basic naming, communication, and data storage services that are used by upper layer services.
- The Distributed Component Management Service (DCMS) supports distributed VO-aware self-* services. DCMS allows the application developer to program self-* functionality of component-based services. In the following, we refer to the latter as self-* code. DCMS is overlay-based and it delegates resource discovery and allocation to the VO management services.
- The VO Management Services include Resource Discovery and Allocation, Membership Management, Application Deployment, and Security services. VO Management Services maintain information about VO users and decide on sharing of VO resources between VO users. It also provides the basic mechanism to start new services within the VO. VO Management Services are overlay-based.

The **Information Service** provides match-making between semantic service descriptions and client requirements.

The **Resource Brokering Service** facilitates interaction between VOs. This service enables applications and VOs to find external resources as they need them. The brokering facility is a resource market place where providers and consumers can meet and trade Grid resources.

Our support for collaborative and federative VOs focuses on data services for sharing storage capacity and content, i.e., a **VO-oriented File System (VOFS)**, a semantic consistency middleware **Telex**, and an **Execution Service** for deploying computation tasks, which are based on a bag-of-tasks model.

Supporting flexible and dynamic VOs requires a novel approach to information sharing. The Grid4All data storage architecture provides three different levels of flexibility. (i) VO users can pool disk space over the network: either offered to each other from their own disks, or acquired on an open market. (ii) A VO has an associated virtual file system, a flexible federation of file names and file contents, exposed by VO users to one another. (iii) A semantic middleware layer allows users to update shared data in a flexible manner. Users may share content in either on-line or off-line mode; the semantic store resolves conflicting updates according to data semantics.

Applications use the lower layers, primarily to obtain computation, storage, and content resources but also to achieve self-* behavior.

## 5   Resource Allocation for Democratic Grids

Applications require resources model computational and storage elements to execute. The available resources on a VO have to be managed internally but they can be also be brokered with other VO at the market place. This adds another dimension to the adaptability of VO to a changing demand or changing conditions of resources beyond the incorporation of additional participants. Resource allocation is a key issue in this dynamic environment that intends to self-manage. This issue permeates mostly all services at all levels and even end-user applications. We need to distinguish between resource management (how resources are contributed and then used) and resource brokerage (when and how resources are offered and obtained from the market place).

### 5.1   Resource Management

The resource management service enables members to contribute resources to the VO and to discover and allocate VO resources. In the context of this service, a resource is a share of computation and storage capacity that supports component deployment; a component is deployed on a single resource.

Contributing resources involves configuring and adding the local Grid4All container or a remote container to the VO. Resource discovery relies on specifying requirements on resource properties; e.g., specifying a minimum CPU speed or memory size. Resource allocation allows reserving discovered resources or parts thereof. Reserving a part of a resource creates a new resource with capacity deducted from the original resource. The service includes support for publishing resource discovery events (e.g., a new resource has joined) and resource parameter change events (e.g., the CPU load of a specific resource has changed). Resource management is used in a VO to regulate the resource usage between services prioritizing based on a policy upon research scarcity.

### 5.2   Resource Brokerage

Brokering concerns arbitration and allocation of Grid resources to virtual organizations. VOs lease resources on need by negotiating at the resource market place.

The Grid4All model of virtual organizations is similar to peer-to-peer networked applications. Members of a VO use resources that belong to the VO. In Grid4All we allow VOs to incorporate resources from non-members. Such resources are expected to be leased from resource brokers that select and match of consumers and suppliers.

The motivation is to adapt to fluctuations in supply and demand with mechanisms to arbitrate which requests for resources should be satisfied and by whom. Priority based, proportional sharing allocations are mechanisms that are useful when the different consumers (applications or users requiring resources) belong to the same organization. In that case, consumers may be prioritized or allocated to shares. This is not the case if applications and users from multiple independent VOs compete for resources. Market based brokering with pricing mechanisms provide fair arbitration, gives incentives and is decentralized.

The minimal GRIMP (Grid4All Market Place) addresses:

- Selection of suitable resources.
- Decentralized feedback from market to aid traders in their negotiation.
- Mechanisms to allocate and establish prices.
- Protocol to establish agreements between consumers and provider.

The resource brokering problem is decomposed into multiple replaceable and extensible components. This allows different scenarios to use a subset of these services to realize their objectives. The platform provides tools that allow traders (consumers and providers) and mediating agents to create ad-hoc auction markets, where they can negotiate with resources. Divergence of prices and hot-spots are risks for market places with simultaneous auctions. For that reason, the GRIMP provides a decentralized publish/subscribe-based information service. This allows trading agents to react to market situations by publishing and subscribing to aggregated (summarized) global information (such as average prices) of the market place. The minimal platform consists of tool-kits and basic services and may be extended to provide added-value, higher-level brokerage, and mediating services. The market-place itself will use the VO run-time services for deployment, monitoring, and other self-management.

### 5.3   Services and Functionality

**Auction Servers.** Its service is accessed through a common market interface. Participants send bids specifying the resources, quantities, time constraints, and budget. The auction determines allocations and the transaction prices. Behind a unique facet (interface), auction servers may implement different mechanisms (rules and policies for bidding, price and allocation determination). The server is designed as a set of Fractal components that separate economic and system concerns. The server is designed as a tool-kit, within which specific allocation and pricing policies and rules may be plugged in. Auction servers are advertised at the Semantic Information System (SIS) which may be queried by traders to obtain candidate lists of active auction markets.

Within this framework two proof-of-concept economic mechanisms have been implemented:

- K-pricing double auction: This mechanism is used to acquire storage resources to satisfy the scenario described in Section 2. This mechanism is computationally efficient for the trading of a resource type amongst multiple consumers and providers.
- Combinatorial auction: This mechanism allows allocation of bundles of computational and storage resources.

**Market Factory.** This is a repository service provided by the market place and offers two sets of interfaces:

- To designers and developers to register implementations for a new type of auction mechanism.
- A mechanism for the selection allows the traders (consumers and providers) to choose a specific auction format and request instantiation of a new auction server.

**Market Information Service.** Obtaining synthetic and summarized information is important in a decentralized market place with a large number of participants and where multiple auctions are executed simultaneously. Examples for such aggregated information are average prices and average demand. This service collects, routes, aggregates, summaries, and delivers global information in a scalable manner to any market participant.

**Currency Management Service.** This is a decentralized account and banking service, which provides basic functions to create accounts and transfer funds between accounts. Technically, it implements a transactional mechanism on top of a DHT to implement decentralized accounts.

## 5.4   Properties

The GRIMP architecture presents the following non-functional capabilities to address the requirements:

**Scalability and Reliability.** The federated architecture allows the market place to scale to thousands of users. Therefore, it has to support as many auction servers as required and to provide a global information system:

- Auction servers are created spontaneously upon need and mechanisms with appropriate properties (computational complexity, efficiency) can be chosen on demand.
- The Market Information Service (MIS) collects, aggregates, summarizes, and delivers in a large-scale the global information of the market. This system allows the participants to be aware and to react on changes of the global market.

**Configurability.** In an open environment, the needed type of applications and resources cannot be fixed. Support for multiple auction mechanisms and tools to select appropriate mechanisms renders the market place configurable. As an example, an application requires both computational and storage resources and it requires combinatorial auctions. An auction mechanisms capable of trading single items is sufficient for an application requiring only a single type of resource (computations or storage).

The architecture based on the Fractal component model presents the advantage of being a single coherent solution to address design, deployment, configuration, and assembly.

# 6    Related and Future Work

There are systems that focus on some aspect of the problem. For instance Tycoon [5] uses auctions and a centralized bank to handle currency circulation. Shirako [4] is based on the idea that different entities, service managers, and brokers trade resource leases to self-manage applications. The SORMA project [8] designs a centralized market, sharing the idea of the Market Information Service, but without a Currency Management as payments are directly applied in real currency. In contrast, Grid4All is proposing a collection of integrated services and an implementation of that architecture to support collaborative, scalable, and adaptable Grid computing applications for everyone based on groups (virtual organizations). This work internally together and share resources for self-interest but they can also trade resources and eventually services across virtual organizations.

Although initial evaluation of each market mechanisms is promising, further work is required to include a wider range of situations. Particularly, the evaluation of the combined mechanisms is important for the regulation effect: auctions, market information, and currency. Another aspect to evaluate is the usefulness of market combinations with a pool of resources. Finally, it is also an open issue how to handle the Self-management of markets: the automatic and dynamic deployment of markets.

# 7    Conclusions

The Grid4All project presents an integrated vision, architecture, middleware, and applications of a public and large-scale Grid for everyone. Furthermore, the proposed market framework supports collaboration among groups of people (VO). On one side, the participants can interact and share work and computing resources among them. On the other side, they can trade resources with other groups. This public Grid self-adapts to the dynamics of the on-line world, which connects networks, computers, and people, who join and leave the community. Therefore, the system needs to self-manage to support applications with varying loads and resource needs.

The market place is a key element as it contains a collection of integrated resource brokerage mechanisms for the global and local regulation across virtual organizations. Limited experiments, which are based on simulations, show that the system has an equitable behavior in the allocation of resources among a range of similar or dissimilar participants. The ongoing development of end-user-oriented, prototyped applications over the Grid4All middleware show how the details of resource allocation and self-management can be partially abstracted out from application developers. Mainly, supporting services, which can gather automatically more resources from the VO and even push them to the VO, can acquire additional resources from the market place. Early results of the evaluation show the need for an integrated approach. Particularly, they show how market places can regulate resource allocation globally with the help from market aware services and self-managing services.

**Acknowledgments.** This work would not be possible without the contributions from the members of the Grid4All project. This work has been partially supported by the EU FP6-2005-IST-5 034567, and the Spanish Ministry of Education with grant P2PGrid TIN2007-68050-C03-01.

# References

1. Foster, I., Kesselman, C., Tuecke, S.: The anatomy of the grid: Enabling scalable virtual organizations. Int. J. High Perform. Comput. Appl. 15(3), 200–222 (2001)
2. Grid5000 project (Page visit May 2008), http://www.grid5000.fr
3. International educational and research network (iEARN) (Page visit (May 2008), http://www.iearn.org
4. Irwin, D., Chase, J., Grit, L., Yumerefendi, A., Becker, D., Yocum, K.G.: Sharing networked resources with brokered leases. In: Proceedings of the Annual Conference on USENIX 2006 Annual Technical Conference, Boston, MA, p. 18 (2006)
5. Lai, K., Rasmusson, L., Adar, E., Zhang, L., Huberman, B.A.: Tycoon: An implementation of a distributed, market-based resource allocation system. Multiagent Grid Syst. 1(3), 169–182 (2005)
6. One laptop per child (OLPC) (Page visit 2008), http://www.laptop.org/
7. PlanetLab, an open platform for developing, deploying, and accessing planetary-scale services (Page visit May 2008), http://www.planet-lab.org/
8. SORMA - Self-Organizing ICT Resource Management (Page visit 2008), http://www.sorma-project.org
9. Zanikolas, S., Sakellariou, R.: A taxonomy of grid monitoring systems. Future Generation Computer Systems 21(1), 163–188 (2005)

# The German Grid Initiative: A Uniform Accounting Service in Multiple Middleware Environments

Jan Wiebelitz[1], Stefano Dal Pra[2], Wolfgang Müller[1],
and Gabriele von Voigt[1]

[1]Regional Computing Center for Lower Saxony, Leibniz Universität Hannover,
Schloßwender Strasse 5, 30159 Hannover, Germany
{wiebelitz,wmueller,vonvoigt}@rrzn.uni-hannover.de

[2]Istituto Nazionale di Fisica Nucleare (INFN), Sez. di Pavola,
Via Marzolo 8, 35131 Padova, Italy
stefano.dalpra@pd.infn.it

**Abstract.** The development of business models is of great importance
for the German Grid inititive D-Grid, which is trying to establish a
sustainable and self-financing long-term operating e-science infrastructure all over Germany. To guarantee the continuity and future growth
of this infrastructure it is necessary to become independent of limited
public funding and achieve the required revenues by chargeable services,
support and developments. The business model of the German Grid Support Organization comprises the development, provision and support of
generic services for the usage by all Grid communities within D-Grid.
The realization of these business models is based on the development of
a comprehensive accounting service that enables a seamless recording of
the usage of all resources. The special challenge lies in the heterogeneous
middlewares, used within D-Grid. The paper describes the development
of a highly integrative accounting system as a component of the service
portfolio of the German Grid Support Organization.

**Keywords:** Accounting, D-Grid, DGAS, Grid, HLRmon.

## 1 Introduction

The German Grid initiative (D-Grid) was launched in 2004 and is funded by
the German Ministry for Education and Research (BMBF). D-Grid currently
comprises 27 projects, embraces over 100 partner organizations from science
and industry, and is part of the high-tech strategy for Germany. In the first
funding period (2004 - 2008), the D-Grid Integration Project (DGI) aimed to
build a sustainable Grid infrastructure with a major focus on the support of
the three widely used Grid middleware packages Globus Tookit [6], LCG/gLite
[2] and UNICORE [5]. At the end of the first phase, a core Grid infrastructure
for the German scientific community was built that provides a portfolio of Grid
services. The activities of the second funding period of the DGI aim to extend

J. Altmann, D. Neumann, and T. Fahringer (Eds.): GECON 2008, LNCS 5206, pp. 208–216, 2008.

and strengthen the production qualities of the infrastructure, and to develop and realize strategies to establish and maintain the D-Grid infrastructure and services even beyond the period of funding.

The focus on the sustainable - and therefore self-financing - operation of a Grid infrastructure requires technical and non-technical solutions. Non-technical issues to be solved are the creation of business models for the communities, and overall business strategies that contain market models for the provision of chargeable services. The technical issues address accounting, pricing and billing.

The D-Grid itself was transformed into a public company under german law, underwritten with the name D-Grid GmbH. After the funding period, it will gather its revenues by membership-fees from Grid resource providers (GRP), Grid service providers (GSP) and the community Grids (CG). Another source of income will be chargeable individual services, such as:

- Customization of generic software components of the Grid infrastructure to meet the individuals needs of the GRP, GSP and CGs
- Support of software components of the Grid infrastructure, including training, consulting, helpdesk and second level support
- Providing of information on new developments, available services and conferences via the Internet
- Consulting services for GSP and GRP concerning the integration of resources, services and applications in the Grid infrastructure with special regards to the open standards
- Development of modifications of software components to guarantee their interoperability with the D-Grid infrastructure
- Consulting services for software engineers concerning the open standards of the OGF
- Providing a test bed for developers in order to evaluate software components, modifications and new applications
- Administration of central components of Grid infrastructures based on D-Grid SLAs
- Modification and adjustment of SLAs according to the requirements of the customers and their software components
- Consulting with providers concerning the setup of their Grid infrastructures with special regards to the compatibility with the SLAs of the D-Grid.

The German Grid Support Organization (DGSE) as a central part of the D-Grid Integration Project will provide these services. Besides these chargeable services provided by the DGSE users of the D-Grid resources have to pay for the resource usage. From this intention arises two requirements. The first requirement is the accounting independant from the used middleware. The second requirement is a comprehensive accounting of all used resources.

As the D-Grid project aims to support the job submission using the three mentioned middleware packages there are two possible solutions to account the resource usage. The first solution is to use multiple accounting systems and consolidate the accounting records to get merged accounting information for every user. The other solution is to apply a uniform accounting system to support the accounting of the resource usage independent of the used middleware package. Because of a missing accounting service in the current deployed release of UNI-CORE it was decided to adapt one existing Grid accounting solution for the development of a uniform accounting service in D-Grid.

In the following section the decision for DGAS as the accounting system for D-Grid is reasoned. Furthermore the challenges for an uniform accounting system are summerized and the necessary modifications that enable DGAS to account all resource usage independant from the used middleware are described. The paper concludes with a description of further steps to a comprehensive accounting in D-Grid.

# 2    Uniform Accounting

One of the fundamental components of a sustainable Grid infrastructure operation is the precise accounting of the resource usage. In the context of the Grid infrastructure, resources can be compute or storage resources, as well as Grid services, applications or datasets. Currently available Grid accounting systems, such as SGAS [4], DGAS [11] or APEL [1] are designed to account the usage of compute resources for a specific middleware. SGAS developed in the Swe-Grid project is the appropriate accounting system for Globus Toolkit. DGAS and APEL are particularly developed for the LCG/gLite middleware. DGAS was developed originally in the DataGrid project. Further development is done within the EGEE project. DGAS is the accounting system of choice in the D-Grid project. Besides the use in D-Grid, the primary deployment of DGAS is in the INFN-Grid, the Italian partner in EGEE.

## 2.1    Challenges of Accounting in Heterogeneous Grid Infrastructures

When supporting the three middleware packages Globus Toolkit, LCG/gLite and UNICORE in the D-Grid project, the challenge arises to account resource usage independent from the used middleware. As most of the Grid accounting systems use the accounting information provided by the batchsystem, which enqueues the submitted jobs to the clusters of the worker nodes, the mapping of the user-account to a unique identifier of the user is the crucial point. In the Grid context the Distinguished Name (DN) of the users X.509 certificate is such a unique identifier. In Grids X.509 certificates are used to authenticate the user and, in conjunction with the belonging private key, to enable resources to act on behalf of the user [14].

The accounting systems DGAS and APEL interpret the gatekeeper logs of the LCG/gLite Computing Element to get information about the user-to-account-mapping as LCG/gLite provides a dynamic mapping to pool-accounts. Whereas SGAS requires the provision of accounting related information in the job description alternatively a mapping file could be used. In UNICORE 5 there is no accounting system implemented.

To comply with the demand of the BMBF of a minimal invasive adaption, DGAS was chosen as the accounting system in the D-Grid project because of three benefits. The first benefit is the scalability reached by the hierarchical structure DGAS offers to build a distributed accounting system. Subordinated Tier 1 accounting servers at several sites are able to submit their accounting records to a superior, central accounting server. The deployment in the INFN-Grid for example comprises 43 sites in a two-layered hierarchical accounting infrastructure. The second benefit is the ability to include benchmarks[1] in the accounting records to gain comparable data of the resources usage, which is an important issue in a heterogeneous Grid infrastructure. For an interpretation of the accounting information it is necessary to get parameters which enable the comparability of different resources of the same type, an interpretation could be the charging of the users resource consumption. The third benefit is the adoption to the requirements in the D-Grid with only marginal changes to the original software.

## 2.2   Deployment in the D-Grid

The DGAS accounting system is actually in the deployment phase and the sites TU Dortmund, FZ Jülich and RRZN from the Leibniz Universität Hannover are currently integrated in the uniform accounting. In the D-Grid infrastructure not all services are deployed to all sites. Generic services like monitoring, VO membership services and information services for example are located at selected sites. Every site in D-Grid has to provide access services for the compute- and storage resources. The access services for the compute resources are installed one dedicated *headnodes* for the three widely used middleware packages Globus Toolkit, LCG/gLite and UNICORE. These headnodes are connected to a central batchsystem server that enqueues the jobs to submit them to a cluster of worker nodes (see figure 1). The DGAS client is installed on the headnode for the LCG/gLite middleware the Computing Element (CE) having access to the accounting data of the batchsystem. The DGAS client merges the accounting information of successfully completed jobs with the users unique identifier, the DN and information concerning his VO-membership into usage records. These extended records are submitted to a central DGAS server and are stored in the *Home Location Register* (HLR), the central accounting database.

In D-Grid, users are mapped statically to accounts with a semi-fixed account name, which is constructed by a two-character prefix describing the organization (the flexible part), a two-character abbreviation of the virtual organization (VO) and a four-digit user-id. To account the resource usage independent of the used middleware, DGAS has to be modified. These modifications affect the mapping from the users account included in the accounting records to the users DN. This is realized by a static mapping of the local accounts to an extended version of the users DN instead of a dynamic mapping that results from the use of pool accounts. The use of this extended DN which includes the users VO membership is necessary because in D-Grid users have the possibility of a multi-VO-membership. The extension of the users DN has no effect to any other applications because of the constricted usage of these extended DN only for the accounting service.

---

[1] SPECint2000 and SPECfp2000.

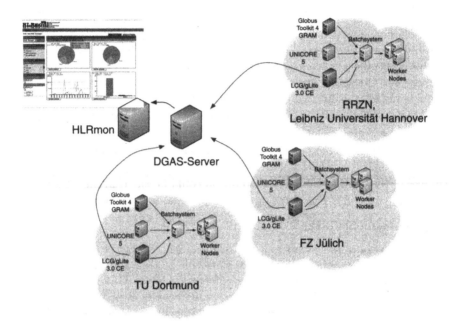

**Fig. 1.** Current accounting infrastructure in the D-Grid project

## 2.3 Visualization of Accounting Information

HLRmon, the visual Web-based component of DGAS, enables access to accounting information for managers, administrators and users [3]. HLRmon gathers the accounting information via the DGAS command line tools to query the HLR accounting database and displays a variety of accounting information like Jobs per VO, Walltime per VO, CPUtime per day. Information is presented in a graphical or tabular form in order to satisfy different user needs.

Due to its ability to authenticate clients through certificate and access rights management, it can a-priori restrict the selectable items range offered to the Web user, so that sensitive information will only be provided to authorized people.

Access to the accounting information, provided by HLRmon, is granted to users whose identity is authenticated through a valid digital certificate, which must be released by a trusted Certification Authority and installed in the client's browser. HLRmon matches user's identity with his access role privileges and preferences. This allows one to directly offer activity reports for the proper subset of information related to role membership, and persistently keeps track of user's preferences (such as date interval or other selections) through subsequent visits. The following four different roles have been defined:

– Regional Operation Center (ROC) Manager
  Can access whole information about activities in every Site, VO and VO
  users (see figure 2).

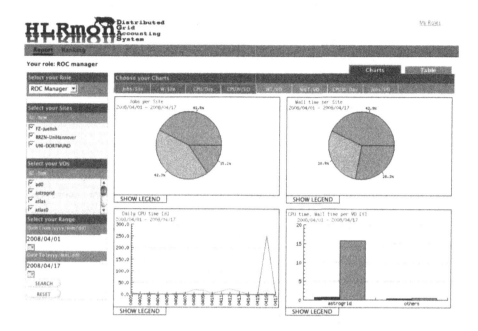

**Fig. 2.** HLRmon - Roc-Manager View

- Site Manager
  Can access whole information about activities of every VO and VO users only on sites where the Site Manager role is granted.
- VO Manager
  Can access information about activities of VOs and VOs users across all sites in the ROC, only on VOs where the VO Manager role is granted.
- VO user
  Can access information about VO user activities only for VOs where the VO user role is granted. This is the only role that can only access information but its own activities.

Another important fact to consider is that the DGAS system is designed to robustly account against transient malfunctioning of Grid components. Assuming for example that a given Computing Element fails to deliver information to his HLR, this information will be retained at CE level and finally transmitted when things are back ok again.

Side effects regarding the visualization of accounting information could be caused due to the fact that these information were assigned to the date as the job execution starts and not when it is finished. To avoid these undesired side effects in HLRmon the nightly update routine is always executed to retrieve latest 60 days of activity in the past (this is of course a configurable parameter), and this makes sure enough that transient effects leave no persistent tracks in HLRmon once passed.

The HLRmon Web interface helps to reveal transient problems at site level by highlighting site names in red, from which no data are collected for six days. Moving the mouse arrow over that site-name, a tooltip would appear telling how many days have passed since the reported activity. A further feature implemented in newer releases of HLRmon permits site managers and VO managers to easily produce a set of monthly or quarterly reports, consisting of a set of twelve or four charts with the same type of chart, each relevant to a distinct month or quarter.

## 3  Future Work

Today the accounting of compute resources usage is provided by every Grid accounting system. The accounting of the usage of storage resources is in progress [13] and has to be extended to support a broader range of storage systems. To provide comprehensive accounting information to enable a seamless charging of resource usage, further accounting metrics have to be identified, and sensors measuring usage have to be implemented. For the identification of these missing metrics the requirements of the scientific and industry Grid resource consumers and resource providers from both ranges have to be inquired.

As resources are not only compute and storage systems, but also for example applications and data, sensors have to be developed to measure the usage of these resources as well. Accounting metrics can be classified as follows [10] (see figure 3):

- Physical resources
  Resources used for compute, storage, network links, but also for example radio telescopes or industrial robots
- Application resources
  Data like images or video for example, which are processed with Grid applications
- Grid core services
  Services that enables Grid computing
- Grid application services
  Software and applications provided for the use by the Grid users

Physical resources and Grid core services are building the Grid infrastructure and have to be accounted by a general Grid accounting service. For a sustainable operation of a Grid infrastructure these metrics must be economically cleared. The application resources and the Grid application services are community specific and must be accounted and cleared within the VOs. To enable a comprehensive accounting by collecting usage information about the resource usage of all these classes, dedicated sensors must be developed that submit the data into a small set of database tables to reach a high standard of comparability. Development of standardized usage records, according to the Open Grid Forum standardized usage records (UR) [7] for compute usage is a necessary task for the near future.

Another focus of future activities is the integration of the resource usage service (RUS) interface [9], [12] to DGAS a deliverable of the OMII-Europe [8]

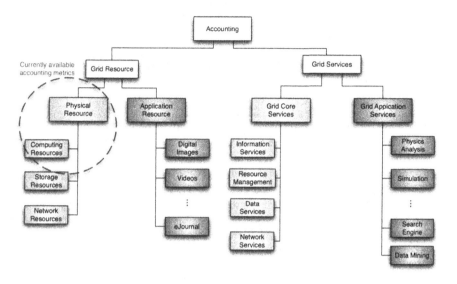

**Fig. 3.** Classification of Accounting Metrics (from [10])

project to ensure the interoperability with other accounting systems. The RUS, in conjunction with the UR, forms the basis of an accounting framework, which enables the integration of small Grids into a national Grid infrastructure.

# References

1. Byrom, R., Cordenonsi, R., Cornwall, L., Craig, M., Abdeslem, D., Ducan, A., Fisher, S., Gordon, J., Hicks, S., Kant, D., Leake, J., Middleton, R., Thorpe, M., Walk, J., Wilson, A.: APEL: An implementation of Grid accounting using R-GMA (September 2005),
   http://www.gridpp.ac.uk/abstracts/allhands2005/apel.pdf
2. Berlich, R., Kunze, M., Schwarz, K.: Grid computing in Europe: from research to deployment. In: Buyya, R., Coddington, P., Montague, P., Safavi-Naini, R., Sheppard, N., Wendelborn, A. (eds.) Proceedings of the 2005 Australasian Workshop on Grid Computing and E-Research - vol. 44, Newcastle, New South Wales, Australia. Conferences in Research and Practice in Information Technology Series, vol. 108, pp. 21–27. Australian Computer Society, Darlinghurst (2005)
3. Dal Pra, S., Fattibene, E., Gaido, L., Misurelli, G., Pescarmona, F.: HLRMON: A Role-based Grid Accounting Report Web Tool. In: Proceedings of Int, Conference in High-Energy and Nuclear Physik 2007, CHEP 2007 (to appear, 2007)
4. Elmroth, E., Gardfjll, P., Mulmo, O., Sandholm, T.: An OGSA-Based Bank Service for Grid Accounting Systems. In: Proceedings of the 2nd international Conference on Service Oriented Computing, New York, NY, USA (November 2004),
   http://delivery.acm.org/10.1145/1040000/1035207/p279-sandholm.pdf
5. Erwin, D.W., Snelling, D.F.: UNICORE: A Grid Computing Environment. In: Sakellariou, R., Keane, J.A., Gurd, J.R., Freeman, L. (eds.) Euro-Par 2001. LNCS, vol. 2150, pp. 825–834. Springer, Heidelberg (2001),
   http://citeseer.ist.psu.edu/erwin01unicore.html

6. Foster, I.: Globus Toolkit Version 4: Software for Service-Oriented Systems. In: Jin, H., Reed, D., Jiang, W. (eds.) NPC 2005. LNCS, vol. 3779, pp. 2–13. Springer, Heidelberg (2005),
http://www.globus.org/alliance/publications/papers/IFIP-2005.pdf
7. Mach, R., Lepro-Metz, R., Jackson, S., McGinnis, L.: Usage Records - Format Recommedation, Draft Recommendation, Global Grid Forum (2003),
http://www.ogf.org/documents/GFD.98.pdf
8. http://omii-europe.org/OMII-Europe/
9. Pace, M.: Preliminary Implementation of a RUS Interface for DGAS (July 2007), http://www.to.infn.it/grid/accounting/techrep/DGAS-RUS-Prototype-1_0.pdf
10. Pettipher, M.A., Khan, A., Robinson, T.W., Chan, X.: Review of Accounting and Usage Monitoring Final Report (July 2007), http://www.jisc.ac.uk/media/documents/programmes/einfrastructure/jisc_aum_final_report_wth.pdf
11. Piro, M., Guaresi, A., Werbrouck, A.: An Economy-based Accounting Infrastructure for the DataGrid. In: Proc. 4th Int. Workshop on Grid Computing (GRID2003), Phoenix, AZ (November 2003),
http://www.to.infn.it/grid/accounting
12. Piro, R.M., Pace, M., Ghiselli, A., Guarise, A., Luppi, E., Patania, G., Tomassetti, L., Werbrouck, A.: Tracing Resource Usage over Heterogeneous Grid Platforms: A Prototype RUS Interface for DGAS. In: Proceedings of the Third IEEE International Conference on e-Science and Grid Computing, pp. 93–101 (December 2007), http://ieeexplore.ieee.org/iel5/4426856/4426857/04426876.pdf
13. Scibilia, F.: Accounting of Storage Resources in gLite Based Infrastructures. In: Proceedings of the 16th IEEE International Workshops on Enabling Technologies: Infrastructure for Collaborative Enterprises, pp. 273–275 (June 2007), http://www.ieeexplore.ieee.org/iel5/4407104/4407105/04407170.pdf
14. Tuecke, S., Welch, V., Engert, D., Pearlman, L., Thompson, M.: Internet x.509 public key infrastructure(PKI)proxy certificate profile. RFC 3820 (2004),
http://www.ietf.org/rfc/rfc3820.txt

# The ArguGRID Platform: An Overview

Francesca Toni[1], Mary Grammatikou[2], Stella Kafetzoglou[2],
Leonidas Lymberopoulos[2], Symeon Papavassileiou[2], Dorian Gaertner[1],
Maxime Morge[3], Stefano Bromuri[4], Jarred McGinnis[4], Kostas Stathis[4],
Vasa Curcin[5], Moustafa Ghanem[5], and Li Guo[5]

[1] Imperial College London, Department of Computing, UK
[2] Institute of Communications and Computer Systems, NTUA, Greece
[3] Dipartimento di Informatica, Pisa University, Italy
[4] Department of Computer Science, Royal Holloway, University of London, UK
[5] InforSense Ltd., UK

**Abstract.** The ArguGRID project aims at supporting service selection and composition in distributed environments, including the Grid and Service-oriented architectures, by means of argumentative agents, an agent environment, a service-composition environment, Peer-to-Peer technology and Grid middleware. Agents are argumentative in that they use argumentation-based decision-making and argumentation-supported negotiation of services and contracts. The integration of all technologies gives rise to the overall ArguGRID platform. In this paper we outline the main components and the overall functionalities of the ARGUGRID platform.

**Keywords:** Grid Computing, Service-Oriented Computing, e-Business.

## 1 Introduction

The ArguGRID project[1] aims at developing a Grid/Service-oriented platform populated by rational decision-making agents that are associated with service requesters, service providers and users. The project also aims at using Semantic Web technologies to support semantic integration of services in distributed environments such as the Grid. Within agents, argumentation [5,15,20] is used to support decision making, taking into account (and despite) the frequently conflicting information that these agents have, as well as the preferences of users, service requesters and providers. Argumentation is also intended to support the negotiation between agents [6,14], on behalf of service requesters/providers/users. This negotiation takes place within dynamically formed Virtual Organisations. The agreed combination of services can be seen as a complex service within a service-centric architecture [4]. We intend to validate this overall approach by way of industrial e-business application scenarios [19].

A high-level view of the ArguGRID vision was presented in [4]. In this paper we outline the ArguGRID platform and architecture, by describing at a high-level

---

[1] http://www.argugrid.eu

J. Altmann, D. Neumann, and T. Fahringer (Eds.): GECON 2008, LNCS 5206, pp. 217–225, 2008.

all its components and by showing how these fit together and provide support for user applications. These components include:

- tools for the authoring and execution of workflows, namely combinations of services, to fulfil the requirements (goals) of users;
- argumentation engines to support decision-making and negotiation;
- an agent platform used to support inter-agent interactions;
- a Peer-to-Peer platform for the discovery of Grid services and agents within the platform;
- Grid middleware.

The paper is organized as follows. In Section 2 we give an overview of the project's aims, scenarios and overall methodologies. In Section 3 we summarise the main components of the ArguGRID platform and describe the integration of these components within the ArguGRID platform. In Section 4 we conclude.

## 2   The ArguGRID Vision

ArguGRID aims to:

- develop argumentation-based foundations for the Grid, populated by rational decision-making agents within Virtual Organisations;
- incorporate argumentation models into a service-centric architecture;
- develop an underlying platform using Peer-to-Peer computing;
- validate the ArguGRID approach by way of industrial application scenarios.

We have chosen a number of e-business application scenarios [19], including

- e-procurement applications and e-Marketplaces,
- e-business for Earth Observation applications.

These scenarios are the outcome of and build upon the extensive field experience of the two industrial partners of the consortium (cosmoONE Hellas Market-site S.A. [2] and GMV S.A. [3], respectively). In [21] we summarise the rationale for the choice of these scenarios to guide the development of and validate the ArguGRID approach to Grid computing and service-oriented architectures.

The envisaged ArguGRID platform is intended to be a multi-layered architecture where: the top layer is about building applications; the middle layer concerns the development of individual agents as well as methodologies for dynamically assembling agents into Virtual Organisations responsible for the negotiation of contracts between service providers and requesters; agents and Virtual Organisations sit on top of the bottom-layer, consisting of Peer-to-Peer and Grid middleware. Each service requester/provider and each user is associated with one or more agents. Agents use argumentation for negotiating on behalf of service

---

[2] http://www.cosmo-one.gr/en
[3] http://www.gmv.com

requesters/providers/users. By means of the top-layer, users can provide input to agents, in terms of their objectives (what they expect to achieve from the service composition performed by the agents) and preferences (either for the specific objectives, or, more generally, as a generic profile of the user).

Within the middle layer, agents negotiate with one another by using argumentation to support their decision making and communication processes. Negotiation takes place within dynamically created and maintained Virtual Organisations, envisaged as societies of agents whereby interaction is regulated by social norms and/or protocols. The outcome of negotiation results in a contract, understood, at the agent level, as a task allocation (in terms of provision of resources/services) to agents. In particular, this contract may include a workflow description that needs to be appropriately executed (within the bottom layer).

## 3   The ArguGRID Platform

The ArguGRID platform consists of four interacting components:

– InforSense KDE: this is a commercial software tool developed by InforSense Ltd [4], and that originates from the Discovery Net e-Science project at Imperial College London [17]. This system provides facilities to build end user application as workflows coordinating the execution of remote web services [3] or Grid services [10]. For the needs of ArguGRID, the KDE system is extended to support semantic workflow authoring and composition and to cater for a semantic registry, which holds higher-level and semantic service descriptions, such as information about their functionality, e.g. QoS, cost, etc. This way, abstract workflows representing user needs can be matched partially or be fully instantiated as concrete workflows and be executed and validated within the grid infrastructure.
– GOLEM (Generalized OntoLogical Environments for Multi-agent systems) [5]: this is an agent environment middleware that can be used to create multi-agent system applications. Applications in GOLEM can be specified declaratively, thus making the deployment of cognitive agents of the kinds envisaged by ArguGRID easier in that perceiving the environment amounts to importing parts of a logical theory [1,2,18].
– PLATON (Peer-to-Peer Load Adjusting Tree Overlay Networks) [6]: this is a Peer-to-Peer platform supporting multi-attribute and range queries [11]. It is developed in the Java programming language and supports mechanisms for load-balancing of peer resources. Load-balancing of resources is necessary in order to guarantee logarithmic querying time using any distributed tree-based multi-attribute Peer-to-Peer platform. In its current release, PLATON has implemented the SkipIndex routing framework by Princeton University.

---

[4] http://www.inforsense.com
[5] http://www.golem.cs.rhul.ac.uk
[6] http://platonp2p.sourceforge.net

- GRIA [7]: this is the Grid middleware that ArguGRID has chosen to use to support its scenarios. The reason for choosing GRIA is that GRIA is a service-oriented infrastructure designed particularly to support Business-to-Business collaborations (such as the ones required by the ArguGRID scenarios) through service provision across organisational boundaries in a secure, interoperable and flexible manner.

The InforSense KDE constitutes the top-layer of the ArguGRID platform, GOLEM supports the middle layer, and the combination of PLATON and GRIA forms the bottom layer.

Within the ArguGRID platform, GOLEM hosts MARGO agents [15,16], running the MARGO argumentative decision-making engine [15], which in turn deploys the CaSAPI general-purpose argumentation engine [7,8,9]:

- MARGO (Multiattribute ARGumentation framework for Opinion explanation) [8], written in Prolog, implements the ArguGRID argumentation framework for practical reasoning about service selection and composition. A logic language is used as a concrete data structure for holding the statements like knowledge, goals, and actions. Different qualitative or quantitative priorities are attached to these items, corresponding to the probability of the knowledge, the preferences between goals, and the expected utilities of alternative actions. MARGO evaluates the possible actions, suggests some solutions, and provides an interactive and intelligible explanation of the choice made. MARGO is built on top of CaSAPI.
- CaSAPI (Credulous and Sceptical Argumentation: Prolog Implementation) [9] is a general-purpose tool for (several types of) assumption-based argumentation. It is written in Prolog. It can support several applications, ranging from decision-making to normative reasoning and goal decision, to e-procurement.

A number of interactions/communications are supported between individual ArguGRID components within the ArguGRID platform, as outlined in Figure 1. Note that this figure should not be interpreted as indicating that the components of the platform are held on a single, local computer. Rather, all components (and the ArguGRID platform itself) will be typically distributed among computer elements residing in distinct locations, connected to a network such as the global Internet.

ArguGRID distinguishes between (Grid) service requesters and (Grid) service providers. Agents may act as service requesters or as service providers (or both). Figure 1 presents the ArguGRID platform from a service requester's point of view, i.e. from the view point of users using the ArguGRID platform in order to obtain (typically composite) services. Users in Figure 1 can be either human users or agents using the ArguGRID platform to achieve their goals.

---

[7] http://www.gria.org
[8] http://margo.sourceforge.net
[9] http://www.doc.ic.ac.uk/~dg00/casapi.html

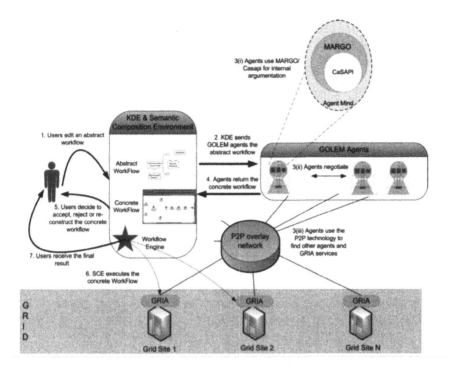

**Fig. 1.** Global Picture of the ArguGRID Platform

Within the ArguGRID platform, WSML [10] is used to provide semantic descriptions of services in registries available to agents. These desciptions are translated onto a logic-based representation, on demand, so that they can be reasoned upon by GOLEM agents using MARGO.

The main interactions used to support user's requests are the following:

1. Users interact initially with the ArguGRID platform by submitting an abstract workflow to the KDE [11]. This is realised through the KDE workflow editing tool. The abstract workflow reflects, at a high-level, the user requirements. In the next Section, we will give an example of an abstract workflow.
2. In its commercial version, the KDE would involve human interaction in order to derive (having as an input an abstract workflow) a concrete and executable workflow, to be executed on the Grid. In the case of ArguRGID, the KDE is extended so that the process of refining an abstract workflow is delegated to intelligent GOLEM agents. Thus, the KDE communicates the abstract

---

[10] http://www.wsmo.org/wsml/

[11] Note that this is only one possible entry point to the ArguGRID platform. Indeed, users may also access the platform by interacting directly with a user agent and specifying either an abstract workflow or some high-level goals that agents need to "translate" into workflows. We omit this other view in Figure 1 for the sake of simplicity.

workflow to a GOLEM agent, acting as the agent representing the user within the ArguGRID platform.

3. Having received the abstract workflow, the GOLEM agent representing the user will start finding which GRIA services should be used in order to derive a concrete workflow, to be executed on the Grid. In order to accoGOLEM agent uses the following capabilities:

   (a) A GOLEM agent uses the MARGO argumentation engine for decision-making, which in turn uses the CaSAPI general-purpose argumentation engine. These are implemented within the mind of every GOLEM agent and work in a way to reason about services and make decisions, aiding the refinement process of the abstract workflow.

   (b) A GOLEM agent can negotiate with other GOLEM agents, sign contracts with them and form Virtual Organisations (VOs) [13]. The latter follow the basic philosophy of the Grid, where VOs are formed in order to solve a common problem or task. In our case, the common problem is the problem of providing a solution to the requirements of the user application, i.e. finding a concrete workflow whose execution will satisfy the application requirements, as stated in the abstract workflow. Interactions amongst GOLEM agents are provided by means of dialectical protocols, using special language structures for agent communication.

   (c) To find out an appropriate GOLEM agent or a GRIA Grid service, GOLEM agents are given the capability to use the Peer-to-Peer platform, linking all available GOLEM agents and GRIA services in a virtual registry that can be queried. Implementation of this virtual registry containing all agents and GRIA services is realised using PLATON. Three types of registries exist: GOLEM registries within the GOLEM platform, Grid registries within PLATON and Semantic registries with the Environment of the KDE.

   Note that all interactions described above as cases a,b,c can be realised in parallel, i.e. we do not imply that there is a strict sequence of interactions. Which interaction to use is a choice determined by the mind of the GOLEM agent, while CaSAPI and MARGO are running.

4. Having carried out its mission, the GOLEM agent representing the user (i.e. the initial agent that received the abstract workflow from the KDE) will return back to the KDE the concrete workflow, constituted by a set of GRIA services to be executed in a certain manner/sequence.

5. At this point, a concrete workflow is provided to the KDE. The user is informed of this solution and is given the choice of either accepting the concrete workflow or rejecting it or deciding to modify the abstract workflow, in order to get a better solution. In the latter case, the abstract workflow will be given again as input to the KDE, repeating steps 1, 2, 3, 4 and 5, until the user either accepts or rejects the ArguGRID concrete workflow solution. In the case of acceptance, the system will follow step 6 below.

6. The workflow engine within the KDE will use its workflow execution service to send the concrete workflow for execution on the Grid infrastructure, running the GRIA middleware.

7. Upon successful execution of the concrete workflow, the user is informed and the execution results/data are returned back to the user.

Of course, more than one user will be able to use the ArguGRID platform at the same time, as the ArguGRID platform follows the philosophy of the underlying Grid, having a distributed nature with multiple service providers and service clients, all using the shared Grid infrastructure at the same time, each client trying to achieve his/hers own goals.

## 4   Conclusions

We have outlined the main components of the ArguGRID platform and their integration to support user-driven applications. We are currently testing components and their integration to support the ArguGRID scenarios of e-procurement and Eearth observation. Preliminary results for e-procurement are described in [16,12].

Overall, the ArguGRID platform affords solutions to problems within these scenarios with the following features: agents automate the process of identifying orchestrations of services (workflows); users and services cooperate (via the agents 'representing' them within the ArguGRID platform) and can negotiate orchestrations of services that require the agents' goals to be flexible; users and services exist within a dynamic and open environment.

Other projects have considered the automated construction of workflows, for example K-Wf Grid [12], which uses agents to support users in authoring workflows. The focus of ArguGRID is the automatisation of the *negotiation* of workflows and contracts amongst agents 'representing' services. Agents are equipped with knowledge, goals and preferences, given to them by users (requesting or providing services), and need to take decisions under 'qualitative' uncertainty. They also use argumentation to 'influence' one another.

To fully support step 3 in Figure 1, we are currently exploring the negotiation of contracts (including SLAs) between users and services (again via the agents 'representing' them within the ArguGRID platform) [6]. We are also studying interaction protocols and strategies amongst agents to support automatic negotiation of workflows and contracts, and the evaluation and use of the trustworthiness of agents (and the services they represent) in order to render these protocols and strategies more effective.

**Acknowledgements.** This work was funded by the Sixth Framework IST programme of the EC, under the 035200 ArguGRID project. Many thanks to anonymous referees for helpful suggestions and to all participants in the ArguGRID consortium for stimulating challenges to the platform design described in this paper.

---

[12] http://www.dps.uibk.ac.at/projects/kwfgrid/

# References

1. Bromuri, S., Stathis, K.: Situating cognitive agents in golem. In: Proceedings EEM-MAS 2007, Dresden, Germany (October 2007)
2. Bromuri, S., Urovi, V., Conteras, P., Stathis, K.: A virtual e-retailing environment in golem. In: Proceedings of Intelligent Environments (IE08), Seattle, US (July 2008)
3. Curcin, V., Ghanem, M., Guo, Y.: Web services in life sciences. Drug Discovery Today 10(12), 865–871 (2005)
4. Curcin, V., Ghanem, M., Guo, Y., Stathis, K., Toni, F.: Building next generation service-oriented architectures using argumentation agents. In: Proc. 3rd International Conference on Grid Services Engineering and Management (GSEM 2006) (September 2006)
5. Dung, P., Mancarella, P., Toni, F.: Computing ideal sceptical argumentation. Artificial Intelligence - Special Issue on Argumentation in Artificial Intelligence 171(10-15), 642–674 (2007)
6. Dung, P., Thang, P., Toni, F.: Towards argumentation-based contract negotiation. In: Proceedings of the Second International Conference on Computational Models of Argument (COMMA'08), Toulouse, France. IOS Press, Amsterdam (2008)
7. Gaertner, D., Toni, F.: CaSAPI: a system for credulous and skeptical argumentation. In: Proc. LPNMR Workshop on Argumentation for Non-monotonic Reasoning, pp. 80–95 (2007)
8. Gaertner, D., Toni, F.: Computing arguments and attacks in assumption-based argumentation. IEEE Intelligent Systems (November/December) (2007)
9. Gaertner, D., Toni, F.: Hybrid argumentation and its properties. In: Proceedings of the 2nd International Conference on Computational Models of Argument (COMMA 2008). IOS Press, Amsterdam (2008)
10. Ghanem, M., Azam, N., Boniface, M., Ferris, J.: Grid-enabled workflows for industrial product design. In: Proc. Second IEEE International Conference on e- Science and Grid Computing (e-Science 2006), December 2006. IEEE Computer Society, Los Alamitos (2006)
11. Lymberopoulos, L., Papavassiliou, S., Maglaris, V.: A novel load balancing mechanism for p2p networking. In: Proceedings of ACM sponsored Conference GridNets, Lyon, France (2007)
12. Matt, P., Toni, F., Stournaras, T., Dimitrelos, D.: Argumentation-based agents for eprocurement. In: Berger, Burg, Nishiyama (eds.) Proc. of 7th Int. Conf. on Autonomous Agents and Multiagent Systems (AAMAS 2008) - Industry and Applications Track, Estoril, Portugal (May 2008)
13. McGinnis, J., Stathis, K., Toni, F.: Virtual organisations as agent societies: Phases. ArguGRID deliverable D.3.2. Technical report, ArguGRID (2008)
14. Miller, T., McBurney, P., McGinnis, J., Stathis, K.: First-class protocols for agent-based coordination of scientific instruments. In: Proceedings of the 5th International Workshop on Agent-based Computing for Enterprise Collaboration: Agent-Oriented Workflows and Services (ACEC 2007), Paris, France (2007)
15. Morge, M., Mancarella, P.: The hedgehog and the fox. An argumentation-based decision support system. In: Proc. of the Fourth International Workshop on Argumentation in Multi-Agent Systems (ArgMAS), pp. 55–68 (2007)
16. Morge, M., McGinnis, J., Bromuri, S., Toni, F., Mancarella, P., Stathis, K.: Toward a modular architecture of argumentative agents to compose services. In: Proc. of the Fifth European Workshop on Multi-Agent Systems (EUMAS), Hammamet, Tunisia, December 2007, pp. 1–15 (2007)

17. Rowe, A., Kalaitzopolous, D., Osmond, M., Ghanem, M., Guo, Y.: The discovery net system for high throughput bioinformatics. Bioinformatics 19, 225–231 (2003)
18. Stathis, K., Kafetzoglou, S., Pappavasiliou, S., Bromuri, S.: Sensor network grids: Agent environment combined with qos in wireless sensor networks. In: Proceedings of the 3rd International Conference on Autonomic and Autonomous Systems (ICAS 2007), Athens, Greece (2007)
19. Stournaras, T., Dimitrelos, D., Tabasco, A., Barba, J., Pedrazzani, D., Yagüe, M., An, T., Dung, P., Hung, N., Khoi, V.D., Thang, P.M.: e-Business application scenarios. ArguGRID deliverable D.1.2. Technical report, ArguGRID (2007)
20. Toni, F.: Assumption-based argumentation for selection and composition of services. In: Proceedings of the 8th International Workshop on Computational Logic in Multi-Agent Systems (CLIMA VIII) (2007)
21. Toni, F.: E-Business in ArguGRID. In: Veit, D.J., Altmann, J. (eds.) GECON 2007. LNCS, vol. 4685, pp. 164–169. Springer, Heidelberg (2007)

# AssessGrid Strategies for
# Provider Ranking Mechanisms
# in Risk–Aware Grid Systems*

Dominic Battré[1], Karim Djemame[2], Iain Gourlay[2], Matthias Hovestadt[1],
Odej Kao[1], James Padgett[2], Kerstin Voss[3], and Daniel Warneke[1]

[1] Technische Universität Berlin, Germany
{battre,maho,okao,warneke}@cs.tu-berlin.de
[2] School of Computing
University of Leeds, United Kingdom
{karim,iain,jamesp}@comp.leeds.ac.uk
[3] Paderborn Center for Parallel Computing,
Universität Paderborn, Germany
kerstinv@uni-paderborn.de

**Abstract.** Grid systems are on the verge of attracting the commercial user who requires contractually fixed levels of service quality. Service Level Agreements (SLAs) are powerful instruments for describing all obligations and expectations within such a Grid-based business relationship. Service selection has so far been based on performance and compatibility criteria while neglecting the factor of reliability and risk.

The EC-funded project "AssessGrid" aims at introducing risk assessment and management as a novel decision paradigm into Grid computing. With AssessGrid, providers are able to express the risk associated with an SLA, and broker services are able to judge the trustworthiness of such provider risk statements. This paper focuses on the provider ranking process where a broker or end-user has to decide which provider to choose from, and consequently which SLA to commit to.

**Keywords:** Grid, SLA, Negotiation, Broker, Ranking.

## 1 Introduction

Advances in Grid computing research have in recent years resulted in considerable commercial interest in utilizing Grid infrastructures for application and service provisioning. However, significant developments in the areas of risk and dependability are necessary before widespread commercial adoption can become reality. Specifically, risk management mechanisms need to be incorporated into Grid infrastructures in order to move beyond the best-effort approach that current Grid infrastructures follow to service provision.

---

* This work has been partially supported by the EU within the 6th Framework Programme under contract IST-031772 "Advanced Risk Assessment and Management for Trustable Grids" (AssessGrid).

J. Altmann, D. Neumann, and T. Fahringer (Eds.): GECON 2008, LNCS 5206, pp. 226–233, 2008.

AssessGrid addresses the key issue of risk by developing a framework to support risk assessment and management for all three Grid actors (end-user, broker, and resource provider) [1]. To integrate risk awareness and support risk management in all Grid layers, new components are introduced: the provider benefits from access to a consultant service that provides statistical information to support both risk assessment and the identification of infrastructure bottlenecks. The broker makes use of a confidence service that provides a reliability measure of a resource provider's risk assessment, based on historical data. In addition, a workflow assessor supports the broker deriving the probability of failure of a workflow from risk estimations of the sub-tasks.

Having risk estimations of single jobs and even workflow jobs available, Grid stakeholders negotiating an SLA have a concrete idea on the risk associated with a particular business activity. Prior to the binding agreement of an SLA, the customer (e.g. the Grid end-user or a Grid broker) usually requests a non-binding SLA quote from one or more providers, which holds all information like price, penalty, or the probability of failure (PoF) of the SLA. This way each party can decide whether or not to accept this risk by committing to a binding SLA. At least if Grid brokers have to map complex workflows to Grid resources, it is common practice to not only request a single SLA quote from a single provider at a time, but from numerous providers in parallel. This way the broker is able to optimize the workflow orchestration according to the particularly available resources at provider side. Such a broadcast request usually results in a large number of non-binding SLA quotes from numerous different providers. Even if the customer is easily able to decide whether the PoF of a particular SLA offer is acceptable, it remains difficult to select the best offer among them.

For supporting the customer in this decision making process, the AssessGrid project will introduce a provider ranking mechanism, which is presented in this paper. After an outlook on related work in section 2, we briefly describe the *getQuote* mechanism in SLA negotiation process in section 3. The main part of this paper focuses in Section 4 on the provider ranking process. A short conclusion ends this paper.

## 2   Related Work

The Grid resource selection from a user's perspective can be separated in two phases. The first phase comprises the discovery of resources that match the user's requirements associated with a job or workflow (necessary condition). The second phase comprises the ranking of these resources so that a user can select the resource with the highest utility/performance.

Resource discovery has been addressed in the past for example with information services like the Globus Monitoring and Discovery Service (MDS) [2]. Performance requirements of the response time are evaluated in [3] and according to data collected by the Grid Index Information Service (GIIS) predications about the response time of queries can be made.

Provider rankings can be based on different utility functions. One obvious criterion is the performance of a provider in terms of resources employed and available. This has been discussed for example in [4] where a framework is described to use Gridbench performance probes to determine resources that are best suited to a user's job. The framework allows the user to individually define filtering, aggregation, and ranking criteria for a custom utility function. A second criterion is of course the price requested by a provider, and projects such as GridEcon [5] define market places for resources.

Given the enormous job failure rates observed in Grids (in DAS-2 more than 10% of all jobs fail [6], in TeraGrid the failure rate is 10–45% [7], and in Grid3 27% jobs fail even with 5–10 retries [8]) it becomes apparent that quality of service and the capability to negotiate SLAs is another key decision factor.

This has been the focus of the AssessGrid project [1] which developed mechanisms to estimate the probability of failure of a job. This estimation can be only be performed from the provider side since it has information about the exact scheduling, planned fault-tolerance mechanisms, and stability of resources which will be used. The confidence service at the broker layer is able to estimate the reliability of the providers' published failure information by setting it into a relation with observed SLA violations [9].

Several papers elaborate on reputation based mechanisms. Elnaffar describes in [10] a ranking mechanism for Grid providers based reputation. The metric employed is a vector of user ranking (a rating entered manually by the user according to the perceived performance), Quality of Service (QoS) conformance (measured discrepancy between asserted and delivered QoS), and fidelity (consistency of delivered performance).

Sonnek and Weissman review in [11] several reputation systems for the Grid and give a quantitative comparison. The reviewed ranking systems comprise the Ebay system. Providers are ranked in a personalized way based on a user's direct experience and other approaches that filter dishonest feedback.

In this paper we define several other criteria that are relevant for the utility of a provider's resources to the user, which are elaborated in Section 4.

## 3    Quote Mechanism in SLA-Negotiation

Grid Service Level management contains QoS descriptions for Web services in the form of SLAs. The Grid community has identified the need for a standard for SLA description and negotiation. This has led to the development of WS-Agreement [12], a language and protocol designed for advertising the capabilities of providers and creating agreements based on initial offers, and for monitoring agreement compliance at runtime. These upcoming standards rely on the Web Services Resource Framework (WSRF).

This WS-Agreement protocol now has been extended to allow flexible SLA negotiation schemes between contractors and service providers. Briefly, modifications consist in the addition of one operation: *getQuote()*. This is only an extension, which allows to change the original single-round acceptance model to a two-phase acceptance model. It introduces the negotiation possibility, in other words the bargaining capability.

The protocol implemented within the EC-funded AssessGrid project is a two-phase commit negotiation. The user first requests a template from the provider, which describes the provider capabilities. The user then specifies his requirements in a quote request. The provider makes an offer by sending a quote based on the request made by the user. The user is then able to accept this quote and sign it. The SLA contract is then signed if the provider accepts the user's signed SLA.

This modification to obtain a flexible and robust SLA negotiation protocol can be seen as a continuation of work within the WS-Agreement specification. The extended protocol answers the requirements where a negotiation before a final agreement is needed.

The agreement mechanism within the WS-Agreement draft specification does not meet the negotiation requirement. The main drawback comes from the single round "offer, accept" agreement mechanism. This has an important consequence: there is no possibility for a service consumer to request offers from different providers so that he can choose the best one among these. In order to do so, he would have to act as the agreement initiator and call *createAgreement()* from several providers to propose some SLA to each. The problem is that he would then be bound to every provider that decides to accept the quote. The concept of "SLA quote" does not exist in the WS-Agreement draft specification: it is not possible for a consumer to simply ask a provider what his terms would be without being committed to the provider by this action. In the real word, a negotiation process usually begins by the initiator asking non-committing questions to the other party.

The solution proposed in AssessGrid is to introduce the concept of "SLA quote" into the agreement mechanism. The *getQuotes()* method offers the end-user the possibility to have a first evaluation of a request for service. Based on this first quote, the user can then decide to accept it using the *createAgreement()* method. If the provider's quote is not satisfactory, a new quote can be requested by entering a new quote request, with slightly different parameters.

# 4  Provider Ranking

The negotiation of an SLA is the first step in the business relationship between a customer and the provider. Even if both parties are interested in a successful execution of an SLA, both are driven by different - often opposing - goals, like high quality service at low cost (customer) vs. maximizing the revenue (provider). In this light, providers may even be tempted to lie regarding their service quality level.

## 4.1  Confidence Service

During the SLA negotiation, the customer may specify the required level of risk in the SLA request. The provider answers this request by publishing the risk level it is able to support. This may either be the risk that the customer demands or lower. At this stage, the customer has to trust the correctness of the provider risk calculation.

For attracting additional Grid jobs and to increase the system utilization and revenue, providers may publish a lower risk than they are actually able to support. For coping with this situation, the AssessGrid broker provides a confidence service, rating the correctness of the provider specified risk value by considering the provider's past reliability [9]. Using appropriate risk models, the broker can deduct the likeliness that a provider performs as announced.

Grid end-users are able to directly request resources from Grid providers. However, the confidence service is a strong incentive for using the services of the Grid broker, because the Grid end-user usually does not have the broker's experience dealing with thousands or millions of SLA-based jobs and workflows and the history behind their specification, management, and outcome, which is mandatory for statistically firm provider ratings. Thus, for the broker the quality of the confidence service is a key argument for attracting customers.

## 4.2   Provider Performance

The information provided by the confidence service is a mandatory key when ranking a list of offerings: all offers having a poor confidence value in the provider specified risk may be filtered, since it is very likely that the actual risk of executing in the context of the SLA in question is not acceptable for the customer. However, the broker's information on provider performance can be further used for not only filtering, but also ranking.

As outlined above both parties are interested in fulfilling an SLA. Hence, AssessGrid will support provider ranking according to the provider's SLA violation rate. Here, the broker is using the floating average of logged provider performance, e.g. focusing on daily or weekly average values. Following this ranking, the Grid end-user is able to select a provider that complies to his risk requirements while showing the best SLA conformance among all offers.

This ranking approach may be enhanced to other parameters. In classic queuing based Resource Management Systems (RMSs), the waiting time of a job indicates how long a job has to wait in the queue until compute resources have been allocated to the job. In general, the smaller the waiting time, the better the service. In case of AssessGrid, the RMS is planning-based and therefore does not use any queues. However, in the case of deadline bound jobs, the provider has a time window ranging from earliest start time (EST) until deadline (DL) for executing the job with a defined runtime (RT). This results in a slack time of $DL - EST - RT$.

In the AssessGrid scenario, the waiting time is reciprocal to the slack time: the end-user is interested in providers offering a small waiting time, so that jobs are started as early as possible after EST. Providers performing with a high waiting time execute the job with only a small slack-time. Thus, the provider executes the job in an SLA-compliant way, returning all results until the specified deadline, but the customer has to anticipate getting results just in time.

## 4.3  Acceptance Rate

As described above, the SLA quote given by the provider has a non-binding character. End-users may request SLA quotes for getting an overview about available resources, mandatory for an SLA-compliant mapping of workflows onto Grid resources. Providers in turn do not have to block resources, answering SLA quotes without any risk or cost.

Providers may exploit this situation by answering SLA quote requests while knowing that offered resources are not available. This is similar to overbooking, where a provider accepts more requests than resources available. Here, the situation is even better for the provider due to the non-binding nature of SLA quotes: the provider may anticipate that resources are available at a later time, when this customer asks for a binding SLA due to the answered SLA quote. Applying a conservative quote policy means the provider would have neither answered the quote request nor got the binding to SLA request, even though resources were available. Hence, providers should be optimistic when answering SLA quotes, but not aggressive, answering quote requests if their fulfillment is unrealistic.

Even if an SLA quote is non-binding and the provider is not obliged to reserve any resources, the requestor should be able to expect that the SLA quote is at least a short term commitment of the provider: if the requestor immediately replies to the request, he may expect the provider to agree to this request.

Using the information on previous negotiations with a specific provider, the AssessGrid broker service is able to determine the ratio of SLA quotes resulting in successful SLA agreements. Moreover, the time between quote and agreement can be considered. Evidently, the ratio decreases with an increasing time span, having multiple customers competing on using a limited set of resources. The more time between non-binding SLA quote and binding SLA request, the more likely it is that resources have been assigned to another request meanwhile. High-quality providers are characterized by a high ratio curve. The higher the probability curve starts and the slower the curve descents, the better for the SLA requestor.

This knowledge is particularly beneficial for brokers mapping workflow tasks on resources, using a two phase procedure. In the first phase an SLA-quote based mapping of tasks to providers is executed, considering time dependencies between consecutive workflow tasks as well as deadlines. If this phase results in a valid mapping, the second phase then focuses on creating binding SLA agreements. SLA offers not resulting in SLA agreements are particularly problematic for the broker at this point, since it impacts the entire workflow mapping, where a single workflow task can no longer be mapped as planned, while other tasks already have binding SLA agreements. In such a case, the broker has to re-enter the first phase for all tasks where no binding SLA has been agreed yet, trying to map the workflow in a different way. As a matter of fact this remapping process may fail, resulting in SLA cancellation costs for the broker.

The AssessGrid broker service is able to use this SLA acceptance ratio curve as ranking or even filtering parameter. Choosing to deal with high-quality providers may be more costly than using low-cost providers, but does pay off at the end due to reduced SLA cancellation costs and an increased service quality level for broker's customers.

## 4.4    Certified and Non-certified Provider Classification

The provider landscape in large scale Grids is extremely heterogeneous, offering all different kinds of resources and services. Also the quality support and administration is very diverse, ranging from high-class compute centers with 24/7 support, over compute resources operated by universities with 12/5 support, up to garage level compute centers with no regular or professional administration at all. Analogously, the quality of hardware resources, the level of redundancy and fault tolerance, or the local security policies also differ significantly.

Obviously the level of support, administration, or other parameters have significant impact on the price of resource usage as well as the provider specified risk value: depending on the acceptable risk, the customer will prefer higher priced SLA offers.

In normal life, classification systems help us in selecting services according to our needs and expectations. In a three star hotel we can expect a color TV in the room, while four star hotels provide 24/7 reception service or a hotel pool. Using data mining methods on the broker information pool, such categories can be established by comparing infrastructure information provided by the provider with the provider's performance data. Obviously, parameters like 24/7 support do have a strong correlation with low risk values and low SLA violation rates. Other parameters like the type of locally used RMS show a strong correlation with acceptance ratio.

Deducting abstract provider classes from these data mining results, may they be specific to a broker or accepted within the entire Grid, help the Grid end-user in ranking and filtering SLA quotes. Similar to the business traveler only looking for business class flights, without really checking the actual services provided to business class travelers, the Grid end-user may select "silver class" providers without checking for detailed services or data.

In this context third-party certificates have focal importance. Even if logfile analysis may reveal contradictions between published data and actual performance (e.g. a provider publishing 24/7 support, only showing 12/5 performance), a provider may lie about other published properties (e.g. policies regarding access security for compute facilities). Here, the provider statements could be certified by a third party. The broker could establish such a certification process for key providers, offering this as additional service for its customers.

## 5    Conclusion

This paper has discussed strategies of the AssessGrid project in relation to ranking mechanisms of SLA offers. The new negotiation process is built on a non-binding SLA request which enables end-users to broadcast an SLA request, and receive and compare SLA offers from a large number of providers. Applying this negotiation mechanism, the end-user requires a ranking mechanism in order to select the best one among them. The history of negotiations recorded by a broker can supplement the ranking mechanisms with several useful metrics such as reliability of estimated failure probabilities, performance (overachieving an SLA) and the acceptance rate of issued non-binding offers. This can help end-users as well as brokers with selecting suitable resources.

# References

1. AssessGrid – Advanced Risk Assessment and Management for Trustable Grids, http://www.assessgrid.eu
2. Czajkowski, K., Kesselman, C., Fitzgerald, S., Foster, I.: Grid information services for distributed resource sharing. High Performance Distributed Computing, 181–194 (2001)
3. Keung, H.N.L.C., Dyson, J.R.D., Jarvis, S.A., Nudd, G.R.: Predicting the Performance of Globus Monitoring and Discovery Service (MDS-2) Queries. In: GRID 2003: Proceedings of the Fourth International Workshop on Grid Computing, Washington, DC, USA, p. 176. IEEE Computer Society, Los Alamitos (2003)
4. Tsouloupas, G., Dikaiakos, M.: Ranking and performance exploration of grid infrastructures: An interactive approach. In: Grid Computing, 7th IEEE/ACM International Conference on, September 2006, pp. 313–314 (2006)
5. Grid Economics and Business Models (GridEcon), http://www.gridecon.eu
6. Iosup, A., Epema, D.: GRENCHMARK: A Framework for Analyzing, Testing, and Comparing Grids. In: CCGRID 2006 Sixth IEEE International Symposium on Cluster Computing and the Grid, pp. 313–320 (2006)
7. Khalili, O., He, J., Olschanowsky, C., Snavely, A., Casanova, H.: Measuring the Performance and Reliability of Production Computational Grids. In: GRID – 7th IEEE/ACM International Conference on Grid Computing (GRID 2006), Barcelona, Spain, September 2006, pp. 293–300. IEEE, Los Alamitos (2006)
8. Dumitrescu, C., Raicu, I., Foster, I.T.: Experiences in Running Workloads over Grid3. In: Zhuge, H., Fox, G.C. (eds.) GCC 2005. LNCS, vol. 3795, pp. 274–286. Springer, Heidelberg (2005)
9. Gourlay, I., Djemame, K., Padgett, J.: Risk and Reliability in Grid Resource Brokering. In: Proceedings of IEEE International Conference on Digital Ecosystems and Technologies 2008 (DEST 2008), Phitsanulok, Thailand (Febuary 2008)
10. Elnaffar, S.: Beyond User Ranking: Expanding the Definition of Reputation in Grid Computing. In: Advances and Innovations in Systems, Computing Sciences and Software Engineering, pp. 381–386. Springer, Netherlands (2007)
11. Sonnek, J.D., Weissman, J.B.: A Quantitative Comparison of Reputation Systems in the Grid. In: GRID 2005: Proceedings of the 6th IEEE/ACM International Workshop on Grid Computing, Washington, DC, USA, pp. 242–249. IEEE Computer Society, Los Alamitos (2005)
12. Andrieux, A., Czajkowski, K., Dan, A., Keahey, K., Ludwig, H., Nakata, T., Pruyne, J., Rofrano, J., Tuecke, S., Xu, M.: Web Services Agreement Specification (WS-Agreement). GRAAP WG - Open Grid Forum (OGF) (March 2007), http://www.ogf.org/documents/GFD.107.pdf

# Author Index

# Lecture Notes in Computer Science

Sublibrary 5: Computer Communication Networks and Telecommunications

Vol. 4357: L. Buttyán, V.D. Gligor, D. Westhoff (Eds.), Security and Privacy in Ad-Hoc and Sensor Networks. X, 193 pages. 2006.

Vol. 4347: J. López (Ed.), Critical Information Infrastructures Security. X, 286 pages. 2006.

Vol. 4325: J. Cao, I. Stojmenovic, X. Jia, S.K. Das (Eds.), Mobile Ad-hoc and Sensor Networks. XIX, 887 pages. 2006.

Vol. 4320: R. Gotzhein, R. Reed (Eds.), System Analysis and Modeling: Language Profiles. X, 229 pages. 2006.

Vol. 4311: K. Cho, P. Jacquet (Eds.), Technologies for Advanced Heterogeneous Networks II. XI, 253 pages. 2006.

Vol. 4272: P. Havinga, M. Lijding, N. Meratnia, M. Wegdam (Eds.), Smart Sensing and Context. XI, 267 pages. 2006.

Vol. 4269: R. State, S. van der Meer, D. O'Sullivan, T. Pfeifer (Eds.), Large Scale Management of Distributed Systems. XIII, 282 pages. 2006.

Vol. 4268: G. Parr, D. Malone, M. Ó Foghlú (Eds.), Autonomic Principles of IP Operations and Management. XIII, 237 pages. 2006.

Vol. 4267: A. Helmy, B. Jennings, L. Murphy, T. Pfeifer (Eds.), Autonomic Management of Mobile Multimedia Services. XIII, 257 pages. 2006.

Vol. 4240: S.E. Nikoletseas, J.D.P. Rolim (Eds.), Algorithmic Aspects of Wireless Sensor Networks. X, 217 pages. 2006.

Vol. 4238: Y.-T. Kim, M. Takano (Eds.), Management of Convergence Networks and Services. XVIII, 605 pages. 2006.

Vol. 4235: T. Erlebach (Ed.), Combinatorial and Algorithmic Aspects of Networking. VIII, 135 pages. 2006.

Vol. 4217: P. Cuenca, L. Orozco-Barbosa (Eds.), Personal Wireless Communications. XV, 532 pages. 2006.

Vol. 4195: D. Gaiti, G. Pujolle, E.S. Al-Shaer, K.L. Calvert, S. Dobson, G. Leduc, O. Martikainen (Eds.), Autonomic Networking. IX, 316 pages. 2006.

Vol. 4124: H. de Meer, J.P.G. Sterbenz (Eds.), Self-Organizing Systems. XIV, 261 pages. 2006.

Vol. 4104: T. Kunz, S.S. Ravi (Eds.), Ad-Hoc, Mobile, and Wireless Networks. XII, 474 pages. 2006.

Vol. 4074: M. Burmester, A. Yasinsac (Eds.), Secure Mobile Ad-hoc Networks and Sensors. X, 193 pages. 2006.

Vol. 4033: B. Stiller, P. Reichl, B. Tuffin (Eds.), Performability Has its Price. X, 103 pages. 2006.

Vol. 4026: P.B. Gibbons, T. Abdelzaher, J. Aspnes, R. Rao (Eds.), Distributed Computing in Sensor Systems. XIV, 566 pages. 2006.

Vol. 4003: Y. Koucheryavy, J. Harju, V.B. Iversen (Eds.), Next Generation Teletraffic and Wired/Wireless Advanced Networking. XVI, 582 pages. 2006.

Vol. 3996: A. Keller, J.-P. Martin-Flatin (Eds.), Self-Managed Networks, Systems, and Services. X, 185 pages. 2006.

Vol. 3976: F. Boavida, T. Plagemann, B. Stiller, C. Westphal, E. Monteiro (Eds.), NETWORKING 2006. Networking Technologies, Services, and Protocols; Performance of Computer and Communication Networks; Mobile and Wireless Communications Systems. XXVI, 1276 pages. 2006.

Vol. 3970: T. Braun, G. Carle, S. Fahmy, Y. Koucheryavy (Eds.), Wired/Wireless Internet Communications. XIV, 350 pages. 2006.

Vol. 3964: M.Ü. Uyar, A.Y. Duale, M.A. Fecko (Eds.), Testing of Communicating Systems. XI, 373 pages. 2006.

Vol. 3961: I. Chong, K. Kawahara (Eds.), Information Networking. XV, 998 pages. 2006.

Vol. 3912: G.J. Minden, K.L. Calvert, M. Solarski, M. Yamamoto (Eds.), Active Networks. VIII, 217 pages. 2007.

Vol. 3883: M. Cesana, L. Fratta (Eds.), Wireless Systems and Network Architectures in Next Generation Internet. IX, 281 pages. 2006.

Vol. 3868: K. Römer, H. Karl, F. Mattern (Eds.), Wireless Sensor Networks. XI, 342 pages. 2006.

Vol. 3854: I. Stavrakakis, M. Smirnov (Eds.), Autonomic Communication. XIII, 303 pages. 2006.

Vol. 3813: R. Molva, G. Tsudik, D. Westhoff (Eds.), Security and Privacy in Ad-hoc and Sensor Networks. VIII, 219 pages. 2005.

Vol. 3462: R. Boutaba, K.C. Almeroth, R. Puigjaner, S. Shen, J.P. Black (Eds.), NETWORKING 2005. XXX, 1483 pages. 2005.